THE
CURIOUS CASE OF
KIRYAS JOEL

THE RISE OF A VILLAGE THEOCRACY
AND THE BATTLE TO DEFEND THE
SEPARATION OF CHURCH AND STATE

LOUIS GRUMET with JOHN CAHER

Published by Chicago Review Press Incorporated
814 North Franklin Street
Chicago, Illinois 60610
ISBN 978-1-61373-500-8

Library of Congress Cataloging-in-Publication Data
Names: Grumet, Louis, author. | Caher, John M., author.
Title: The curious case of Kiryas Joel : the rise of a village theocracy and
   the battle to defend the separation of church and state / Louis Grumet,
   John M. Caher ; foreword by Judith S. Kaye.
Description: Chicago : Chicago Review Press, 2016. | Includes bibliographical
   references and index. | Description based on print version record and CIP
   data provided by publisher; resource not viewed.
Identifiers: LCCN 2015048469 (print) | LCCN 2015048056 (ebook) | ISBN
   9781613735015 (PDF edition) | ISBN 9781613735039 (EPUB edition) | ISBN
   9781613735022 (Kindle edition) | ISBN 9781613735008 (hardback)
Subjects: LCSH: Kiryas Joel Union Free School District (Monroe,
   N.Y.)—Trials, litigation, etc. | Satmar Hasidim—New York (State)—Kiryas
   Joel—Trials, litigation, etc. | Satmar Hasidim—Legal status, laws,
   etc.—New York (State)—Kiryas Joel. | Religion in the public schools—Law
   and legislation—New York (State) | Jewish religious education of children
   with disabilities—New York (State)—Kiryas Joel. | Jewish religious
   schools—New York (State)—Kiryas Joel. | Freedom of religion—United
   States. | Church and state—United States. | BISAC: LAW / Constitutional.
   | LAW / Legal History. | HISTORY / United States / 21st Century. | HISTORY
   / United States / State & Local / Middle Atlantic (DC, DE, MD, NJ, NY,
   PA). | POLITICAL SCIENCE / Government / Judicial Branch. | RELIGION /
   Judaism / Conservative.
Classification: LCC KF228.K565 (print) | LCC KF228.K565 G78 2016 (ebook) |
   DDC 344.73/0796—dc23
LC record available at http://lccn.loc.gov/2015048469

Interior design: Jonathan Hahn
Author photos: Louis Grumet, photo by Megan Groppe; John M. Caher, photo by
   Robert D. Mayberger; Judith S. Kaye, photo courtesy of *New York Law Journal*,
   Rick Kopstein, photographer

Printed in the United States of America
5 4 3 2 1

To a friend, unsung hero, and inspiration: Dr. Hannah Flegenheimer, who devotes her life to providing children of all potentials and all capabilities with the chance to succeed, and through her commitment and life example reminds me regularly of the role education plays in nourishing our democratic republic and sustaining our Constitution.

CONTENTS

FOREWORD

————

TALK ABOUT THE intervention of fate! Though I had agreed to consider writing a foreword for a new book coauthored by my friends Lou Grumet and John Caher, the manuscript sat temptingly on a table in my office, but it was a long reach across several piles of documents with due dates on them. Then very early one Friday morning, I found myself at home sprawled on the hallway tile floor, having taken a bad fall while racing from the bedroom to answer the cell phone plugged into the kitchen wall. When I finally made it to a doctor, he pronounced no disaster and ordered light pain medication, lots of ice for the knees and forehead, and my legs raised whenever possible. The perfect prescription for plunging into the manuscript. There I was, Friday afternoon through Sunday evening—from sofa to armchair to bed, always with the manuscript in hand.

Not for a moment do I suggest that you pursue such a pathway into this book. Just pick it up the usual way. It's a treat, not a treatment.

In writing this foreword, I now put all personal involvements aside, most especially my own participation in the fascinating *Kiryas Joel* cases as a judge of the Court of Appeals of the State of New York. So, what precisely makes this book such an engaging read for each of you?

I begin with the fact that the book is a great introduction to a world we all should know much more about: our government—each of the three branches and their interactions with one another, from the principles envisioned by our founders centuries ago to the implementation and protection of those principles every single day by our contemporaries in a radically changing society. That's hardly a day at the beach, I admit, and most of us, regrettably, avoid it, satisfying ourselves with merely grumbling and complaining. But this book is a compelling introduction to the subject told through a single lens, and it could not be more beautifully or articulately illustrated, with good, solid introductions to each of the participants, from our nation's founders to today's governors, legislators, political leaders, and judges, and the human beings actually impacted by their choices.

Second, the lens itself is a subject of immense interest. The particular focus of the book is on Satmar Hasidim, a religiously homogenous, politically muscular group situated in Orange County, New York, and on education services for their many, many children with disabilities and special needs. This subject embraces a rainbow of fascinating issues, from First Amendment constitutional protections ("Congress shall make no law respecting an establishment of religion, or prohibiting the free exercise thereof"—in other words, freedom to and freedom from), to political deal makers and courts generally settling (and unsettling) the reach of these fundamental concepts, and ultimately to the power of relentless persistence.

Never is the reader left in the clouds on these mind-wrenching, yet critically important, issues. Each matter is graphically tied to people captivatingly described (and actually quoted) in great detail, offering a unique, singular view into the operation of their hearts and minds. You're on the scene from day one, meeting the Satmar and their neighbors, strategizing with Satmar leaders on how to educate Sheindle Silberstein and other Satmar children with similar difficulties in the comfort of their religious and cultural tradition. You're at the table through meetings with state and federal political leaders, ultimately securing actual state legislation to enable the Satmar to establish their own special school district. You're in several courtrooms, both presenting and hearing oral argument. You're even in the conference room of the Supreme Court of the United States for heated inside exchanges and decision dynamics among the justices (thanks to the writings and notes of Justice Harry Blackmun).

It is, of course, no surprise that long after the Supreme Court's decision in this case, the swinging pendulum of legal and human entanglements on similar "freedom to and freedom from" issues has remained in perpetual motion in Satmar and other communities, and in courts around the nation. I will say no more than to endorse first my friends' view that *Kiryas Joel* was a crucial benchmark at a crucial juncture, and second the closing words of their book: "Eternal vigilance is indeed the price of liberty."

Looking back to that fateful Friday fall that took me deep into the manuscript, I cannot recall any accident in my life that yielded such a rich reward.

Judith S. Kaye, the first woman to serve on New York's highest court and the state's chief judge for fifteen years, went on to become of counsel to the Manhattan law firm of Skadden, Arps, Slate, Meagher & Flom. She passed away in 2016.

citizens. These interviews added significant context, essentially putting meat on the skeletal bones of the legal papers.

Additional sources included myriad published accounts—primarily newspaper articles—on the case as it worked its way up and down the judicial ladder.

PROLOGUE

"CURIOUS" JOEL

I**T WAS THE** first Sunday in November 1994, and I had the distinct impression that I had fallen down a rabbit hole to a world where nothing was real and nothing made sense.

There I was, an obscure, liberal Jewish lawyer from Upstate New York appearing on the most watched program on television to explain my lengthy and seemingly endless battle with an Orthodox Jewish sect and with a man who was to me a mentor, a friend, a brilliant constitutional scholar, and a liberal icon: Mario Matthew Cuomo, then governor of New York and darling of the national Democratic Party.

I would tell Ed Bradley of *60 Minutes* how an extremely insular group of Hasidic Jews had bought up land in a rural area, populated it exclusively with members of their sect, founded a village composed of members of their religion, and then exerted extraordinary political pressure to persuade Cuomo and the New York State Legislature to create a publicly funded school district catering to the interests of their sect—marking the first time in American history that a governmental unit was established for a religious group.

I tried to explain why Governor Cuomo had signed legislation that he must have known was unconstitutional, and why both houses of

1

the New York State Legislature were continuing to make an end run around the entire court system and the Constitution, even after the US Supreme Court had spoken. But several months after the Supreme Court issued what should have been the last word, the story was still unfolding and would continue to develop for many years. Before the last chapter was written, the dispute had weaved its way through seven trial courts, thrice visiting the New York Court of Appeals, the most esteemed state high court in the nation.

This is the full story.

It is a story of personalities, religion, culture, religious apartheid, government, politics, soul selling, and constitutional law, all centered on a small community of Satmar Hasidic Jews that chooses to be so far outside the American mainstream that it cannot assimilate. Yet this group was oddly blind to the fact that by inviting (actually insisting upon) government accommodation and financial support, it was undermining the very instrument that protects its traditions and customs from government interference: the First Amendment to the US Constitution. It is, to me, an object lesson on the critical importance of church-state separation with implications far beyond the village of Kiryas Joel* (pronounced KIR-yas Jo-EL), and a beaming illustration of the concerns Thomas Jefferson expressed two centuries earlier when he argued forcefully for a "wall" of separation between church and state. If the Satmar could obtain for themselves a public school district, why couldn't a group of neo-Nazis or Islamic extremists do exactly the same thing: buy up a bunch of farmland, subdivide it to their members, and form an exclusive school—and then force the public to pay for it with no voice in how it is run?

The Satmar Hasidim has its roots in the city from which its name derived, Satu Mare ("St. Mary"), now in Romania. After World War II,

---

* Kiryas Joel maintains an extensive website detailing its history, current news, photographs, and other materials: www.kjvoice.com/faq.asp.

members of the group followed a charismatic leader and Holocaust survivor, Grand Rebbe Joel Teitelbaum, to the United States and settled in the Williamsburg section of Brooklyn. Their numbers grew geometrically over the decades, and they became one of the most powerful voting blocs in New York City. Since Brooklyn is the most populous Democratic county in the state, this made the Satmar one of the state's most potent pressure groups, for the simple reason that they vote strictly as directed by the rebbe. There is no loyalty to any particular political party or politician, only to their spiritual leader. So the leader is in a position to promise—*and deliver*—virtually all of the votes in the community. Despite their relatively small numbers, by voting as a group the Satmar can, and do, determine the outcome of close elections. Their collective clout far exceeds their numbers.*

But the group is independent not only of the political parties but of the Jewish establishment as well. As fierce opponents of Zionism[†] who do not support the state of Israel, the Satmar are on the fringes of the Jewish community, a subculture and in some ways modern-day Pharisees.[‡] Yet on select issues, when choosing to mobilize the collective power that comes from bloc voting, the small, insular group is a political wrecking ball. This can happen only to the extent that the Satmar can maintain their unique identity and their leaders can govern with

---

* Consider the congressional election of 2006. A six-term Republican congresswoman, Sue Kelly, who had won her seat with strong Satmar support, was up for reelection and vulnerable for a number of reasons. Because she had not, in the eyes of the Kiryas Joel leadership, provided the "pork" to which they felt entitled, the leaders threw not only their support but that of the entire village behind Kelly's challenger. John Hall, a former rock star, was elected with 88 percent of the village vote, which accounts entirely for his narrow 4,760-vote victory.

† A photograph published in the *Village Voice* on March 4, 2015, accompanying an article titled "Ultra-Orthodox Jews Protest Netanyahu's 'Provocative Politics' Outside Israeli Embassy," shows Satmar Hasidic demonstrators, one of them holding a sign that reads, ZIONISM IS ANTITHETICAL TO JUDAISM. See http://blogs.villagevoice.com/runninscared /2015/03/thousands_of_satmar_protestors_speak_out_against_netanyahu_speech.php.

‡ "Pharisee" comes from the Hebrew word *perisha*, which translates to "separated ones."

authority unchallenged by outside influences and, therefore, deliver their votes.

In 1975 Grand Rebbe Joel Teitelbaum, increasingly doubtful of his ability to keep American culture at bay in New York City, suggested the sect expand into an isolated community in Upstate New York, where their children would not be distracted by such cultural pollutants as sports and blue jeans. They began buying up land in the town of Monroe, Orange County, about an hour north of the city, and set out to build their community. Once they had the requisite five hundred inhabitants to legally form their own village, they did so. The village of Kiryas Joel ("Joel's Village," named for the grand rebbe) was established in 1977. The Brooklyn community remained—to this day, some fifty thousand Satmar live in the borough—but Kiryas Joel emerged as its large and growing cousin.

The village was governed largely as a theocracy. The children were educated in private yeshivas (religious schools), and civil disputes were resolved by Jewish law, not the laws of the State of New York. Residents generally spoke Yiddish, not English. Television, radio, and newspapers were eschewed if not banned outright. There was no baseball, no jeans, no sneakers, no birth control, and no private interaction between males and females prior to marriage, which was arranged and always within the sect. Religious leaders and religious tradition ruled virtually every hour of every day, and night, of the citizenry.

"We want isolation," said Rabbi Elliott Kohn, who was dean of the village's religious school for girls. "That's why we have no TVs or radios. We don't want to expose our kids to the entire society, to the entire world. We want to keep our tradition."

Kohn continued. "The boys never, never meet any girl. They only have boy friends. They never meet girls or see all those things on television."

A sign welcoming visitors to Kiryas Joel admonished visitors to "maintain gender separation in all public areas"—although apparently

not in private areas. In order to expand and further populate and perpetuate their community, the Satmar procreated with gusto; many
families had a dozen or so children, and the community's population
continues to double every decade.* With some degree of inbreeding
inevitable—the group was so small and exclusionary that many married couples would unknowingly share recessive genes—a dispropor-
tionate share of the children had disabilities.

And therein is the root of the problem.

Children with disabilities require a wide variety of intensive services. Under state and federal law, children are entitled to special
education services even if they are enrolled in private school. Special
education, however, is very expensive, and the schools in Kiryas Joel
were not able to provide the services to which the children were legally
entitled. Understandably, and appropriately, the Satmar demanded that
the local school district, Monroe-Woodbury, provide and fully fund
those services. But they insisted that these services be provided only on
terms they deemed consistent with their religious and cultural practices.

Initially, Monroe-Woodbury sent its public school teachers to provide the necessary special education services in an annex to one of the
religious schools in the village. But a year later, in 1985, the US Supreme
Court, in *Aguilar v. Felton*, struck down a New York City program in
which public school teachers were sent to parochial schools to provide remedial education—which is what was occurring in Monroe-
Woodbury. When Monroe-Woodbury stopped providing the services
in accordance with the court decision, the parents of children with disabilities in Kiryas Joel reluctantly consented to having their offspring
bused to the local public school.

It was an unmitigated disaster.

---

* In his 2014 book *The Pious Ones: The World of Hasidim and Their Battles with America*
(New York: Harper Collins, 2014), Joseph Berger tells the story of Yitta Schwartz, a
resident of Kiryas Joel who died in 2010 at the age of ninety-three—leaving behind some
two thousand descendants.

With their atypical clothing and habits, the children did not fit in, and neither the parents nor the Satmar community had any desire for them to do so; they did not want their children exposed to secular culture in any fashion. They would not permit their daughters to be taught by men or their sons by women. They objected to women driving school buses. They were unreasonably and unceasingly demanding. But Monroe-Woodbury also showed incredible insensitivity, on one occasion bringing the children to McDonald's—hardly a *glatt kosher** establishment—and on another casting a disabled child from Kiryas Joel as Rudolph the Red-Nosed Reindeer in a Christmas pageant. The parents withdrew their children from Monroe-Woodbury and refused to send them back.

And who could blame them?

"We look different—like a person from a different planet," Rebbe Teitelbaum explained. "These children feel hurt if they go to a different school. They are broken children anyway."

Against that backdrop, the village leaders successfully lobbied in 1989 for legislation to establish a public school district within Kiryas Joel, one that would serve only members of the Satmar Hasidic community who lived there. That legislation was enacted in secret, in the dead of night, and sent to Governor Cuomo for his approval.

At the time, I was executive director of the New York State School Boards Association. The association viewed the legislation as a violation of both the state and federal constitutions, and I personally viewed it as a threat to my own religious freedom. Who knows better than a Jew, especially one who grew up in West Virginia, the insidious danger of church-state entanglement?

I went to see Governor Cuomo. I had served as his special assistant for three years before he became governor, and I greatly admired his

* *Glatt kosher* technically refers to meat from animals with defect-free or smooth lungs. Today, it generally means meat processed under a strict standard known as *kashrut*.

intellect and principles. I assumed he was largely unaware of the legislature's mischief (not knowing until years later about the governor's secret political role in the bill's preliminary stages), and I urged him to veto the bill.

"Do you know how insensitive the public schools have been to these people's religion?" Cuomo asked. "These people don't ask for much, Luig,* they just want to send their children somewhere where they won't be insulted. It's our duty to protect these immigrants."

I agreed, entirely. The Satmar children had been treated atrociously. They were entitled to special education services at taxpayer expense (the parents, after all, were taxpayers), and I absolutely agreed that the government had an obligation to help resolve the crisis. However, I thought that the bill was an illegitimate solution to a legitimate problem. I understood the political implications: if the governor vetoed the bill, he would offend a large and powerful voting bloc in New York City, his stronghold. But I argued that the bill was so flagrantly unconstitutional that the courts would strike it down. Since the governor had served as a law clerk to a judge of the state's highest court, had only half-jokingly suggested he'd rather be chief judge than governor, and viewed himself (quite legitimately) as a legal intellect and constitutional scholar, I argued that he would look quite foolish. Cuomo shrugged me off with a wave of his hand and suggested no one would dare, or perhaps bother, to challenge him.

"Who's going to sue?" Cuomo asked dismissively and, I thought, rather arrogantly as he escorted me out of his office.

"*I* will," I responded. The governor smiled at me with a condescending grin that I had seen many times when I worked for him. He clearly didn't view a former bureaucrat running a largely obscure state association of school boards as much of a threat.

---

* Although I always addressed Cuomo by his title—and called him "Governor" even after he left office—he often referred to me as "Luig," an Italianized version of my name. I got a kick out of it and had always considered it an expression of affection and friendship.

Ten days later, Cuomo signed the bill over the objections of every one of his top advisers, telling them, too, "These people don't ask for much."*

The *60 Minutes* story was filmed in the summer of 1994 but aired two nights before the November election, in which Governor Cuomo lost his office to then state senator George Pataki. As an assemblyman, Pataki was the initial sponsor of the original legislation to create the unconstitutional school district in 1989. The television segment showed Cuomo campaigning for reelection in the village of Kiryas Joel, where he promised to enact whatever legislation was necessary to keep the school district running and vowed to push and push and push until the courts finally gave in.

I was stunned and terribly disappointed in the governor's disdain for the judicial process. He had always spoken so eloquently and, I thought, sincerely about the rule of law. But here he was, essentially saying that he's all for the rule of law as long as he gets what he wants.

It was only the latest in a long series of disappointments. Since the legislation was first enacted half a decade earlier, I had slowly begun to understand how a seemingly simple squabble between a religious sect and the broader community escalated into a major national dispute that pitted the New York political leadership against the state court system, the US Supreme Court, and the media. I saw how national religious and educational organizations distorted the fact patterns in the litigation to fit their agenda of the moment, ignoring the enduring legacy of the Establishment Clause ("Congress shall make no law respecting an establishment of religion"). But mostly, I was devastated that people I

---

* Actually, they ask for, and receive, a great deal, with a huge percentage of the population, and the community itself, receiving government subsidies.

admired would so cavalierly abandon the Constitution when it didn't fit their needs.

What follows is the inside story of the decadelong battle that ensued, told from the perspective of someone who was there every step of the way and witnessed the extraordinary and terrifying power that a small religious conclave, which votes heavily and contributes heavily, can exert over our political system and our government.

1

A NEW HOMELAND

The United States of America should have a foundation free from the influence of the clergy.

—George Washington

WHEN ANN KRAWET and her husband, Dave, moved from New York City to Monroe, New York, in 1968, they weren't looking for anything unusual—just a nice, safe home and a smaller, more manageable community. Ann and Dave, a Reform Jewish couple expecting their third child, had been living in a one-and-a-half-bedroom walk-up apartment in Brooklyn and were desperate for more space.

Upstate in Orange County, they found a classic cedar-shingle home in a little subdivision that had been neatly cut into a tree-covered hill so that all of the homes remained surrounded by woods. Ann thought the small round windows on the second level—just under the eaves—were "darling." A living room at the far end of the house had huge sixteen-pane windows that looked over a large lawn bordered by trees. They had found their paradise in a town named in honor of our fifth president, James Monroe, officially a Virginia Episcopalian but more likely a deist.

Monroe, an old colonial town west of the Hudson and about an hour northwest of the Bronx, had approved several subdivisions in the 1960s, including the one where Ann and Dave found their home. They had been attracted to Monroe for a few reasons. First, it was about equidistant between Dave's job at the old US Custom House in lower Manhattan (a two-hour commute) and Ann's parents' home in Sullivan County (west of Orange County, on the border between New York and Pennsylvania); second, since Monroe necessitated a long commute to Manhattan, the prices were cheaper than in closer suburbs (Ann and Dave were able to buy in a subdivision with two-acre lots); finally, the presence of the old town of Monroe added a touch of authentic "small-town" feel to the benefits of good public schools and bucolic splendor offered by such bedroom communities.

Orange County was named after the Dutchman William of Orange, who took over England at the end of the seventeenth century. Originally owned by the Dutch, New York was called New Netherland until the British kicked them out and, in keeping with the reign of King Charles II and his family, renamed it after the Duke of York, brother of the king. About fifteen years after taking over New Netherland from the Dutch, Charles's family lost control of England to the Dutch leader, William. This occurred as part of the "glorious revolution of 1688," when the Protestants took England back from the Catholics one more time. William was married to Mary, daughter of the English king, and invaded successfully. Religious disputes have always weighed heavily in the area. Although William didn't change the name back to New Netherland, he didn't protest when some appreciative Dutch colonists named the southwest area of the Hudson Valley "Orange County."

When the town of Monroe was chartered in the early eighteenth century by Queen Anne, the area of mostly high, rocky hills and swampy valleys was sparsely populated, and the situation wasn't much different eighty years later when the American Revolution was sweeping the colonies. The region saw a fair amount of action during the wars at the end of the eighteenth century. Along with the Mohawk's great chief Joseph

Brant, Claudius Smith and his "cowboys" were particularly active in the area around present-day Monroe, defending loyal British from the "American" paramilitary operations. In fact, during his retreat toward Pennsylvania after the disastrous Battle of Brooklyn, George Washington stayed in a farmhouse in Orange County. With its tactical advantages and commanding plateau overseeing the Hudson River, Orange County has been home to the US Military Academy at West Point since 1802.

Monroe was built on a relatively level raised plain in a region of marshy farmland that few farmed because nobody knew how, until some Poles and Volga Germans showed up at the turn of the twentieth century, found it familiar terrain, and immediately began to grow onions. Before the arrival of these hardy farmers, this part of Upstate New York had clung to a way of life that would have been recognizable to Diedrich Knickerbocker. These days, bridges have replaced ferries, bringing the west bank of the Hudson within easy reach of Manhattan; the empire of the automobile bought out the onion farms, and the landscape has become a patchwork of suburbs and outlet malls, interspersed with the few remaining colonial towns and a large regional airport.

When Ann and Dave Krawet arrived in the late 1960s, agriculture still dominated a landscape that was ever so slowly evolving into rural suburbia. Cow crossings continued to bring traffic to a standstill on Highway 17, the major east-west corridor, as the cattle were ushered to the milking barns where Velveeta cheese, the 1917 invention of a Swiss immigrant who had settled in Monroe, was still made. The Krawets loved the charm of the area. It seemed they had arrived just at the right time.

Ann resigned her job as a social studies teacher to concentrate on raising the family's three children but soon found she had time on her hands. She started volunteering for a variety of activities at Temple Beth-El, the local Reform synagogue. The temple had been founded during the days when Monroe was just a vacation rental area for people on their way to the big resorts in the Catskills (known as the Borscht Belt because of the primarily Eastern European, Jewish clientele). It was during those first few years volunteering at the temple and for school activities that Ann made lasting friendships in town and was introduced to the whole panoply of local government and community issues with which any vibrant town buzzes. Things were going great: the older kids loved the schools, Ann felt at home in the community, and Dave, despite the long commute, was proud that he could provide his family a lifestyle that, in comparison to the postwar Brooklyn where he had grown up, was one of pastoral luxury.

Then one day a mysterious real estate developer from Montreal purchased about three hundred acres of a recently cleared wasteland north of Highway 17, in Monroe Township. The land near Stewart Air Force Base had been deemed suitable for industrial use. When those plans collapsed, the land was on the market, and relatively cheap. Rumors spread, one of the more accurate beginning at the local Lions Club, where a member who was a state trooper let it be known that he had inspected several different vans that week that had been parked illegally along Routes 44 and 17. In each case, he said, the van had been full of strange men with big beards and some kind of religious cult outfit. The trooper's account was soon confirmed by someone at the chamber of commerce, who knew someone whose nephew worked at the county records office.

Who were these people, with their odd appearance and customs, and what did they want with such a large parcel of land?

Many people understand Hasidic Jews to be "ultra-Orthodox" or some other label that indicates rigid adherence to (even preoccupation with) divinely designated rules for Jewish living. That is not wholly inaccurate, but it is simplistic and unfair and does rather miss the point of Hasidism, which began as a reform movement in Eastern European Jewry in the eighteenth century.

The Hasidim follow a kind of religious life advocated by Rabbi Yisroel ben Eliezer, known as the Baal Shem Tov, a man who lived in Eastern Europe in the late 1600s. The Baal Shem Tov, though quite a brilliant scholar himself, felt that the benefits of Judaism, the benefits of that special relationship with God, belonged to all Jews—not just great scholars. He wanted to shift the focus of Jewish devotion from scholarship and asceticism to prayer and rejoicing. Of course, this was still Judaism, so study of holy scripture and strict attention to the laws laid down in those scriptures remained central to the life of the community, but what changed was the goal of the religious life: for the Jewish community to recognize and joyously participate in God's actual presence in the entire world.

Not without controversy, but definitely with success, Eliezer's reforms swept through the Jewish enclaves of Eastern Europe. Dynasties of revered rabbis in the new Hasidic tradition exercised total control over the communities they led. Competition was fierce, with disaffected heirs taking adherents off to start new congregations throughout the pale of settlement in Eastern Europe.

One branch of the complicated Hasidic dynasty settled in the city of Satu Mare in Hungary, near the Transylvanian border. Satu Mare had been an important metropolis for centuries, and by the outbreak of World War II, more than fifty thousand Jews lived there under the rule of Rabbi Joel Teitelbaum, a Talmudic scholar who had become its rebbe in the early twentieth century, and later became grand rebbe.

The grand rebbe himself was saved from concentration camps and sent to Switzerland, where he survived the war, but the vast majority of his community perished in the camps. Not being a Zionist*—in fact, Rebbe Teitelbaum became famous throughout the Orthodox community for his scholarly refutation of Zionism—the grand rebbe stopped

---

* To this day, the Satmar oppose the state of Israel on the grounds that Jews are supposed to remain in exile until their deliverance with the arrival of the Messiah. According to a November 11, 2012, article in the *New York Post* ("No to Israel, Yes to Obama" by Gary Buiso), residents of Kiryas Joel were instructed to vote for President Obama and against his challenger, Mitt Romney, because the former was deemed less friendly to Israel. That in itself obviously puts the Satmar at great odds with mainstream Jewish organizations, as well as most Jewish people.

only briefly in Jerusalem after the war before making his way to Brooklyn, where other Hasidim had preceded him, in 1946.

Although there was a thriving Hasidic community in Brooklyn before the war, popular culture and assimilation of the various strands of the Jewish community into the New York City melting pot had— at least in a very limited way—encroached on their customs, and the stricter devotees of the sect had, to some extent, given in to what might be described as moderate zealotry. Who could tell what would happen to the rich Hasidic traditions and way of life in a generation, or three? What was the long-term threat to the Orthodox hegemony?

Grand Rebbe Teitelbaum had one goal in later life: to rebuild in America the lost cultural community of Satu Mare. By virtue of his position, Rebbe Teitelbaum was something of an autocrat—a benevolent one to be sure, but an autocrat nonetheless—and he used that power quite effectively.

When Teitelbaum suggested that all Satmar relocate to New York City, they came from all over the world. When he taught that his followers should have absolutely nothing to do with American culture (no baseball games, no radio, no TV, no English-language newspapers, no hamburgers, no golf, no blue jeans), they fervently accepted that too. And when he suggested that, in order to repopulate, married couples should have as many children as possible, they conformed (the *average* Satmar family has more than eight children). When he taught that young Satmar boys should be trained the way they had been in Satu Mare—studying the Torah and Talmud at yeshivas from 7 AM to 7 PM, starting around the age of five and continuing until a few years after marriage—yeshivas sprang up all over the Brooklyn neighborhood.

But by the mid-1970s Rebbe Teitelbaum had grown increasingly skeptical that American culture could be kept at bay, especially with all the temptations in New York City. Because he feared *ausgegrunt* ("the green wearing off," or the lost zeal of younger generations that is endemic to devotional sects; witness the second generations of the Puritans in England and America) and lacked faith in the ability of any of his potential successors, he suggested that the community buy a large plot of upstate land and start building an even more isolated community of insular purity—unwittingly following in the tradition of American religious utopias upstate (including secular, socialist Zionist Jewish camps). On the way to the summer bungalows in the Catskills, the elders of the community had noticed a sparsely populated area off Route 17.

That would do nicely.

Monroe locals had a lot of fun arguing over whether the strange appearance of Satmar was a good or bad thing.

Many of the suburbanites had lived in New York City at some point in their lives, and these former New Yorkers fancied themselves sophisticates and sought to demonstrate their liberal open-mindedness by making an ostentatious show of their commitment to diversity, noting how nice it would be to get kosher meat and relating to anyone who would listen their worldly experience with Hasidic shops or neighborhoods in the city of New York. A fair number of those who had moved to Monroe from such "outposts" as Syracuse, Buffalo, and Rochester listened to the sophisticates with curiosity and anticipation.

The naysayers, on the other hand, were excited because they had something to complain about: it was the end of the "traditional community" as far as they were concerned. They feared the newcomers would destroy property values and ruin the school district, and they warned everyone about doing business with the untrustworthy Satmar.

Ann and Dave Krawet were certainly not fear-stricken, nor were they predisposed to dislike the Satmar. But they were nervously curious, because the area where the Satmar were building was near their own subdivision, and the Krawets remembered family members and other adults complaining about the Hasid as *shanda fur die goyim*: doing something embarrassing to Jews in the presence of non-Jews.* They soon met a few Satmar and found them pleasant and interesting people. The Satmar claimed that they wanted to be good neighbors and the Krawets, with a shrug, were more than willing to give them a chance.

As was Sotirios "Steve" Lagakos, owner of the classic Monroe Diner. A short, tough man with a deep Mediterranean tan and a razor-sharp triangular mustache, Lagakos had arrived in America in the late 1960s, fresh out of the Greek air force and able to speak only halting English.

After working tirelessly for a few years at a diner in Manhattan, saving every cent so he could eventually own his own diner, one night Lagakos found himself driving around upstate in the first automobile he ever owned, a destined-for-the-junk-heap Chrysler he got for twenty dollars. He was searching for a location for his dream diner but had no idea where he was going. His rather erratic driving caught the attention of two state troopers, who pulled him over on Route 17. Upset that he had embarrassed himself while searching for his place in the American Dream, Lagakos started crying. The officers initially suspected he was nuts or drunk and asked him to accompany them to the station (or, as he put it, "the brig"). With one trooper driving ahead and one

---

* That has remained an issue. When the local media reported in mid-2014 that 93 percent of the residents of Kiryas Joel were on Medicaid, a blogger at the *Jewish Worker* opined, "This is driving animosity for Orthodox Jews as they are being looked upon as drains on the government treasury. . . . In the past Jews (including Orthodox Jews) have been looked upon as a model population in the US, educating their children and contributing/succeeding economically. Now the picture has changed radically and Orthodox Jews are looked upon as a drain on society. I don't know how much longer this can go on" (http://jewishworker.blogspot.com/2014/06/93-in-kiryas-yoel-on-medicaid.html). As a Jew myself, I too worry about backlash.

following close behind, Lagakos made his way to the barracks. Along the way, he saw a shuttered diner with a FOR SALE sign. He slammed on his brakes, causing the trooper to rear-end his Chrysler. He excitedly jumped out of the car—it was raining by this time—and hastily scribbled down the information from the sign. The troopers took this as further evidence that he was crazy, and when he tried to explain by pointing vigorously at the sign and shouting, "I buy diner! I buy diner!" they were convinced of it.

The troopers ("They treat me very nice") released him to his brother, after giving him a cup of coffee and an hour to "sober up." But Lagakos came back to Monroe a few days later. He walked into the local Chase Manhattan bank branch, announced he was buying the diner and dumped more than $70,000 in $100 bills onto the loan officer's desk. It was all the money he had in the world, a combination of his mother's life savings and the cash Steve and his brother had literally stashed under a mattress. He scraped and saved to afford improvements to the restaurant, sleeping on a blanket in the basement for a year.

It was the 1970s, the heyday of the American diner, and Steve did a brisk business. By the end of the decade he was well on his way to having five diners throughout the region, owning a large home, sending his kids to college, and employing his entire extended family.

Lagakos remembers welcoming the new Satmar residents and businessmen, wanting to give them the same chance that he had been given. After all, when he arrived in town, he was as foreign as the Satmar, but the community had fully embraced him, respecting his work ethic and the quality of his business sense. Didn't the newest arrivals deserve the same? Steve thought so—as long as they played by the rules, as he and other immigrants had done.

True to everyone's expectations, the Satmar quickly began to develop the big subdivision they had purchased, giving the streets

Hasidic-sounding names and redeveloping a strip mall to serve their need for religious-oriented items. People were both a little surprised at the speed with which the Satmar were moving in and a little disappointed that they didn't see much of their exotic neighbors. After the first six months or so, however, rumors spread. The houses going up in the Satmar subdivision began to look strange—in fact, they were row houses! Some were three stories, and many of them seemed to be duplexes. One particularly large building looked like a condominium. Some of the local tradesmen who had worked on the subdivision told stories of supposedly single-family homes with four or five kitchens and as many bathrooms. Plumbers told of odd sewer hookups.

It was obvious to anyone who drove by the area that the Satmar were flagrantly breaking building regulations and zoning ordinances. The houses did not meet code. The roads did not meet code. The wells and sewers did not meet code. It was beginning to look like . . . Brooklyn!—the borough from which many local residents had escaped.

Public sentiment that had been indifferent to or had even favored the "interesting" Satmar turned to panic. The town council, the school board, and the PTA had an emergency meeting. County politicians were called in. "Who the hell do these people think they are?" became the universal outcry.

The locals had been anticipating something attractive and pastoral—something along the lines of a Jewish version of Amish communities and their roadside markets. Kugel stands, perhaps? Nobody was expecting an Eastern European shtetl or ghetto. And beyond the important emotional fact of disappointed expectations (however fanciful and ill-formed), there were the rules to think about. It may have been the late twentieth century, but the double-barreled sobriety of this half-Yankee, half-Dutch community retained a capacity to be offended at the idea that anyone would intentionally break the rules. Rules, after all, are rules. Those who weren't swept into the anti-Satmar camp in defense of the principle of the laws came in defense of the spirit of the law—"We didn't move out here to have to look at urban blight!" It was one thing to break a rule here or there, but to completely subvert the pastoral character of the area was something else entirely. On the practical side, folks were not at all sure that the sewer system and water supply could handle development on the scale the Satmar seemed to be contemplating.

Those who had warned about the Satmar from the beginning were turned to for advice, but they only provided horror stories—tales of a town called New Square, and of East Ramapo—once-happy suburbs and school districts that had, according to the tales, been torn apart by Hasidic or ultra-Orthodox development. They multiply like rabbits! They'll vote down the school budgets! They'll tap the wells dry! Others—especially some secular, Zionist Jews from the area—spread even more far-fetched rumors: the Satmar would throw stones at the cars of those with whom they disagreed, and do the same to immodestly dressed women. They would riot if men and women swam in the lake together.* Rumors and speculation passed far beyond sinks per square foot and storm-gutter placement.

About this time, Ann Krawet recalls, she woke up to an unfamiliar sound.

Ann's street, Mountain View, is a narrow one-lane road in the town of Monroe, slightly outside the village of Kiryas Joel but close enough that some of the Satmar were buying houses near hers with a plan toward expanding the village. The topmost branches of the trees on either side of the road almost touch as they reach out across the pavement. Narrowing the street further, extra family cars are frequently lined up along the curbs. This was the last place Ann expected to see

---

* In fact, one of the agreements that the Satmar made with the town before being granted permission to develop their land was that they would keep a pond open to swimmers (the tradition of swimming in public ponds remains alive throughout the rural Northeast). But the pond had already been filled with construction rubbish, and the more cynical of the skeptics were sure this had been done on purpose to prevent men and women from swimming together.

three forty-foot buses grunting up the street in noisy low gears. Dumb-founded, she watched as the buses crawled along, stopping in front of the homes of her Satmar neighbors just long enough to let a small stream of men of various ages pile in for their daily commute to Man-hattan, where some worked in the Forty-Seventh Street diamond dis-trict and others owned stores selling cameras and other wares. When the first bus reached the end of the road, it executed a groaning three-point turn. Now heading back down the street, it edged past the other two, each of which then executed the same clumsy 180-degree turn and drove away.

That was odd, Ann remembers thinking. When the same thing happened the next day, and the next, she grew concerned and made inquiries of her neighbors, who said they knew nothing about it. When the same thing happened every day for a week, she started complaining. No one had anticipated an unregulated municipal bus system. It's dan-gerous! It's noisy and smoggy and inappropriate for this street! But the buses kept coming. Her Satmar neighbors—especially the wives—told Ann privately that they really did agree with her about the buses, but that when they had complained, their leaders told them that it "was good for Kiryas Joel" and so there was nothing more they could do. Finding the situation intolerable (and disappointed by what she saw as the spinelessness of her Satmar neighbors in the face of their leader-ship), Ann decided to complain at the next meeting of the Monroe Town Council.

That was when Ann was introduced, firsthand, to the community crisis that the Satmar had precipitated.

One woman complained that a Satmar neighbor had, without a permit, built a swimming pool, visible from the front yard, and had hung eight-foot-high, electric-blue curtains around it. Ann stood up and complained about the buses. A group of three homeowners, whose lots bordered the village of Kiryas Joel, followed Ann and complained that their wells, which they had dug decades ago, had run dry. A fourth person was complaining about used tires and an old refrigerator that had been left for weeks on the lawn of a Satmar neighbor.

The town council members were squirming. It was obvious that the new residents didn't give a whit about zoning, deed restriction, sanitation, and utility rules that applied to everyone else. But the council was torn between citizenry who insisted that the town enforce its rules equally and a Satmar community that was crassly willing to exploit the Holocaust: Every time someone stood up to lodge a complaint, a group of Satmar would jump to their feet and shout them down. "This is just how the Nazis talked!" "That's what they said before the Holocaust!" "Can you believe we came to this country which is supposed to be free from anti-Semitism, but it is just like the old country? It will be back to the ovens before we know it!" One elderly Satmar man had rolled up his sleeve and was pointing at the faded tattoo on his arm and shouting about his experiences in a concentration camp.

As a Jew, Ann was appalled and disgusted at the notion of being accused of anti-Semitism by people who seemed to her to be self-righteous cultists and who failed to realize how much of their non-Hasidic audience was Jewish. She was embarrassed to be in the presence of anyone who could dare to compare zoning disputes to genocide and livid that people of her own faith would so cavalierly invoke the Holocaust to excuse the dumping of trash in their yards or using long-haul commuter buses like taxis on suburban cul-de-sacs!

Even more infuriating was to see the effect of the Satmar's fulminations on the secular or Christian members of the community. Any self-respecting liberal would be terrified by such accusations of anti-Semitism and would have no idea how to proceed—which is presumably just what the Satmar wanted.

Ann recalls talking to one of the political leaders of the Satmar about the bus problem on her street. "I went up to him very quietly—he was in the back watching or directing the meeting—and I asked, 'How come you can't compromise, use smaller buses? Why does it have to be these gigantic buses?' And he told me, 'Because we get these buses for free from the government.'" They were surplus retired buses from larger municipalities.

As the Satmar population grew—and it grew rapidly, both from a high birth rate and a high influx from Brooklyn—so grew the influence of the Satmar in local elections. This is natural in a democracy, of course, but Ann and other like-minded citizens in Monroe felt that the Satmar had purchased a double standard with their votes. They noticed that the town council looked the other way whenever a Satmar failed to follow "ordinary" rules of suburban life, whether it was putting the wrong kind of trash out on the wrong day or failing to seek approval for remodeling or drilling wells. "All we wanted was for them to follow the rules," she recalls, "but there were never any consequences. And they just kept growing!"

Ironically, it is the complaint against their growth that the Satmar found most difficult to understand: the *point* of Satmar organization is to increase the number of Satmar Jews. Hasidic culture simply lacks any pejorative connotation to population growth. Positive, even divine, associations with genetic expansion go back to the biblical era, to the foundational covenant with Abraham.

Of course the Satmar were interested in the low crime and larger houses that living in the suburbs afforded them, but they didn't seem to associate those things with all the other principles of suburban planning. Since they have virtually no crime within their community (or, perhaps more accurately, no reported crime; the sect deals with its troublemakers on its own terms), the Satmar didn't understand how they could be seen as bad neighbors. Suburban aesthetics—timely trash disposal, taking deed restrictions seriously, controlling development—simply meant nothing to most of them.

Community leaders prepared to take the Satmar community to court, but a funny thing happened on the way to the courthouse.

Under an obscure provision in the New York State statutes, any group of people who live contiguously can band together and declare themselves a village when they reach a population of 500. In 1977, when the Satmar community grew to 525 people, they did just that, naming their new development Kiryas Joel. Instantly, a brand-new village— one in which virtually every single resident was aligned with a single religious sect with a very specific agenda—appeared on the map. The implications were clear: villages have their own mayors, the power to tax and spend, and the authority to establish their own zoning regulations and building codes. The ordinances and rules of the surrounding town no longer necessarily applied. The Satmar were now free to build just about anything they wanted, any way they wanted.

The citizens of Monroe felt bullied, cheated, hoodwinked, abused, and angry.

Very, very angry.

Although the residents of Monroe had heard of Rebbe Teitelbaum, few had seen him. In 1979, just two years after the village was incorporated, Teitelbaum died. More than a hundred thousand Jews are said to have attended his funeral. To this day, if you ask just about anyone in town about the Satmar, they will respond with some version of what happened when the rebbe died. They'll tell you that there were so many cars and buses that mourners could not find parking places, so they simply left their cars on the highways and walked. Some will give hugely inflated numbers: up to two hundred thousand mourners—every Orthodox Jew in the eastern United States!

In any case, the grandness was a sign of respect to the great rebbe but also a commemoration of Rebbe Teitelbaum as a symbol for something more than himself. His was the passing of one of the last great scholars in the old tradition, someone who had been born and grew to manhood in the nineteenth century, who had seen Eastern European

Jewry at the height of its sophistication as a civilization, and who had not only survived the Holocaust but also personally sown the seeds for the incredible rebirth of that civilization in outposts scattered throughout the West and the Levant. More than anything that had led up to it, the observances of the grand rebbe's passing impressed upon the suburbanites of Orange County the magnitude of both the Satmar community and the Satmar's plans for Kiryas Joel.

After the grand rebbe's burial in Kiryas Joel, the village's population continued to soar, but the tensions between the communities settled somewhat. There were occasional blow-ups—especially when the Satmar bought and annexed a second large parcel of land. Ann Krawet and some of her friends from the town council and the Reform synagogue started Save Monroe, an organization dedicated to forcing the town leaders to hold the Satmar to the laws of the land; a village, though it enjoys considerable autonomy, it is still part of a town. "All we wanted," she remembers, "is that the rules be applied to everyone the same. But no matter what, whenever the town tried to hold the Satmar to the rules, they reacted as if they were being punished for being Satmar. I mean, hello, how can it be anti-Semitism when all anyone is asking is for you to obey the law?"

Save Monroe had some early successes by publicizing some of the more blatant abuses. For instance, the Monroe council agreed to enforce a town-wide ban on oversized vehicles on suburban streets. The victory, however, was short lived, as the Satmar realized that the ban did not apply to municipal vehicles, and—sure enough—buses are municipal vehicles.

In time, the Satmar adopted a more tactical approach—due in no small measure to the emergence of Abraham Wieder as the key temporal leader of Kiryas Joel.

Elected mayor and head of the United Talmudic Academy (the

organization in charge of the yeshivas in both Kiryas Joel and Williamsburg), Wieder was a very smart, politically savvy man. He saw
the mistakes that the Satmar had made in the early clashes with the
community, and he preferred to work behind the scenes, using the
overwhelming and undeniable demographics of his community to get
what he wanted.

In the 1970s Wieder had bought Monroe Wire and Cable, an old
wire-manufacturing company, and set about transforming it into a
powerhouse of military contracting. By the mid-1980s Monroe Wire
and Cable was benefitting from the largesse of major US Navy contracts
(including the contract to produce wires for nuclear submarines), and
the Satmar had been placed on the affirmative action fast track for
military contract bids (by President Ronald Reagan, at the behest of
New York senator Al D'Amato and local congressman Ben Gilman, the
chair of the House of Representatives Committee on Foreign Relations).
With this political assistance, Abe Wieder became the largest employer
and wealthiest person in the Satmar community.

He was also far too sophisticated, and connected, for Save Monroe
to handle. No matter how much attention Ann and her group drew to
the double standard in Monroe or the blindness of the town council
in the face of blatant rule-breaking by the Satmar, nothing seemed to
change. Once every few years, Save Monroe would shame the town into
passing an ordinance or enforcing a zoning rule, but as soon as a single
Satmar was held accountable, members of the town council would be
replaced or would mysteriously change their votes at the next election,
and it would be back to business as usual. Kiryas Joel was growing fast,
it voted as a bloc, and now in Abraham Wieder it had a leader who
knew exactly how to exploit those advantages.

By the late 1980s the Satmar were approaching the ability not only
to control a majority of the town council and a local assembly district (sending a friendly non-Hasidic member to the state legislature
in Albany) but also to heavily influence the local state senate seat. Only

a few short years after the village was established, Kiryas Joel had the votes and know-how to influence both local and state politics.

Many local residents began to believe that the state, county, and town government officials gave the sect whatever they wanted, including the attendant funding. As Lagakos, the diner owner, puts it, "It's this way. They go to the politicians and say, 'We have this many votes and we want such and such. Is it yes or no?' And for them, the answer is *always* 'Yes.'"

2

WHO MOVES IN?

I contemplate with sovereign reverence that act of the whole American people which declared that their legislature should "make no law respecting an establishment of religion, or prohibit the free exercise thereof," thus building a wall of separation between church and state.

—Thomas Jefferson

TO MALKA SILBERSTEIN, whose family had been Satmar for at least four generations, the laws of her faith were not a burden at all but a wonderful, magical blessing, a code of honor that she proudly observed.

True, the sect strictly adhered to the six-hundred-plus commandments of Jewish observance and obediently followed laws governing everything from diet to sexuality to keeping the Sabbath. True, that strict adherence separated the Satmar from the Reform and Conservative branches of Judaism. True, the group's anti-Zionist stance further distanced them from the other descendants of Abraham. But it was exactly that uniqueness, that collective spirit, that allowed the Satmar, nearly destroyed by the Holocaust, not only to survive but to thrive and to rebuild their community on another continent. Malka's own parents were Holocaust survivors.

In her faith, Malka found a joy and unity with God that she loved to share with her family and her community, reveling in the opportunity to devote her life to raising Hasidic children in concert with rules and traditions laid down thousands of years before and interpreted by the great Rebbe Joel Teitelbaum.

Malka Silberstein, who grew up in Williamsburg, Brooklyn, in the same neighborhood and on the same block where her parents had lived after they fled Europe in the wake of World War II, had a dozen children, the last one born in 1982 when she was in her early thirties. When the grand rebbe first moved to Kiryas Joel, she remembers envying the early colonists who moved up there with him. But Malka and her husband weren't quite ready to uproot their family and venture outside the Williamsburg cocoon that constituted their entire universe; neither of them had ever spent more than a weekend away from their Brooklyn neighborhood. Although in the 1970s and '80s New York City was growing increasingly dangerous and seemed poorly managed, and popular American culture was becoming much more difficult to suppress, the prospect of leaving their tiny, cramped, urban cosmos was daunting.

Her daughter Sheindle made the difference.

The last of the Silbersteins' children, Sheindle has Down syndrome, a condition not that unusual among the Satmar, who, because they regularly marry within the sect and also regularly bear children well into their forties, experience a high rate of developmental disabilities—including not only Down syndrome but also deafness. The Satmar had made little progress in integrating their disabled members into society. When one's place in the community is all important and that place depends on demonstrations of piety, and piety depends on practicing and understanding a complex and ancient tradition, there's not much of a framework for dealing with the needs of those who suffer disabling conditions.

Even so, Malka desperately wanted Sheindle to be part of their community—the only community her family knew, the only community they understood. At first, she simply longed to bring Sheindle with her to weddings, but fearing the gossip often typical of such an extraordinarily tight-knit community, she was reluctant to do so on her own. So she gathered a group of other mothers of children with disabilities who agreed to bring their kids to important events and parties.

Although this was real progress, it wasn't enough to overcome the obstacles facing Sheindle—the biggest of which was school. The Satmar in Williamsburg, eager to ensure that outside cultural elements not spoil the purity of the Hasidic experience, sent their boys to receive an education that consisted almost entirely of Torah study in private yeshivas and the girls to special private academies to learn the things necessary for their lives as mothers and homemakers in the community. But children with severe disabilities might be unable to grasp the Torah or master the art of being a good Hasidic woman.

Simultaneously, beginning in the mid-1970s, state and federal education officials were enforcing new federally mandated requirements for special education, requiring that children like Sheindle receive appropriate schooling at substantial public expense. New York had enacted its legislation in 1976, and I was part of the team that had drafted the legislation as a representative of then secretary of state Mario Cuomo. In late 1977 I was offered the position of "assistant commissioner of education for the education of children with handicapping conditions." I was the third person to hold the position, and my mandate was to enforce the new legislation. In accordance with the new laws, we curtailed funding for seventy-five of the three hundred private schools serving severely disabled children with tax dollars, and moved five thousand children with disabilities from the public schools to less restrictive learning environments. We also engaged in a huge crackdown on the New York City school system to ensure adequate services for children with special needs.

Malka was encouraged but also troubled—eager for anything that would promote the growth and development of Sheindle and others like her, yet very mindful that in a public school, these children would surely be exposed to the perceived corrupting influences of American society. They would discover the existence of rock stars, junk food, animated superheroes, and all the trappings of popular culture. Nevertheless, the Silbersteins and other parents reluctantly agreed to give it a try, and with considerable trepidation they sent their special needs children to New York City public schools to receive the education they needed and deserved, while struggling to keep the outside influences at bay.

But it was unworkable, as Sheindle found it impossible to live in two diametrically opposed cultural worlds. What was exciting and interesting at school was taboo at home; what was expected and normal at home was foreign and unintelligible to the non-Satmar children at school. Sheindle and other Satmar children with disabilities were now overwhelmed by the prospect of adjusting to two quite different ethoses.

Then, in the mid-1980s, Malka learned that Kiryas Joel was planning to open a private school that would serve the disabled children of the village. It seemed like the perfect solution to her problems. At a private Satmar school, Sheindle would receive the government-mandated education without being tainted or taunted by American culture.

The Silbersteins decided to move. They bought a home in the newly developed village of Kiryas Joel. It seemed a godsend. Vistas of the Catskills replaced the Brooklyn cityscape outside their kitchen window. Their children went off each and every morning to the yeshivas or girls' institutes, and the Silbersteins were at last able to rest easy. In all probability, their children would not have to see or be seen by a single non-Satmar child in their new community. They would never again pick up a USA Today they found on a bus, or come home with the words of a crass popular song spewing from their innocent lips. Questions that should not be asked or answered would not be asked or answered. And Sheindle would be safe and secure, embraced with the opportunity to become all that God would enable her to become.

But it never came to be.

The leaders of Kiryas Joel came to the realization that special education is extraordinarily expensive, far too costly for this tiny village to fund and support. Besides, the residents of the village were already paying school taxes to the local Monroe-Woodbury Central School District, and both state and federal law made abundantly clear that children, even those enrolled in private schools, are entitled to special education services. It was the district's responsibility and obligation to provide for these children.

Monroe-Woodbury recognized its obligation, and for a short while sent its teachers to Kiryas Joel to provide special education services at an annex to Bais Rochel ("House of Rachel"), the girls' school in the village, named after a prominent biblical figure. That worked well enough, but only for about a year until 1985, when the US Supreme Court held in *Aguilar v. Felton** and *School District of the City of Grand Rapids v. Ball*† that sending public school teachers into private schools violated the Constitution.

That left the Monroe-Woodbury school board in a bit of a bind. The school district had to raise taxes every year to make ends meet, and its constituents were growing angry and less inclined to divert funds they thought should be spent on their own children to provide special accommodations for a small, aloof minority group that didn't want

---

* In *Aguilar v. Felton*, 473 US 402 (1985), the US Supreme Court ruled against, as a violation of the First Amendment, a New York City program in which public school teachers were sent to parochial schools to provide remedial education services to disadvantaged children. The court found that the program violated the constitutional bar on excessive church-state entanglement. *Aguilar* was later overruled in *Agostini v. Felton*, 521 US 203 (1997).

† In *School District of the City of Grand Rapids v. Ball*, 473 US 373 (1985), the Supreme Court held that state aid to religious schools violates the Establishment Clause when it has the primary effect of advancing religion.

anything to do with them anyhow. In the minds of many, the leaders of Kiryas Joel pushed their luck a little too far when they insisted not only that the public school district educate their special needs children in private schools but that they do so in Yiddish.

On the other hand, Kiryas Joel—or "KJ," as it was becoming known to outsiders—was something of a cash cow and powder keg all in one. It provided millions of dollars in tax revenue to Monroe-Woodbury while costing the district relatively little. The school board did provide busing for the five thousand Satmar children, but the vast majority of them were educated by the United Talmudic Academy and Bais Rochel, both of which operated schools at several sites throughout the village. And, critically, the village was growing to the point where the leaders could muster a voting bloc that just might shoot down any budget presented and oust the members of the school board. That had happened before in communities with large Hasidic and ultra-Orthodox populations, including the town of East Ramapo in nearby Rockland County, and it was apparent that the leaders of KJ were quite willing to exert their voting bloc power.

The inevitable standoff had nearly come to a head the year before, when Abe Wieder confronted the school board, introducing himself as mayor of the village of Kiryas Joel, pointedly reminding the board members of the district's legal responsibility to provide transportation for the Satmar children—and then asserting that the KJ children could not be driven by bus drivers of the opposite sex. Wieder insisted that the boys not be subjected to or exposed to women operating such vehicles.

"None of our children can ride in a bus driven by a woman," Wieder told the school board. "Women do not drive in our community. At all. We do not want our children to think it is all right or even possible for women to drive machines like that."

The board initially considered compromise.

"Well . . . could we maybe put a curtain around the bus drivers so they wouldn't be seen?" one of the school board members asked.

Abe rejected the idea out of hand, along with every other suggestion, and the community was infuriated. The notion that a sect whose
children were getting free busing to private schools could dictate the
gender of publicly employed bus drivers was beyond the pale. But the
school board was able to duck the issue: the contract with the bus drivers' union allowed the drivers to choose their routes by seniority; ironically, all of the senior bus drivers were female, and they all had chosen
KJ routes. "You'll have to take it up with the union."

And Wieder did just that, challenging the union all the way to New
York's highest court—and losing resoundingly every step of the way.
Ultimately, the male students would begin walking to school rather
than riding in buses driven by women.

The 1985 US Supreme Court decisions rekindled the tensions,
especially after the school board refused to accommodate the Satmar
children with special needs anywhere other than in the local public
school. Abe, whose daughter was deaf and in need of special services,
went back to court, attempting to force the district to educate KJ's disabled children at a segregated facility in the village. Monroe-Woodbury
could have done that. In 1988 the New York Court of Appeals ruled
that while the district did not have to provide the accommodations Abe
demanded, it could do so if it wished. But the school board was fed up
with Abraham Wieder and, by this point, was spoiling for a fight that
it desperately hoped would be over before the Satmar had enough votes
to wrest control of the entire school district.*

---

* To this day, Kiryas Joel is viewed suspiciously by many of its neighboring residents
in Orange County, who have long suspected that the community routinely games the
system. For instance, in 2011 the *New York Times* reported that according to census
figures, Kiryas Joel is the poorest municipality in the United States, where 70 percent of
the residents claim to live below the poverty line and half the inhabitants receive food
stamps. Yet they used their political clout to obtain $10 million for a "luxurious" postna-
tal maternal care facility where women can recuperate for two weeks after giving birth.
To many critics, the members of the sect, through self-dealing and outright deception,
avail themselves of numerous benefits at public expense. William Helmreich, a sociology
professor at City College specializing in Judaic studies, told the *Times*, "I cannot say as

Meanwhile, Malka Silberstein was torn. She loved the isolation of Kiryas Joel and the cultural sanctuary it provided for her family. But they had moved to KJ for Sheindle, and it appeared that the only way the girl would receive the education and services she would need to be a content and contributing member of her community was to enroll in the local public school. Reluctantly, the Silbersteins and the parents of a dozen other special needs children sent them to Monroe-Woodbury.

The result was disastrous.

Not only were the children exposed to cultural shock, they were teased, goaded, ridiculed, and humiliated. Some of the staff, through indifference, resentment, or almost unimaginable ignorance, were incredibly insensitive. There was a feeling that the community was taking out its frustration with the Satmar on the children it was meant to be educating.

"They would go out to lunch at McDonald's, and our children are not supposed to eat at McDonald's," Malka told the *San Francisco Chronicle*. "My daughter's retarded. How can I explain to her that eating kosher is very important to us?"

One day in the fall of 1989, Malka was at the school for a meeting with school administrators when she made an unannounced visit to Sheindle's classroom. There she saw the students rehearsing for a Christmas pageant, and all their attention was focused on one child decked out in antlers and a big red nose while the other kids pointed and laughed, mockingly singing "Rudolph the Red-Nosed Reindeer." It was Sheindle.

And it was the last straw.

"My child was learning about pagan and Christian holidays," Malka complained. "My child could not be part of our family, she could not be part of our community, she was not here and not there."

a group that they are cheating the system, but I do think they have, no pun intended, an unorthodox way of getting financial support." See Sam Roberts, "A Village with the Numbers, but Not the Image, of the Poorest Place," *New York Times*, April 20, 2011.

Within days of Malka Silberstein's witnessing her daughter sub-jected to this humiliation, the rage of the Satmar had spread to much of the Hasidic and Orthodox community in New York State. The outcry had been heard by the governor and senators, by congressmen and mayors. And the town of Monroe, a town that had survived about eight wars, four monarchs, and forty presidents, was facing demographic and budgetary Armageddon.

Naturally, the Silbersteins first turned to Abe Wieder with their prob-lems. As horrified as Wieder was to learn of the Rudolph incident, he seemingly grasped its political utility. Wieder was the go-to guy for dealing with the multitude of governmental officials within the state and, indeed, at the federal level. For almost ten years he had been one of the leading men in Kiryas Joel. Wieder had developed a business with a nationwide reputation and had important government connections. He learned from the battles over zoning issues and pushed for the creation of the village as a solution to those problems. He spent the better part of four years in a losing fight with the Monroe school district, first over busing and then the location of special education services, battles in which he had relied entirely on the US legal system. Wieder had come to believe that all of the issues faced by KJ—from busing, to care for the disabled population, to zoning disputes—came down to one thing: freedom of religion. It seemed, perhaps because the religious life and culture of the Satmar are inseparable, that he could not easily distin-guish between the right to freedom of religion and the more theoretical concept of separation of church and state. Nor did he try.

Wieder viewed every attempt to thwart the growth of Kiryas Joel and the public funding of its services as either a denial of the right to freedom of religion or an expression of anti-Semitic bias. When the town said that a single-family home could not include second cousins or that city-style housing could not be built under rural zoning laws,

Wieder saw anti-Semitism. When the town refused to provide only male drivers on buses carrying male students, he saw a denial of freedom of religion. When the school district refused to teach KJ's disabled children at a site in KJ, he saw both. Look at the Saint Nicholases in the schools! Look at the Christmas stories they read in grade school. If the Christian children could run around shoving store-bought *Saint Valentine's Day* cards into heart-decorated boxes on their classmates' desks, how dare anyone question his right to a simple thing like male bus drivers! There was little question in his mind about what constituted religious discrimination.

It's easy to deride the inability of the Satmar to see what has long been obvious to most Americans (including American judges): Rudolph the Red-Nosed Reindeer, Santa Claus, and Saint Valentine are expressions of secular American culture, their religious or semireligious roots all but obliterated by department store razzle-dazzle. But the propriety of Christian symbols or the appearance of the word "God" in or on various public instruments is a two-sided coin. It forces us to acknowledge that there is no neutral cultural ground: religious sentiment is so integral to Western culture that expressions, symbols, and images of religion are inescapable. To those who care, no matter what their religious beliefs happen to be, this is serious stuff. On the flip side, it's frivolous, because not only can nothing be done about it but the offense caused by religious references in the Pledge of Allegiance, holiday decorations, and the presence of "God" on money is perceived by many to be so insignificant (and, from a legal perspective, "ceremonial" rather than spiritual) that only a publicity hound or a zealot would haul the government into court over such issues. Yet the court system has spent an enormous amount of time trying to figure out how many angels are dancing on the heads of these pins.

Wieder was staunchly protective of his community—especially its children, especially after the reindeer incident. But the courts had disappointed him in the past, and Wieder didn't want to waste his time with another lawsuit. Rather, on the advice of other leading Satmar, he turned to the politicians who had come through for him in the past. His assistant dialed, in quick succession, Congressman Ben Gilman; local state senator Art Gray (the first Democrat elected in the area since the Civil War, who slipped into office when his predecessor was thrown in jail for corruption); George Pataki, Kiryas Joel's assemblyman in Albany; George Shebitz, Abe's politically connected lawyer; and Roberta Murphy, the president of the Monroe-Woodbury school board. A meeting was scheduled for the following day at Roberta Murphy's home.

Everyone knew that Roberta was a potent force. Since the Monroe-Woodbury school board was one of the more active boards in the state, she was well known among education professionals throughout New York. Murphy's reputation rested largely on her indifference to the distinguishing characteristics of the national parties and her obvious enthusiasm for brass-knuckled local politics, which had carried over from her formative years spent in Brooklyn. Roberta approached school board elections with a seriousness that major parties rarely gave to even congressional elections, fervently parsing the sub-sub-microtrends of suburban Orange County by households.

Once everyone had assembled on the back deck of Murphy's cedar-sided house, lawyer George Shebitz, speaking for Wieder, explained that Kiryas Joel wanted an immediate political solution to settle all current and future disputes within the Monroe-Woodbury school district over school budgets, special education, and busing. Shebitz reminded everyone how such disputes had turned his own school district, East Ramapo, into a virtual war zone between the Orthodox community and the board of education. The Monroe-Woodbury superintendent, Daniel D. Alexander, had previously been an assistant superintendent in East Ramapo, and was quite familiar with the threats that Shebitz was subtly articulating.

Alexander had a solid career in educational administration and was well known and highly regarded statewide, deemed a growing force by the state education officials. When he was at East Ramapo, ultra-Orthodox Jews had moved into the community in large numbers and begun demanding more and more funding for their children, who were mainly educated in yeshivas. When the school district, which was one of the largest and most successful in the state, resisted, the Hasids joined with the ultra-Orthodox to defeat a series of school district budget votes. They also began running candidates for the East Ramapo school board and eventually got the majority, which shifted resources to the private yeshivas. The East Ramapo school district morphed from a coherent, thriving school district to a cauldron of religious controversies.

Alexander had written his doctoral dissertation on the Ramapo situation and was determined to prevent history from repeating itself in Monroe-Woodbury.

Murphy doubted that the Monroe community was willing to give an inch on any of Wieder's concerns, despite the threat KJ voters posed to the school budget. The congressman and the state legislators debated a variety of possible options, from Albany or Washington, to little effect. There was some discussion of asking the state education department to intervene, using its significant power to enforce education laws and regulations (when I was the assistant commissioner in the department, we had actively intervened to secure student services that a district refused to provide). But no one thought the administrative route would work. The group, it seemed, had no answers.

And then, George Pataki had a brainstorm.

When he was the mayor of Peekskill, a small city in Westchester County, Pataki had been frustrated by the fact that the school district boundaries didn't match the political district lines in the area. Because different parts of the city belonged to different school districts, Pataki had a difficult time addressing the interests and complaints of constituents—to say nothing of ensuring consistent standards throughout the city. He helped introduce several measures designed to change the school district borders so that all Peekskill schools would be within one district contained within the city's borders. Recalling this earlier solution to a similar problem, Pataki suggested that the Satmar ask Albany to draw a new school district coterminous with the village of Kiryas Joel. He didn't point out that no other village in the state had responsibility for educational services. Indeed, it was a responsibility not afforded to any county, town, or city, either—except for the school districts in the state's largest five cities (New York, Buffalo, Rochester, Syracuse, and Yonkers). The provision of education had always been kept separate from the politically responsive municipal jurisdictions, precisely to preserve the independence of educational decision making.

At first Pataki's idea was rejected outright, not only by Senator Gray, who thought it impractical, but also by Wieder, who was not keen on the idea of running a secular school district. Being forced to send special needs children to public schools was one thing, but being forced to conform to the state's decidedly secular curriculum was something else entirely. Wieder was not at all sure the village could run a school district and abide by the voluminous rules of state education law while still remaining true to Jewish law.

But the discussion was all about political expediency. Neither the First Amendment to the US Constitution nor the so-called Blaine Amendment* to the New York State Constitution ever came up;

---

* Many states, including New York, passed a "Blaine Amendment," named after former Speaker of the US House of Representatives and unsuccessful 1884 presidential candidate James Blaine, during a wave of anti-Catholic bigotry. Blaine could not persuade Congress to pass his amendment barring the use of government funds at "sectarian" schools (although he came within four votes), but dozens of states carried his torch. The New York State Constitution, as ratified in 1894 and amended in 1938, reads, "Neither the state nor any subdivision thereof shall use its property or credit or any public money, or authorize or permit either to be used, directly or indirectly, in aid or maintenance, other than for examination or inspection, of any school or institution of learning wholly or in part under the control or direction of any religious denomination or in which any denominational tenet or doctrine is taught, but the legislature may provide for the transportation of children to and from any school or institution of learning."

seemingly nobody gave a thought to whether the plan would violate church-state prohibitions.

Also absent from the discussion was the unmistakable fiscal impact on the Monroe-Woodbury district. Excising the village from the surrounding district was bound to result in a loss of millions of dollars of revenue. Under the current system, thousands of nondisabled students were being privately educated in the village at little cost to the district. If the village left the school district, the Satmar would no longer be paying property taxes to the Monroe-Woodbury district, and the state and federal aid generated by their presence in the district would be lost.

Nor did the group consider the state master plan for school districts, which had been adopted by the New York State Board of Regents, with legislative approval. This plan called for consolidation of existing districts, not the creation of new ones. The idea was to improve administration, as well as to provide more comprehensive educational services. Indeed, no new districts had been formed in decades.

As the afternoon wore on and nobody came up with a better idea, Pataki's plan became more and more appealing. By the end of the meeting, only Roberta Murphy remained uncommitted—because of reservations about whether the school board would back it. But Murphy had an ulterior motive. She knew that following the decennial redistricting coming up in 1990, a seat in the county legislature would be available, and she wanted it for herself. She was also certain that she could dominate the county as she dominated the school board.

When the meeting drew to a close and all but Wieder had left, a pact was made. Murphy reminded Wieder of all the power that comes with running a school district—the power to tax, the power to control staff and to some degree curricula, the power to control the bus and transportation funds for all of the students in the district, including those in private schools. And she mentioned to him that the county legislative lines would be redrawn after the upcoming redistricting, and wouldn't it be nice if there was a new district that encompassed only

Kiryas Joel and a few other homes—such as hers? Wieder was sold, and Murphy saw a bright political future in her tea leaves.*

All that remained was figuring out a way to make it happen in Albany.

And Pataki had a plan.

---

* Indeed, Murphy was eventually elected to the county legislature and rose to the chairmanship. She enjoyed the unbridled support of Kiryas Joel.

3

WHO GOVERNS?

Our history vividly illustrates that one of the specific evils feared by those who drafted the Establishment Clause and fought for its adoption was that the taxing and spending power would be used to favor one religion over another or to support religion in general.

—Chief Justice Earl Warren, *Flast v. Cohen**

I N THE 1980s, as today, the Williamsburg section of Brooklyn was a veritable melting pot, with enclaves of Italians, Dominicans, Puerto Ricans—and tens of thousands of Hasidic Jews of varying, and sometimes competing, sects. It remained a center of Satmar activity, and the sect's leaders exerted enormous influence there. But Joseph Lentol, the area's popular assembly representative, was a force himself;

---

* *Flast v. Cohen*, 392 US 83 (1968), was an important decision establishing that taxpayers have a right to bring a federal court action challenging an alleged violation of the Establishment Clause. The case arose because Congress had appropriated money to assist private and public schools, including parochial schools. In a concurrence, Justice Potter Stewart added, "Every taxpayer can claim a personal constitutional right not to be taxed for the support of a religious institution."

as Brooklyn's principled warrior for often-lost causes, he was their man in Albany.

By the end of the decade, Joe Lentol's district, which he had served faithfully since the early 1970s, was suffering. Decades of infrastructural isolation and dwindling manufacturing jobs had dealt a terrible blow: in 1961 the Williamsburg section alone had ninety-three thousand manufacturing jobs; by 1989 fewer than fifteen thousand remained. The economic collapse merged with a social collapse as AIDS and crack cocaine devastated the community. Joe did his part, bringing the bacon back from Albany, protecting what businesses he could, dealing with the specific local problems that occasionally arose, and, most of all, maintaining his position among the Brooklyn Democrats, which was so important to delivering to his constituents enough of a share of the ever-dwindling state coffers.

Lentol's ability to deliver was tied directly to his local connections. Being an assemblyman for Brooklyn meant being a Democrat, and being a Democratic politician in Brooklyn meant Lentol was part of the power structure. The Democrats might fight among themselves, but at the end of the day it was a Democrat, and only a Democrat, who prevailed. Occasionally, albeit quite rarely, a "reform" Democrat from outside the mainstream club would actually win an election, usually after the incumbent got indicted for something. But in general, the machine churned out, and kept in office, its own. And Lentol was one of its own.

One day in the summer of 1989, Joe arrived late at his office on the ground floor of a three-story tenement on Lorimar Street, across from the Catholic Veterans Society building and about thirty yards from the hulking swoop of the Brooklyn-Queens Expressway, the highway that in 1957 had cut his neighborhood in half. The office walls were a testament to the representation Joe had provided over the years. There were pictures of Joe with various governors and other political heavyweights, Joe with orphans, Joe with teachers, Joe with nuns, Joe with

Hasidic Jews . . . Joe took the coffee his secretary had prepared for him and told her that he expected some special visitors and was unavailable to talk to anyone else. He walked into his inner office, where he was soon joined by some men in black hats, men who, from what the assemblyman had heard, had been extremely busy in Albany and New York City throughout that hot and rainy August.

About a month earlier, Anthony Genovese, an assemblyman from Canarsie, Brooklyn, and leader of the most powerful Democratic club in the county, was driving through some foggy weather on his way back to Albany. The car raced easily up I-87 past the tattered remnants of East Coast agriculture and industry—half-suburbanized onion farms and poisoned river towns, which remained as yet untouched by the gentrification that would shortly ignite a frenzy of renovations throughout the Hudson Valley.

As his car passed through the northern reaches of Orange County, not far from the village of Kiryas Joel, Genovese thought long and deep about his curious meeting with Hasidic constituents the day before. At that meeting was a man who had come with an intriguing request, and Genovese instantly saw how the political angles fit together, and what they potentially spelled for his career.

Genovese was one of the most powerful politicians in New York, and 1989 was a big election year for him. He was one of Brooklyn political boss Meade Esposito's* "Green Berets," charged with enforcing the Brooklyn machine's will and using its power of persuasion on everyone from school principals to presidential candidates, getting them to toe the line and pay appropriate homage—and frequently kickbacks—to the local Democrats. But Esposito, who reigned over Brooklyn politics for a quarter century, was tainted. A year earlier, Esposito had

---

* Amadeo Henry Esposito was a onetime bail bondsman who wrested control of the Brooklyn Democratic club, delivered votes to Governor Nelson Rockefeller, advised Bobby Kennedy, and took full advantage of the favors he earned. He was convicted of graft in 1988 and died in 1993. See his *New York Times* obituary, September 14, 1993.

been convicted in an influence-peddling scandal, and Genovese and the other generals of the Brooklyn Democratic army were vying for control of the clubhouse. They well knew the cost of loyalty: patronage.

For much of the twentieth century, New York was under the control of a series of powerful governors. Al Smith, Franklin Roosevelt, and Tom Dewey all won their national party's nomination for president. Averell Harriman ran in several presidential primaries, narrowly losing to Adlai Stevenson twice. Nelson Rockefeller, who was and still is arguably the most powerful governor in New York history, became vice president in the Ford administration.

Richard Nixon once said that Rockefeller was among a very small handful of people in American politics—including, of course, himself—who really understood the use of power. And like no governor before or since, Rockefeller treated the New York State Legislature like a wholly owned subsidiary. He got what he wanted, and he bought legislative support by sending pork to his friends. And when a politician is as unabashedly ambitious as Nelson Rockefeller, *everyone* is his friend. Unlike other governors, his ability to deliver was not constrained by the state treasury. He could and would reach into the family fortune when necessary.

But if "Rocky" was the most prominent of New York's buy-the-legislature governors, he was also the last. A period of fiscal austerity and near bankruptcy began in the 1970s, just as Rockefeller was leaving office, and since that time there has never been enough money for a governor to buy the rest of the government with pork and patronage. Failing cities fought for the remaining scraps of state funding as the big corporations that had defined New York business for a century—and had paid for a large portion of the politicians' largesse—left the state. Huge employers up and went. Governors, even Rockefeller, didn't have the money to buy off, or scare off, legislators, and the legislature began to flex its muscle.

Simultaneously, the character of the legislature was changing. Once a part-time job for farmers and others who would devote a few months a year to the people's business before heading home, the legislature had essentially become a full-time occupation for lawyers and others who dabbled in their profession while spending more and more time, and more and more capital, on politics.

Party leaders in the legislature, who controlled fundraising and the distribution of party funds to local election campaigns, used that power to build lockstep coalitions. Anyone who ventured out of line would not only lose party campaign funds but also see his or her district cut off from government projects. The Democrats were in control of the New York State Assembly, the lower house of New York's bicameral legislature, leveraging the plurality of seats from Brooklyn into control of New York City, and leveraging control of New York City into control of the state assembly. The Democratic majority in the assembly was often so numerically superior that it could, whenever the Speaker wanted, override a gubernatorial veto. So the Speaker had enormous power, sometimes more than the governor himself.

Meanwhile, the Republicans solidified control of the New York State Senate with a coalition of upstate and Long Island conservatives. That left one house of the legislature in control of entrenched Democrats and the other in control of entrenched Republicans. The status quo became all-important in a devil-you-know way, and the two houses traded gerrymandering favors to ensure the incumbents in both houses and both parties would retain their seats in perpetuity. Each party in each house carefully avoided the chaos of democracy by selecting leaders who could control their members through lucrative committee assignments and the distribution of pork to their district. They had learned something from Nelson Rockefeller.

In short, the Speaker of the Assembly became the most powerful Democrat in a Democratic state. But that power depended on the support of the rank and file assembly members. For twenty-five years, the Brooklyn Democratic leader had been the power behind the throne, the one person who could herd the cats of the party conference and ensure their support of the Speaker. But there were changes playing out in the Brooklyn leadership, creating a void that Tony Genovese planned to fill.

And so in 1989 Genovese was driving to Albany and pondering the peculiar request—or demand, really—of the man with the black hat, the long beard, and a presence that suggested he was used to getting his way. On the surface, the Hasidic man had no leverage to demand anything. The people he represented were few in number. They had no money to speak of, no connection to the Democratic Party, and they lived a hundred miles from Tony's Brooklyn district. But the Satmar understood power politics in a way that would have delighted Rockefeller, and they voted in a bloc. And in Brooklyn, that bloc could deliver around fifty thousand votes in a primary and virtually control an election.

Tony had recently visited several Hasidic communities in Brooklyn, hoping to secure their vote for his candidate for New York City comptroller, Frank J. Macchiarola, the former New York City Schools chancellor. Genovese had a stake in the election because the comptroller has the power to audit every public official and every dollar spent in the city, and having a "team player" in that position—someone who owed him something—would be useful as he solidified his power. The Satmar Hasidim in Brooklyn agreed to support Macchiarola, on one condition: that Genovese help pass Assembly Bill 183. Though Genovese knew nothing about the bill, he promised to support it wholeheartedly and do what he could to get it through the legislature.

Genovese arrived in Albany and headed directly to a meeting with George Pataki, the young, ambitious, and popular Republican assemblyman from Peekskill whose district included parts of Orange County. Pataki, it seemed, was the man behind the request that had put all of New York's bosses into an uncustomary position. Under normal circumstances, Genovese would barely acknowledge the existence of a junior Republican lawmaker in a chamber controlled by senior Democratic lawmakers. But Pataki's office in the state capitol was close to Genovese's, and they had become friends.

A second-generation Hungarian American, George Elmer Pataki is an American success story. Pataki's father, Louis Pataki, was a mailman in Peekskill and, of course, wanted his children to benefit as much as possible from the opportunities in America. When George's older brother was admitted to Yale, it seemed as if the father's dream had come true, except the acceptance came with no money. Tuition at Yale, even in the days before the outrageous inflation of recent decades, was far too steep for a mailman. Distraught, Louis Pataki visited the local school principal, who told him, "Whatever it takes, you send your kid to Yale."

So, George Pataki remembers, "what my father did was leave work at the post office and went up to Yale in his mailman's uniform and sat outside the admissions office. The receptionist asked if he had an appointment, to which, of course, the answer was no. 'Well, why are you here?' And my father said, 'I want to talk to the admissions officer.'

"He waited all day until they finally let him go in and talk to the admissions officer. He showed the officer the acceptance letter and said, 'I thought people at Yale are supposed to be smart. Well, you accepted my son to Yale, which means, I assume, you want him to go here. You know I'm a mailman and what I earn and you didn't give him a scholarship. Now, how can you accept somebody that he can't go here? You're supposed to be smart.' And the guy was just blown away by my father's working-class logic and called the Westchester Alumni Association, because Peekskill is in Westchester, and said, 'You gotta raise the money for this Pataki kid.' And they wrote the check to Yale so that my brother could go."

Until his brother found his way into the Ivy League, George had been planning on going to Notre Dame. But George admired his brother and was determined to follow his footsteps. After graduating from Yale, he entered Columbia Law School. The combination of his middle-class upbringing and elite education left Pataki with a working-class bonhomie tempered by Ivy League civility.

Pataki had parlayed his charm, cleverness, and intelligence into a political career. He became mayor of Peekskill but was looking beyond the borders of the small city. He got himself elected to the New York State Assembly, but as a Republican in a regime controlled by Democrats, he was powerless; Republicans in the assembly are lucky to even discover what the legislature's agenda is, much less have the opportunity to advance any bills of their own. Pataki had no chips, but he did have an ace in the hole—and that ace was a little village in his assembly district: Kiryas Joel.

Pataki knew the Satmar voted as a bloc, and that the little enclave in his district was an entrée into the much larger enclave in Brooklyn. If he could influence the Brooklyn Satmar, he could influence the state's Democratic stronghold, and begin making a mark. The Satmar had strategically positioned themselves as the swing vote in Republican Orange County and a major force in Democratic Brooklyn. They had no loyalty to either political organization or to any political philosophy.* Their sole, unapologetic calculus was and is who could get them what they wanted.

Pataki's chance came in the late summer of 1989.

The Satmar of Kiryas Joel needed help. If Pataki could deliver, and the Satmar viewed him as a friend, he could establish a career-making alliance. The implications of a young, obscure Republican lawmaker from the hinterlands having the power to influence politics in the Democratic stronghold were profound, and immediately clear, for the ambitious politician.

---

* On the Kiryas Joel official website (www.kjvoice.com/faq.asp), it is stated, "The citizens of Kiryas Joel take their participation in the election process very seriously. As a community, they feel an obligation to show their appreciation for individuals who support the community or stand up for the issues and ideals shared by the residents. At times the community has supported Democrats and at other times Republicans, but have generally spoken with one voice to have the greatest impact. The community views voting as a privilege in this country and realizes the importance of electing officials who share their vision for family and community. The so-called 'bloc vote' that is manifested on Election Day in KJ is no different than the endorsement made by the teachers union or other labor organizations throughout the Country."

The Satmar grasped Pataki's idea and wanted an amendment to the state education laws that would allow Kiryas Joel to secede from the Monroe-Woodbury school district and create its own independent district, complete with the powers to tax and to place children in educational programs at government expense. Pataki was willing to support them, but as a minority lawmaker with no power and little ability to get legislation introduced, he needed a Democratic sponsor to carry his bill. He went to see Assemblyman Joe Lentol.

Lentol, with his huge Satmar constituency and every political incentive to ingratiate himself with the group, agreed to be the Democratic face for Pataki's bill, to sponsor the legislation. Thus was the Republican assemblyman from an upstate district able to introduce a bill in the city-dominated, Democratic-controlled New York State Assembly.

Passing it, however, would be another matter; even Lentol couldn't get it to the floor of the assembly for a vote without the permission of Mel Miller, a Brooklyn lawyer who succeeded the legendary Stanley Fink* as Speaker of the Assembly and, as such, was the most powerful person in the chamber. Nothing got to the floor for a debate without his approval, and when it did get to the floor there was no sense in debate, because his members would vote as told and the Republicans lacked the votes to do anything at all.

Miller exploited his power,† as he learned from Fink, by employing everything from arm-twisting to the invocation of curious procedural rights with which the members of the assembly had cloaked their

---

* Fink was the first modern Speaker of the post-Rockefeller era and defined the job for his successors, turning his maverick Democrats into a cohesive and formidable bloc.
† Miller was convicted of federal fraud charges (later overturned) in 1991. His successor, Saul Weprin, was succeeded by Sheldon Silver, who was convicted November 30, 2015, on federal honest services fraud, extortion, and money laundering charges. According to the Brennan Center for Justice at New York University School of Law, "The New York State legislature is nationally notorious for its dysfunction and subservience to special interests, who wield their power through campaign donations" (www.brennancenter.org/issues/new-york-reform).

leader. For instance, no bill can be voted on until it has been assigned a number. And since only the Speaker can assign a number, nothing gets voted on without his approval.

The Speaker of the Assembly has extraordinary power, but only as long as he keeps the majority of members happy. Maintaining the leadership position requires the Speaker to play ball with the most influential members of his caucus—people like Tony Genovese—because when the party conference gets an incentive, it can reject the Speaker and his agenda. In a sense, the Speaker functions as a funnel and filter, not unlike the committee system functions in Washington.

"The beauty of the leadership system," Miller explains, "is you can reconcile your conference, so it doesn't balkanize into warlord committees where a chair in one committee can control how you spend all your money because he controls the committee and there's nothing to rein him in. In a leadership system, if the head of a committee doesn't necessarily represent the views of all the Democratic members in this state, you don't have to leave the decision to a chairman. Instead, you're going to have a conference and let the chair advocate for his position, but at the end of the day, it's the conference and the Speaker that will make the decision."

Miller did not approve of the Pataki-Lentol bill and, normally, that would be the end of it. But this was not a normal situation. Miller knew the Satmar community was under the control of religious authorities. He knew that giving them a school district to run would violate the constitutional principle of separation of church and state. All of his attorneys told him so, and as a lawyer, he had no trouble grasping what was legally and constitutionally obvious. He felt strongly about the issue and was quite vocal.

But Pataki's brainstorm and his collaboration with Tony Genovese had seemingly yielded a have-your-cake-and-eat-it-too political bonanza. Pataki persuaded Genovese, and Genovese persuaded Miller, that there was next to no chance Governor Cuomo, the constitutional scholar, would sign the bill, and even if he did, the courts would provide cover by shooting it down. So they could collect all the political benefit of ushering the measure through the legislature and win the undying gratitude of the Satmar with a bill that had no chance of becoming law. Perfect!

"Look, I was sure it was not constitutional—facially, applied, whatever, it was not constitutional, but we looked at it again and I probably thought that we could get points for passing something, even though we should have been resolving it administratively," Miller recalls. "As sure as I'm sitting here, I thought it was going to be vetoed, and if not vetoed then knocked out by the courts. Sometimes you make these political calculations—it's just politics."

The bill was drafted hastily and with no input from the state education commissioner. Orange County assemblywoman Mary McPhillips, who went on to become a major political power in in the county, opposed the bill. It is extremely rare in Albany for a bill that has mainly local impact to be passed over the objections of a local assembly member. It is almost unheard-of that a bill would pass by an otherwise unanimous vote, with the sole dissent coming from the local legislator. There was almost no public discussion of the proposal, neither in Albany nor in the Orange County area. The bill passed 149–1 in the assembly and was buried in a large package of bills before the state senate.

In the waning hours of the last day of the legislative session, the senate approved the Pataki-Lentol bill with no fanfare, no publicity. The vast majority of state legislators had absolutely no idea what they were voting on.

Indeed, those of us who were closely following the bill did not know it was on the (largely hidden) agenda for a vote. I was awakened at 5 AM by staff who called to tell me it had been passed into law.

4

WHO EDUCATES?

There is one upstate place with a whole lot of clout in our region—the Village of Kiryas Joel. It votes as a bloc and wields that voting power like an electoral sledgehammer. But please don't blame Kiryas Joel for its clout. The folks there are doing what every district in our region would like to do. . . . They're using their political clout to get what they want.
> —Rep. Steve Israel, D-NY, chair of House Democratic
> Congressional Campaign Committee

WHEN I LEARNED that the legislation had been passed, I was flabbergasted, appalled—and a little chagrined and angry with myself. I had gravely miscalculated by viewing the bill as such a dead-on-arrival proposal that I really didn't take it seriously. I felt as if I'd dropped the ball as the executive director of the New York State School Boards Association and let my members down.

Further, on a personal level, I was deeply offended as a committed 1960s civil libertarian. I intensely believe in both desegregation and church-state separation. I had grown up in West Virginia and had lived in a district that desegregated only after the US Supreme Court forced it to with *Brown v. Board of Education* in the 1950s. I had been riveted to the news media during the battles to open southern schools. I went to college in Washington, DC, and sat in the US Senate galleries and watched the Humphrey-Russell debates that led to the Civil Rights Act of 1964. Probably more important, I was one of the few Jewish kids in a steel town in West Virginia, and I knew what it was like to be discriminated against in school due to one's religion. I understood how crucial it was to protect the right of all individuals to determine their own choices, and to not allow any group to make the determination for them.

The recently enacted legislation violated some of my core beliefs. It enabled a politically powerful group to determine that government funds could be spent to ensure that a religious group could be segregated from the broader community. I did not think it was relevant whether the source of the discrimination was outside that group or inside; the effect was the same.

I had left West Virginia and moved to New York to get away from actions that undermined desegregation and religious tolerance, and I was stunned that it was happening in New York, which I thought was the closest we had to a state that believed in the same things I did. I was especially shocked to see that this situation was being supported by both political parties and by a governor whom I revered.

As I pulled out of my driveway the morning after the vote, I began to work out a plan of action. It seemed obvious to me that the law violated the First Amendment to the US Constitution as well as the Blaine Amendment to the New York State Constitution. But the legal fight would come later, if necessary. First, I had to figure out the politics. How in the world had this stealth bill passed? It was my job as executive director of the School Boards Association to know the answer to things like that, and I didn't have it, yet. I had struggled to make the association a player in Albany politics, and I felt I had fumbled.

The New York State School Boards Association, founded in 1896, was a $5 million not-for-profit corporation run by an elected board of directors. It had a membership of about 750 school boards, representing almost five thousand individuals, equivalent to one-half of the elected officials of the state. Its members each had an equal voice on policy issues; each had one vote in a governing body. Thus, the smallest district had the same authority as New York City. The political power of the association was directly related to the relationships its members had with the legislature and the press. It made no political contributions.

Let me take a step back. In order to understand the politics of public education, it's necessary to understand that schools are essentially a business—a very, very big business.

New York State *alone* spends nearly $60 billion annually on education. That's nearly twice as much as Coca-Cola grosses worldwide. It's enough to buy every major league baseball franchise. And the education "industry" is loaded with tentacles and offshoots. Practically every kid in the country goes to school for ten or twelve years. Those kids go to school in buses owned by private contractors. They go to buildings built by private contractors and financed by public debt. They sit in chairs and at desks manufactured by private companies. They learn from things written on boards, projected on screens, printed into books, or accessed through computers—and all of those things were made by private companies. Millions of those kids are fed by private contractors with food supplied by other private companies (the contract to provide milk to a school district is enormous). The waste generated by those kids is carted off by private contractors. Those kids are taught by hundreds of thousands of professionals, all of whom make decent middle-class wages and most of whom have generous pension plans, more than eight weeks of vacation, and family health insurance, from which the insurance industry makes a handsome profit. The pension plans are serviced by powerful financiers. In other words, that little elementary school in your neighborhood may seem less complex than the million-square-foot corporation in the industrial park, but don't be fooled; it's part of a system that is every bit as complex, labyrinthine . . . and profitable.

Unlike other gigantic government programs, the cost of education is overwhelmingly raised and spent at the local level. In New York State, education funds are raised and distributed, more or less, at the discretion of school boards composed of people elected at what are supposed to be nonpartisan special elections. Being a school board member is not a full-time job, and none of the members are politicians in the ordinary sense. They think of themselves as members of the community since they do not run with political party labels like Republican or Democrat, and in fact are barred from doing so.

In my experience, most school board members conform to one of five distinct characters: Character 1 is just there to keep taxes low. Character 2 loves to hear him- or herself talk and to feel important. Character 3 thinks the school district ought to be teaching Mandarin Chinese and the details of Hiragana Buddhism to sixth graders, and that there should be a dressage team for ninth grade girls. Character 4 thinks the school should not teach students that animal species are created by a natural process of evolution. Character 5 is the parent of a child in a special population, and is there to assure that the child gets the services the parent thinks he or she needs. A school board contains people of several of these characters and attempts to come to a compromised consensus to keep the schools operating. So, while the individuals do unquestionably have competing agendas, the boards themselves are—theoretically, anyhow—there to advance a single agenda of advocating for schools and the kids.

When I took over the School Boards Association, it was a sleepy, poorly funded, poorly organized lobbying group that was forever steamrolled by the energetic, richly endowed, and brilliantly organized teachers' union. Three years later, we had some clout in Albany, frankly because we were learning how to use public opinion and the media to advance our agenda and obtain fairly widespread and penetrating coverage. We never could have bought such coverage through any sort of formal advertising or public relations campaign. But we still didn't have much money, certainly compared to our sometime adversaries in the teachers' union, so we had to pick and choose our fights strategically and judicially. When I first heard of the Pataki-Lentol bill, it appeared to be something the teachers' union would oppose, so I figured I'd let them fight that battle.

New York State United Teachers (NYSUT) was formed in the 1960s by Al Shanker and Tom Hobart to rectify the horridly inequitable pay scales and working conditions that were then in effect. It gained strength, power, and credibility after going on strike in New York City for several months and forcing the power brokers to play ball. And then it emerged as power broker in its own right. It became a major political campaign contributor, and not only in dollars and cents. It summoned thousands of teachers, through the largest phone bank in the state, to blast calls to lawmakers. It built a huge headquarters and hired hundreds and hundreds of people, all for the benefit of teachers (or, more accurately, their union).

The other major player in education politics was, of course, the New York State Education Department, overseen by the New York State Board of Regents, which dates back to 1794. Members of the board of regents are selected jointly by the two houses of the state legislature. It is the regents, not the governor, who appoint the education commissioner. Over the centuries, the board's power has increased substantially, and it now oversees all education from birth to death, vocational rehabilitation programming, museums and cultural institutions, and most licensed professions.

In light of the passage of the Kiryas Joel legislation, however, I felt that my association needed to take its own stance and abort this monstrosity before it was delivered. The governor hadn't signed the bill yet—nor was he likely to do so, I thought, as long as he knew what the bill was about. But I was also concerned about my board and membership, and how they would feel.

Of the approximately 750 school boards that belonged to the association, some were from tiny school districts like Raquette Lake with fewer than two dozen students, and some were from enormous districts like New York City, with well over a million students. As with most organizations of such diverse makeup, it was the middle-sized members that controlled the association—wealthy, suburban districts from places like Long Island and Orange County. In fact, Monroe-Woodbury was one of the association's most active members. I was concerned that the district might be in favor of the bill, because I knew that the non-Hasidic citizens in the area resented the Satmar and I could easily see the Monroe contingent selling out the Constitution in order to get the Satmar out of their hair, despite the loss of significant tax revenue. What's more, since I and several of the association's board members were Jewish, I was concerned about being accused of starting a religious dispute with the Satmar.

Even more important, I was unsure what to expect from two prominent and powerful members of my board, Judy Katz from suburban Buffalo and Georgine Hyde of East Ramapo. Judy was extremely active on a number of western New York and national Jewish not-for-profit boards, many of which might have problems with the School Boards Association being involved in a lawsuit involving Hasidic Jews. Georgine was a survivor of the Auschwitz and Theresienstadt concentration camps and was very active in state and national discussions on the impact of the Holocaust. She was also the longtime school board president of East Ramapo, the district that had suffered its own battles with an active Hasid and ultra-Orthodox community over school finances and priorities. I knew it would take yet another act of courage for Georgine to be supportive of litigation.

I arrived at my office at 119 Washington Avenue in a state of brain rush, but I had already formulated a few plans of attack. There was a message waiting for me on my desk: call Tom Hobart.

Hobart was not only the cofounder of the NYSUT but also its president. He was the grandson of Garret Hobart, President William McKinley's first vice president, who predeceased McKinley and was succeeded by Teddy Roosevelt, who in turn succeeded McKinley when the latter was gunned down in Buffalo. As a young man Tom Hobart, a political savant, arranged for the upstate teachers' association—a "professional organization" rather than a "union," largely because teachers at that time thought of themselves as "professionals" not in need of union protection—to merge with the NYC-based United Federation of Teachers, a union run by the brilliant labor organizer Albert Shanker.* With Hobart holding the political strings and Shanker organizing strikes, the newly created NYSUT won its first string of labor victories in the 1960s.

Then, a Republican state assemblyman from Long Island decided to test the teachers' newly discovered clout. He cut a deal with Governor Rockefeller over the budget, including a provision extending the probationary period for teachers from three to five years (meaning teachers would have to work five years for tenure rather than three). Hobart raised $150,000 overnight, offered the Republicans in Suffolk County $25,000 to oppose the assemblyman in the next primary, and knocked the incumbent out of the legislature.† If Hobart had previously made NYSUT an organization that politicians respected and took seriously, from that point forward it was a group to be feared. Nothing gives lawmakers more angst than the thought of an incumbent losing. Hobart's strategy was childishly simple: lavishly support every incumbent of both parties, but kill the career of anyone who gets out of line. I don't mean to say that he got everything he wanted (though he came close). But he was almost always able to derail any legislation the union opposed.

---

* Albert Shanker (1928–1997), a junior high math teacher from Queens whose mother was a labor activist, became the president of the United Federation of Teachers from 1964 to 1985 and led the American Federation of Teachers from 1974 to 1997. He was a legendary labor leader and activist who was posthumously awarded the Presidential Medal of Freedom by President Bill Clinton.
† The leader of the GOP was so shocked at the proposed payoff that he accepted "only" $20,000. In Albany, that passes for principle.

So, assuming that Hobart would oppose the Pataki-Lentol bill, and knowing that if he did it was a dead duck, I was not concerned. I reached Hobart in his office on Wolf Road, a suburban "miracle mile" of offices, shops, car dealerships, a mall, and restaurants just outside of Albany. After we commiserated with each other about the bill and agreed that it was totally unacceptable, Tom made a confession: he was uncharacteristically hamstrung and had relied on the assumption that I would oppose the bill. Although Tom didn't think much more of the bill than I did, his members in the Monroe-Woodbury area were passionately in favor. Ironically, since both of us assumed the other would oppose it, neither of us had done much of anything right away. But neither of us thought it was too late. Mario Cuomo was a friend, and his door was open to me. I was certain that the governor, as a committed constitutionalist, would see the glaring defects, and as a legal scholar, would realize what would obviously happen when it got to court. Just as important, Cuomo was a pragmatic politician.*

Back in 1974, when I was a fledgling public servant at the Office of Local Government (an agency created by Governor Rockefeller that was every bit as bureaucratic as it sounds), Hugh Carey, a Democrat, surprised everyone by winning the race for governor. The executive mansion had been dominated by the Republican Rockefeller from 1959 to 1973, but the labor-backed Carey (supported especially by the newly omnipotent NYSUT, without the help of which Carey could not have won) beat Rockefeller's chosen successor, Malcolm Wilson. Wilson had been an assemblyman from Westchester, and was lieutenant governor

---

* It was years before I learned that Cuomo was not only very familiar with the bill but that he had cut a deal with Hobart and the teachers' union, getting them to agree not to stand in its way. Hobart being Hobart opted to view the deal *literally*—oh, yes, he agreed that NYSUT wouldn't oppose it. But that didn't mean he couldn't encourage *me* to go to war against the governor, and he did just that.

when Rockefeller left. Because of the surprise victory, for a few days in Albany things were chaotic. The outgoing Republican governor had been so confident of victory that he had scheduled budget hearings for the next year to be held in the days following the election.

The governor's office, scrambling and embarrassed, invited Carey to send a representative to assist in the transition, but Carey didn't yet have any officially appointed representatives in Albany. At the suggestion of former New York City mayor Robert Wagner (whose son had become friendly with me while I was working on the mayor's New York State Commission on the Powers of Local Government), I was asked to attend the budget hearing on behalf of the new governor.

When I arrived, dozens of reporters and several TV cameras were expecting this unknown, twenty-nine-year-old bureaucrat to speak on behalf of Carey, but I explained that I had never met the new governor, was connected to the election only through having voted, and was there only because an adviser thought I could "keep my mouth shut and take notes." The next day the papers were abuzz with the story of "the first new Carey man to emerge." That was news to me, but within a few weeks I was asked by the new administration what I wanted as a reward for having worked on the transition team. I was interested in the gobbledygook of policy and wonk-like concepts such as "intergovernmental policy projects" and "local governance initiatives," and asked for such a position. The team looked at me with glazed eyes, suppressing yawns, and told me to report to my new boss, the freshly appointed secretary of state and the first real Carey man to emerge: Mario Matthew Cuomo. Cuomo had been the Democratic designee for lieutenant governor but was defeated by Mary Anne Krupsak. As something of a consolation prize, Carey, who was Cuomo's close friend— both were alumni of St. John's University School of Law—made him secretary of state shortly after taking office in January 1975.

Cuomo had made a name for himself in Queens as a young lawyer resolving housing disputes. In the late 1960s and early '70s, New

York was awakening to the harsh reality that segregation was not just a southern problem. When it came time to erect public housing in middle-class or upper-middle-class neighborhoods dominated by white professionals, egalitarian rhetoric flew out the window, and NIMBY-ism ("not in my backyard") became the universal response.* Having calmed a dispute in Corona, a strongly Italian neighborhood, Cuomo was asked to act as mediator for Mayor John Lindsay in his proposal to site public housing in the Jewish-dominated enclave of Forest Hills, Queens. Since Reform Jews were the backbone of the liberal wing of the Democratic Party in New York City, none of the people in the mayor's office expected a struggle—especially because black and Jewish voters were seen as a single bloc, with no real policy disagreements. The firestorm that resulted from the Lindsay proposal destroyed that myth.

In any case, Mario Cuomo was energetic, restless, engaged, and ambitious and would never be content in a do-nothing or dead-end job. True, the secretary of state position had become pretty obscure since the halcyon days when Al Smith† appointed Robert Moses to the post. But Cuomo was intent on restoring prestige and power to the office, and Carey was willing to let him. So, with the transition team's advice, Cuomo consolidated a variety of Rockefeller programs (including the Office of Local Government) into the secretary of state's portfolio.

Over the next few years, I became Cuomo's go-to "bleeding heart"—handling issues related to poverty, integration, Native Americans, people with disabilities, and similar matters. It was some of the most enjoyable work of my career, and I had a near worshipful

---

* The situation reminded me of the words to a Phil Ochs song: "And I love Puerto Ricans and Negroes, as long as they don't move next door. So, love me, love me, love me, I'm a liberal!"

† Al Smith was a legendary New York governor from the 1920s, a rip-roaring Democrat who appointed Robert Moses as his secretary of state. Moses became known as the "great builder" who remade New York and positioned it for further economic progress through the erection of bridges, roads, dams, highways, and byways—no matter what the cost or opposition.

relationship with Cuomo, whom I saw as a brilliant lawyer and committed progressive politician. Though I left in 1977 to become the state assistant commissioner of special education when Cuomo made an unsuccessful bid for mayor of New York, we stayed in contact over the years. I had worked again for Cuomo briefly during his first term as governor, leaving that post in 1984 to head the School Boards Association.

So, in view of my relationship with the governor, and given Hobart's constraints, it was up to me to pay a visit to Cuomo.

I left my office and headed down Washington Avenue to the New York State Capitol to meet with the governor. From a distance, the state capitol, with its Romanesque/Renaissance/Victorian "style," looks something like a grand French château. It is both elegant and monumental, but neither martial nor religious looking. It has a palatial quality that is lacking in the Greek- and Roman-inspired buildings in Washington.

At the time of its completion in 1899 (thirty-two years after the ground-breaking),* it was by far the most expensive public building in the Western Hemisphere, costing an astounding half billion dollars. In form and construction it was an architectural and institutional allusion, not to some classical cradle of democracy but to the ancien régime. It is oddly lacking a dome, but not by design: by the time they got to that point, the capitol was already grossly over budget and literally going downhill. It was beginning to slip down the incline of State Street, so they had to add a sixty-six-foot-long exterior staircase to support the facade. At the bottom of the grand exterior staircase is a

---

* The New York State Capitol is a peculiar blend of three architectural styles reflecting the influence of three different teams of architects over the years of its construction. The first floor is Classical Romanesque, the next two floors are in the Renaissance Classical style, and the fourth floor is in a Victorian-Romanesque style. See Jack O'Donnell, *Bitten by the Tiger* (Chapel Hill, NC: Chapel Hill Press, 2014), 20.

statue of Civil War General Philip Sheridan, his mount facing away from the capitol with its derriere facing the statehouse.

In any case, while the capitol lacks a dome—one of only eleven statehouses nationwide without such an accoutrement—it is loaded with ghosts from the political graveyard. George Clinton (the fourth vice president); John Jay (the nation's first chief justice); Chief Justice Charles Evan Hughes; Presidents Martin Van Buren, Grover Cleveland, and Theodore and Franklin Roosevelt; and almost-presidents William Henry Seward, Samuel Tilden, Al Smith, Tom Dewey, Averell Harriman, and Nelson Rockefeller had all been New York governors, and their aura haunts the capitol.

As I ascended the interior Great Western Staircase, also known as the Million Dollar Staircase (it took more than $1 million, and fourteen years, to construct the 444 stone steps), I glanced at some of the seventy-seven famous faces so beautifully carved into the sandstone, including Washington, Lincoln, Grant, and Susan B. Anthony. I considered Mario Cuomo their intellectual equal and felt confident that he would instantly see the constitutional infirmity in this bill about to reach his desk. I was right, sort of. He did see the problem; he just didn't care.

"But, Luig," Cuomo said, calling me by the nickname he had devised for me years earlier, "it's just a school for thirteen poor, retarded immigrant children."

Dumbstruck, I swiveled in my chair as a new set of angles arranged themselves in my mind. As I did so, I glanced, not without sentimentality, at the portrait of Saint Thomas More, patron of lawyers, which Cuomo had kept in his offices as long as I had known him. It's a print of the one by Hans Holbein (the original can be seen at the Frick Collection in Manhattan). More is in three-quarter profile; he looks implacable and rich. Cuomo had identified with More and his speeches to revolutionary stepchildren about the "rule of law."

Cuomo's simple recitation of the facts revealed that he already knew all about the bill. That surprised me. If, I reasoned, Cuomo had already known even this much about the bill, could he have been involved in its passage all along? Finding that hard to believe, I handed the governor a copy of the bill to read, just to make sure we were on the same page. The bill read as follows:

> The territory of the Village of Kiryas Joel in the Town of Monroe, Orange County, on the date when this act shall take effect, shall be and hereby is constituted a separate school district, and shall be known as the Kiryas Joel Village School District and shall have and enjoy all of the powers and duties of a union free school district under the provisions of the Education Law. (L.1989, ch. 748, § 1.)

To me, this is what it meant:

> The territory of the Village of Kiryas Joel *(a theocracy inhabited only by members of the Satmar sect of Hasidic Judaism, a reclusive, exclusive group of religious fundamentalists whose dearest wish is to re-create an Eastern European ghetto in rural New York and to remain completely separate from all aspects of American culture except for receipt of an extraordinary amount of government funds)* in the Town of Monroe *(an old colonial town full of mainly non-Jewish people who are not comfortable with the Hasid and who are, collectively, willing to give the Satmar anything they want in hopes that they will go away)*, Orange County, on the date when this act shall take effect, shall be and hereby is constituted a separate school district *(never mind that under the First Amendment, "Congress shall make no law respecting the establishment of religion")* and shall be known as the Kiryas Joel Village School District *(even though New York is in the middle of a decades-old drive to cut the number of school districts by more than half, as we the legislature gladly set this precedent of giving school districts to religious fundamentalists because they vote unanimously and loudly)* and shall have and enjoy all of the powers *($$$$)* and duties *($$$$$$$$)* of a union free school district *($$$$$$$$$$$$$$$$)* under the provisions of the Education Law *(never mind that under*

New York's Blaine Amendment, "Neither the state nor any subdivision thereof shall use its property or credit or any public money . . . directly or indirectly, in aid or maintenance . . . of any school or institution of learning wholly or in part under the control or direction of any religious denomination").

I told Cuomo that the bill violated not only the federal Constitution but also the Blaine Amendment. He first took the high road, blaming the xenophobic, possibly anti-Semitic neighbors of the Satmar for the problem: "Do you know how insensitive the public schools have been to these people's religion? How insulting?"

I did not need to be convinced on the merits. Having been the assistant commissioner of education for five and a half years, I knew not only the education laws but also the lay of the land better than Cuomo did. I wondered aloud whether it was a good idea to bypass the US Constitution because of a few insensitive teachers and school board members. I also promised that, if Cuomo would veto the bill, I would personally see that every Satmar kid in the district was placed in a suitable educational environment at public expense. I was well acquainted with service providers who could easily accommodate thirteen kids from Kiryas Joel, and I knew it would be no problem to find appropriate placements.

Cuomo's temper flared: If I thought it was such a damn moral crusade, I should have said something about the bill before it passed both houses of the legislature. He accused me of sitting on my hands so I could grandstand before the press after the bill passed!

This was vintage Cuomo behavior. When seemingly cornered, he got defensive, and offensive. Still, to an extent he was right. I really hadn't done anything to stop the bill's passage through the legislature, nothing to prevent this hot potato from landing on his lap. (On the other hand, Pataki and Lentol had whipped the bill through at near record speed, and it is highly unlikely I could have done anything at the time to stop it.) Still, I couldn't help but see the point that the governor was more than hinting at: if he vetoed the bill now, he would have to shoulder all of the political blame from a powerful voting bloc in New York City, the governor's stronghold. It would have been easy for Cuomo to scuttle the bill before passage; now it would be a much bigger sacrifice.

Bearing this in mind, I asserted that if the governor signed it, the courts would knock it out. And, with a very obvious glance at the portrait of More, I noted that this would be a huge embarrassment to the great "constitutionalist" governor. Cuomo didn't like that and proceeded to usher me out of his office, with the dismissive rhetorical question "Who's going to sue?"

Ticked off, I said that *I* would, and then marched down the Million Dollar Staircase.

Although the brief debate had been carried on in the usual half-serious tones of combat that the governor and I had often engaged in, I felt that this one had been more serious. Also, I was sick at the thought of a man I admired as much as Mario Cuomo treating the Constitution as just another political chip as long as he thought no one would sue— which is to say as long as he thought no one would notice. The more I thought about it, the angrier I became, even though, having spent my life in public policy, I had certainly seen many worse examples of political disdain for constitutional principles. Now sadly certain that Cuomo would sign the bill, I was trying to decide if I could make good on my threat to sue. What might my board of directors think? It was their organization, not mine. Would they really let me take on the governor of the state of New York?

Ten days later, Cuomo indeed signed the bill. Every one of his highest advisers urged him in writing to veto it, and, in each case, the governor insisted on signing it, telling his counselors, "These people don't ask for much."

5

WHO IS WORSHIPPED?

———————

*Congress shall make no law respecting an establishment of religion, or pro-
hibiting the free exercise thereof.*

—First Amendment, US Constitution

I N SIGNING THE bill into law, Governor Cuomo was establishing
the first governmental unit in American history that was created
solely to serve the needs and interests of only one religious group. Other
units have had a large majority of individuals from one group, such as
Utah Mormons, but no other unit had ever been established with the
intent of only dealing with the needs of one religion. Never before had
a religious sect been given a public school to run. In my mind, this
could not go unchallenged.

As a lawyer and a history buff, I fully appreciate the freedom *of* versus freedom *from* religion debate that has continued since our nation's
birth. Our Founding Fathers—particularly Thomas Jefferson and James
Madison—began the debate more than two hundred years ago, and
to this day it has not been firmly resolved by the US Supreme Court.
Certainly, the court decides Establishment Clause cases all the time,

frequently relying on stare decisis (precedent), but this is an incredibly shaded debate and different courts in different areas and different eras have come to different conclusions on what the First Amendment really means. Perhaps that is because it meant one thing to Jefferson and something a little different to Madison. In short, where Madison was focused on protecting religion and the religious from government interference, Jefferson was intent on protecting government and individuals from religion.

But the Jefferson and Madison viewpoints were not diametrically opposite by any stretch. Both of them believed in freedom of *and* freedom from religion, and their differences were relatively nuanced.* The Constitution artfully embraces both concepts in the eloquently simple prose of the First Amendment: "Congress shall make *no* law *respecting* an establishment of religion [Jefferson] or *prohibiting the free exercise thereof* [Madison]" (emphasis mine). Note that the clause is absolute, permitting *no laws* of either sort. To me, *no* is not an ambiguous word. Over the years, the Supreme Court has acknowledged the validity of the Jeffersonian and Madisonian arguments but has never firmly chosen one and rejected the other. So one ruling may seem to flow directly from Madison's reasoning, another from Jefferson's, and many seemingly coming from a compromise between the two.

Our founders clearly did not want religion meddling in the affairs of government, nor did they want government interfering with an individual's right to worship (or not worship) however he or she saw fit. And for good reason. They were well aware that when religion and government mixed, oppression and/or bloodshed was frequently the result.

---

* In a 1787 letter to Jefferson, Madison wrote, "No distinction seems to be more obvious than that between spiritual and temporal matters. Yet whenever they have been made objects of Legislation, they have clashed and contended with each other, till one or the other has gained the supremacy." See James Madison, *The Writings of James Madison*, vol. 5, *Correspondence, 1787–1790* (New York: Putnam, 1904), http://oll.libertyfund.org /titles/1937.

Many of our ancestors came here specifically to escape religious persecution, and the colonies they established reflected their beliefs: Massachusetts was envisioned by the Puritans as their shining "city on a hill"; the Quakers, under the leadership of William Penn, settled in Philadelphia; Maryland was established by Lord Baltimore as a colony where religion and state were separate and Roman Catholics could peacefully prosper alongside their Protestant neighbors; eastern Virginians were committed largely to the Church of England, while western Virginia was Methodist territory. Ironically, and hypocritically, these were generally not very tolerant groups, and they were not above persecuting those who did not share the beliefs of the dominant majority. Citizens were forced to attend government-sponsored, tax-supported churches, most of the colonies eventually had an official religion, and religious tests for public officials were standard.

After the revolution, there was considerable controversy over the role of religion in government, especially as Baptists, Presbyterians, and other minorities escaped to the new country, lured by the promise of religious freedom. The battle reached fever pitch after Patrick Henry, in 1784, proposed a bill for tax-supported religion in Virginia, spurring Madison and Jefferson into action. Madison, in his "Memorial and Remonstrance Against Religious Assessments," drew a line in the sand in 1785:

> Because we hold it for a fundamental and undeniable truth, "that Religion or the duty which we owe to our Creator and the Manner of discharging it, can be directed only by reason and conviction, not by force or violence." The Religion then of every man must be left to the conviction and conscience of every man; and it is the right of every man to exercise it as these may dictate. This right is in its nature an unalienable right. It is unalienable; because the opinions of men, depending only on the evidence contemplated by their own minds, cannot follow the dictates of other men: It is unalienable

also; because what is here a right towards men, is a duty towards
the Creator. It is the duty of every man to render to the Creator such
homage, and such only, as he believes to be acceptable to him. . . .
Who does not see that the same authority which can establish Chris-
tianity, in exclusion of all other Religions, may establish with the
same ease any particular sect of Christians, in exclusion of all other
Sects? . . . What influence in fact have ecclesiastical establishments
had on Civil Society? In some instances they have been seen to erect
a spiritual tyranny on the ruins of Civil authority; in many instances
they have been seen upholding the thrones of political tyranny; in
no instance have they been seen the guardians of the liberties of the
people. Rulers who wished to subvert the public liberty, may have
found an established clergy convenient auxiliaries. A just government, instituted to secure & perpetuate it, needs them not. Such a
government will be best supported by protecting every citizen in the
enjoyment of his Religion with the same equal hand which protects
his person and his property; by neither invading the equal rights of
any Sect, nor suffering any Sect to invade those of another.

Jefferson meanwhile had proposed a "Bill for Establishing Religious
Freedom":

Well aware . . . that Almighty God hath created the mind free . . . that
all attempts to influence it by temporal punishments, or burthens, or
by civil incapacitations, tend only to beget habits of hypocrisy and
meanness, and are a departure from the plan of the holy author of
our religion, who being lord both of body and mind, yet chose not
to propagate it by coercions on either, as was in his Almighty power
to do. . . . No man shall be compelled to frequent or support any religious worship, place, or ministry whatsoever, nor shall be enforced,
restrained, molested, or burthened in his body or goods, nor shall
otherwise suffer, on account of his religious opinions or belief; but

that all men shall be free to profess, and by argument to maintain, their opinions in matters of religion, and that the same shall in no wise diminish, enlarge, or affect their civil capacities. . . . We are free to declare, and do declare, that the rights hereby asserted are of the natural rights of mankind, and that if any act shall be hereafter passed to repeal the present or to narrow its operation, such act will be an infringement of natural right.

Madison, who wrote the First Amendment, drew heavily from Jefferson's "Bill for Establishing Religious Freedom," incorporating both the freedom *of* and freedom *from* concepts. Jefferson, while he certainly favored religious freedom and most definitely opposed government interference ("It does me no injury for my neighbor to say there are twenty Gods, or no God"), saw the institutions of religion and government on entirely different, never intersecting orbits. He called for a "wall" of separation between the two, with neither having any influence on the other.* That, perhaps, was overly optimistic, even for Jefferson. As two-hundred-plus years of Supreme Court cases show, there is no end to the ways in which government and religion inevitably interact, and often collide, as Madison clearly foresaw.†

---

* Jefferson used the "wall" metaphor in a letter he sent to the Danbury Baptists on January 1, 1802. It has been cited by the US Supreme Court on several occasions. See Reynolds v. United States, 98 US 145 (1878); Everson v. Board of Education, 330 US 1 (1947); McCollum v. Board of Education, 333 US 203 (1948).

† In an 1832 letter to the Rev. Jasper Adams, Madison wrote, "I must admit moreover that it may not be easy, in every possible case, to trace the line of separation between the rights of religion and the Civil authority with such distinctness as to avoid collisions and doubts on unessential points. The tendency to a usurpation on one side or the other, or to a corrupting coalition or alliance between them, will be best guarded against by an entire abstinence of the Government from interference in any way whatever, beyond the necessity of preserving public order, and protecting each sect against trespasses on its legal rights by others." See James Madison, *The Writings of James Madison*, vol. 9, *Correspondence, 1819–1836* (New York: Putnam, 1910), http://oll.libertyfund.org/titles/madison-the-writings-vol-9-1819-1836.

Even after the adoption of the Bill of Rights in 1791, a number of states kept established churches (the last state to abandon the practice was Massachusetts in 1833), and in the first century following the ratification of the Constitution there was very little Establishment Clause jurisprudence. During that period, immigration brought millions of individuals to America, increasing dramatically the religious diversity of the nation. The first groups, from northern Europe, were Protestant; the southern Europeans were mainly Catholic, as were the Irish; the eastern Europeans were either Eastern Orthodox or Jewish.

The large tide of immigration brought many antiforeigner sentiments, and it spurred the growth of a public school system dedicated to Americanizing the new arrivals. The schools promulgated Protestant ethical values, even when they stopped short—often *just* short—of proselytizing for a particular denomination. This led to the establishment of parochial schools, especially among the Catholic populations. In a countermovement, many states passed constitutional amendments that prohibited public funding for parochial schools. Adoption of children by prospective parents of a different faith was prohibited in many states. Nevertheless, there were no movements to gerrymander local or state boundaries along religious lines. Even when the Mormons decided to establish the new state of Utah, the Utah Constitution prohibited state spending or actions aimed at helping religious groups. Still, a number of states did require citizens to belong to and support a religion.

The first major test of the Establishment Clause occurred in 1878, after George Reynolds of Utah, a member of the Church of Jesus Christ of Latter Day Saints, took a second wife while he was still married to the first. There was no question at all that he had committed polygamy, and no question that polygamy was illegal in the United States. Reynolds did not dispute that he had broken federal law. Instead, he asserted his First Amendment right to the free exercise of religion, arguing that his religion not only tolerated polygamy but encouraged it.

In *Reynolds v. United States*, the Supreme Court held that while Congress could not outlaw a *belief* in the correctness of polygamy, it could outlaw the *practice* of it. It said that with the First Amendment, "Congress was deprived of all legislative power over mere opinion, but was left free to reach actions which were in violation of social duties or subversive of good order." The court made clear that people cannot evade the law because of their religion: "Can a man excuse his [illegal] practices . . . because of his religious belief? To permit this would be to make the professed doctrines of religious belief superior to the law of the land, and in effect to permit every citizen to become a law unto himself. Government could exist only in name under such circumstances." The ruling also noted that since religion was not defined in the Constitution, it was necessary to look back to both Jefferson and Madison for an understanding of what was meant by the First Amendment.

Some sixty years later, in the 1940s, the court returned to the issue of church-state separation in *Everson v. Board of Education*, permitting a New Jersey school district to reimburse parents for the cost of transporting their children to and from parochial schools. The court stood strong for separation of church and state but held that in this scenario busing did not impact on religious ideas one way or another. In the 1960s the Supreme Court expanded upon the meaning of separation and prohibited the use of prayers in public schools. In 1968 the court overturned a law prohibiting, for religious reasons, the teaching of evolution; the ruling indicated that by enforcing religious views, the Arkansas State Legislature was establishing religion.

With the sheer number of Establishment Clause cases making their way into court and the obvious confusion in the courts and in the country, the Supreme Court in the 1971 case of *Lemon v. Kurtzman* attempted to draw some guidelines on just where the line falls. In a dispute over state aid to help parochial schools pay their teachers, the court enacted a three-part litmus test for Establishment Clause analysis: (1) the law must have a secular purpose, (2) the law may neither advance nor inhibit religion, and (3) the law must not excessively entangle religion and government. But, as always, the devil was in the details, and the *Lemon* attempt to achieve clarity was not successful.

The country was in the midst of massive change regarding church-state separation as the proliferation of governmental services raised all kinds of new questions. Government safety nets were reaching into areas such as civil rights, serving the mentally ill and developmentally disabled, planned parenting and abortion-related services, communicable disease prevention and services, and increased standards for public schools—all of which potentially involved religious issues or organizations.

Many of the newly offered government services had in the past been provided by religious groups and religious-supported nonprofits, and the new governmental actions were intruding on their turfs. Political groups pushed for abortion and planned parenting or related services, but strident and angry countervailing forces organized and pushed back. As the costs of serving developmentally disabled children and adults skyrocketed and those impacted saw their rights dramatically expanded, huge battles broke out among service providers, many of which were religiously based. When courts and legislatures decided to shut down inhumane, warehouse-like institutions and shift resources to small, less restrictive community residences and group homes, religious affiliates quickly filled the need. Billions of dollars were channeled to groups like Catholic Charities and the Jewish Federation of Philanthropies, and such organizations suddenly became the largest providers of the new services.

Meanwhile, public education was at a low point in the 1970s. Desegregation and busing and the resultant racial tension and riots took a toll on educational quality. Schools lowered standards and pushed kids from grade to grade whether they could read or not. Parochial schools began to grow rapidly in evangelical Protestant groups, and Conservative and Reform Jewish groups were also forming religiously based schools.

By the late 1970s voters were convinced society was breaking down. The cultural pendulum that had veered far leftward in the 1960s and '70s swung not only back toward the center but well over to the right. By the 1980s "Government is not the solution but the problem" became a familiar mantra of the Reagan Revolution. Public support for government services dropped dramatically, and at the same time support for private enterprises—including churches and synagogues—increased. Religious groups capitalized on their societal resurgence and became masters of political pressure. Coalitions grew among the evangelical Christians, the Catholic Church, and the Hasidic Jews. Groups such as the Moral Majority and Pat Robertson's 700 Club exerted unprecedented influence in matters of governance and public policy.

We were reaching a point Jefferson had feared we would reach and Madison had so fervently hoped to avoid with his careful drafting of the First Amendment. As Madison observed in "Memorial and Remonstrance Against Religious Assessments": "The same authority which can force a citizen to contribute three pence only of his property for the support of any one establishment, may force him to conform to any other establishment in all cases whatsoever." Our founders feared that religious liberty would ultimately be the victim if government could use its taxing and spending powers to aid religion. The First Amendment—just those few short words in a remarkable document—were all that stood between us and Madison's worst nightmare.

So, it was in this context that I considered how to legally challenge the statute that created the Kiryas Joel Village School district, as well as the political and public relations consequences.

Many small religious groups that have intensely held views are valuable political allies because they tend to vote as a bloc. But the Satmar, who vote in almost unanimous accord, are especially potent, partially because, unlike other religious groups, they do not subject politicians to an ideological litmus test. While Catholics, for example, may well withhold support from anyone who does not share their view on, say, abortion, the Satmar rarely concern themselves with the politician's ethical or legal positions. What they want are specific dollars-and-cents services, not philosophical or spiritual accord. They remember the politicians who deliver and, just as strongly, don't forget those who don't.

Cuomo, admittedly, was in a difficult position, and though suffering more than a hint of political paranoia, he had reason to feel ambushed. Hardly anyone had spoken out against the bill until it was on his desk, leaving him to shoulder the entire political weight of the issue: sign the bill and receive tens of thousands of votes; veto the bill and lose the same number or more. It was that simple.

I understood this political reality, but I thought Cuomo was not giving enough weight to the possibility that for every Hasidic vote he won in Brooklyn or Orange County, he would lose more Reform Jewish votes in places such as Forest Hills, the Upper West Side, and Riverdale. Separation of church and state was a gut issue for most Jews, who for obvious reasons instinctively oppose any steps toward involving government in their parochial concerns. I knew the Kiryas Joel statute would divide the Jewish community, and that there were likely many more Jewish voters who would oppose the measure than would support it. In addition, many New Yorkers—Jews and non-Jews alike—had traditionally opposed changing the Blaine Amendment (and had indeed defeated an effort to excise it from the state constitution). The problem, of course, is that the Satmar vote as a bloc, whereas others do not necessarily do so. Consequently, while support for Cuomo from the Satmar was a virtual sure thing, support from other groups and individuals was far less certain.

At first glance, it might appear that Cuomo and Kiryas Joel held the higher moral ground, because the underlying issue—educational services for children with disabilities—was entirely legitimate. Who could argue that these unfortunate kids should be denied services that are provided to everyone else? It's hard to persuade the public with abstract talk about the Constitution when the other side accuses you of shortchanging deaf or developmentally disabled kids.

But after years of fighting to ensure and expand services for children with disabilities, I was ready to face such rhetoric, and quickly formulated a two-pronged approach. The first spike would be a lawsuit seeking to shut down the school district as unconstitutional on church-state grounds. That was the legal attack. Second, and equally important, was the PR skirmish. We needed to win both battles to prevail in this war, and I knew that managing the public relations aspect would help the legal effort. Although they are supposed to be independent and divorced from popular opinion, the courts are—and must be—attuned to public sentiment.

I don't mean to suggest that judges (most judges anyhow) rule with a finger-to-the-wind abandon. But they do understand that their decisions must have if not public support then at least credibility with the public. Consider, for example, the Supreme Court's momentous decision in *Brown v. Board of Education*, which held that separate schools for black and white students were inherently unequal and unconstitutional. I suspect that if the greatest Supreme Court justices in history came together and were handed the exact same case a decade earlier, they would not have come to the result reached in 1954—and if they did, the public would have been outraged and the credibility of the Supreme Court would have been compromised. Obviously, the decision would have been just as right in 1924, 1934, or 1944 as it was in 1954, but neither the court nor the public was ready for such a leap in an earlier era.*

---

* I hope it is clear that I am not comparing the particulars of the Kiryas Joel case to *Brown v. Board of Education*. My point is simply that the courts can't take society where it's unwilling or unready to go, and that public acceptance is crucial to jurisprudence.

I reasoned that if we could win the battle in the press, it would pave the way for a victory in the courts as well. To my thinking, courts, no less than legislatures, track the media's attention to and reporting of policy issues. My view was born of a career serving inside complex modern bureaucracies and closely observing government decision making from all angles—as a young Democratic National Committee employee in the days of Lyndon Johnson, as a clerk doing legislative research in Senator Jacob Javits's law offices, as a state urban development administrator, as an aide to powerful appointees and politicians, and now as the executive director of an organization representing many elected officials. I had lobbied and I had been lobbied; I had advised and been advised; I had felt both sides of the media's double-edged sword. If I had learned anything, it was that politicians rarely take significant action until forced to do so by a vigorous press and/or by vigilant citizens or pressure groups. And, like it or not, judges are politicians.

First I had to determine the level of support I could expect from my board of directors. The board was made up of seventeen individuals elected from the various geographic regions of the state. This made for a somewhat diverse set of ideological philosophies, making it fun to work with but difficult to coalesce. The board officers were elected for one-year terms, though many served for two terms. At the time, Judy Katz from suburban Buffalo was the president. She was a model board member and the type of person every executive director dreams of working with. She had served on many other boards, including those of prominent Jewish groups. Experienced, articulate, and well connected, with excellent judgment, Judy fully understood the church-state issues involved in Monroe-Woodbury. But I was concerned that she would not support a lawsuit that might open the association up to charges of anti-Semitism. It turned out I was wrong in that concern—dead wrong. She was immediately and incredibly supportive.

The president-elect was a retired state worker from rustic western New York who was very conservative and represented rural areas quite well. Al Hawk, a strong advocate for protecting the public schools from religious encroachment, would be the president at the start of the lawsuit. He was willing to be listed first as the named plaintiff.

Gordon S. Purrington was a vice president. A professor of education at the State University of New York at Albany, Gordon was an extremely religious Mormon and the father of two special needs children.* A strong advocate for public education in an integrated setting, Gordon was in full support of challenging the Kiryas Joel measure.

Georgine Hyde was the board member with the most at stake. As president of the school board in East Ramapo, she had already witnessed the danger of a religious community voting down school budgets and ousting school board members who did not support their educational demands. Georgine had been the school board president there for thirty-five years, and she was well known and widely beloved. She spoke often on her years as a prisoner in Theresienstadt and Auschwitz, and was a noted author on ethics issues. Georgine knew well that if she signed on to our lawsuit, she would be viewed in some segments of her community as a Benedict Arnold and would forever lose their support and respect. But without hesitation, and as a monument to her political courage, Georgine never flinched in giving me her support.

In fact, not one single board member opposed filing a lawsuit; the board unanimously endorsed litigation filed under the auspices of the association and in the individual capacities of Al Hawk and myself.

First hurdle cleared.

But how could we possibly afford to hire an attorney with the skills, acumen, and time to take on what could be a long and exhausting legal battle against the weight of the New York state attorney general (who had roughly five hundred lawyers at his disposal) or the Washington-based litigators I was sure the Satmar would retain? In my mind, we already had our man—a young, exceptionally bright, overworked and underpaid in-house counsel right down the hall.

---

* Gordon S. Purrington's obituary in 2012 described him as a "warrior for people with special needs." It is an apt description. See *Deseret News*, April 29, 2012, www.legacy.com/obituaries/deseretnews/obituary.aspx?pid=157308557.

6

WHO LITIGATES?

Litigation is the pursuit of practical ends, not a game of chess.
      —Justice Felix Frankfurter, *Indianapolis v. Chase National Bank*

JAY WORONA WORKED in a narrow office with one drafty window that faced a parking garage, a threadbare carpet, chintzy fluorescent lighting, and walls decorated with cheaply framed Chagall posters. Though it wasn't exactly glamorous, Worona was grateful for every day he spent in that office.

A native of Poughkeepsie, Jay had graduated from Albany Law School in the early 1980s into a dismal national economy and what seemed like a withering industrial core in New York. He was languishing in a job at a law firm in Schenectady, unhappy and unfulfilled but unwilling to relocate. He went to law school because he was fascinated with the Constitution. I could certainly relate to that: The majesty and brilliant yet simple prose of the Constitution has an almost spiritual quality that entices the intellect and nourishes the soul. To me, and I'm sure Jay, it borders on sacred scripture.

Unfortunately, for most lawyers the Constitution is something of an abstraction, likely because of the tension between the inviting flexibility of the document and the rather mundane and mechanical way in which the courts (quite sensibly) actually use it. For example, a guarantee of "due process" or "equal protection" is both romantically abstract and platonically concrete. To an extent, the living, growing, and expanding document, and the fact that it was ratified, is a monument to the power of ideas. Applying those ideas and principles to real life is endless labor for the Supreme Court, and a frustrating exercise in semantics for many law students. Worona was quite the exception.

In law school, Jay excelled at constitutional law, having a natural feel for the semipolitical, quasi-legal issues worked out by the Supreme Court. But, as many a student in his position has discovered, the opportunity for practicing constitutional law is limited. Out of school and in legal practice, the academic affection for the Constitution can wither. So Jay, somewhat disillusioned with the practice of law, continued a somewhat despondent shuffle through his days at the firm in Schenectady, becoming increasingly miserable and inventing plans of escape. He'd had just about enough when he was summoned to defend a man accused of fondling himself in a car and was directed by his boss to argue—presumably, with a straight face—that the defendant was actually swatting at a bee in his parked car. This was not why Jay went to law school. He quit on the spot, and within a week was sitting in front of me, being interviewed for a job.

Worona didn't have—and I couldn't afford—government experience, or much experience at all. I was hoping to find a promising young lawyer, someone I could mentor, someone creative and innovative, as well as intelligent and energetic, someone who was willing to push the envelope. I told Worona that my strategy for expanding the power of the School Boards Association would be to file lawsuits, mostly constitutional challenges, in New York, as well as to weigh in on similar issues in the rest of the country. I said that I wanted to use the law and the Constitution to resist some of the more destructive demands of those who wanted to attack the core of public education as an equalizing tool in society. His eyes lit up. I had my lawyer.

In the next few years, Jay and I indeed raised the organization's profile by filing amicus briefs* in major education cases throughout the country. Indeed, we filed more amicus briefs than any other organization in the state. The 1980s was a time of growing discontent with the public school system. In particular, the Reagan administration's landmark report "A Nation at Risk: The Imperative for Educational Reform" documented the failings of our public education structure, alarming parents, spurring fundamentalists into lawsuits and homeschooling, and terrifying an industry that was thoroughly wedded to the status quo. Though some portions of the administration's document were quite irrational, the report was truly a bellwether event in education reform.

One of the earliest cases Worona and I participated in by submitting a brief stemmed from a group of conservative legal organizations challenging the literature curriculum in a public school in Tennessee. These fundamentalists had been shocked into action when they learned that the school was teaching *The Diary of Anne Frank*. The passage in which Anne says, "Peter, I wish you had some religion to hold onto, it doesn't matter what it is, just some faith," antagonized local Christian fundamentalists, who couldn't handle the prospect that theirs wasn't the one true faith, to which all who seek God's approval must adhere under threat of eternal damnation. It was a Tennessee case with no direct link to New York, other than that the Constitution affects all of us. Still, in order to file an amicus brief, Jay had to get permission to practice in federal courts in Tennessee.

---

* An amicus curiae is an individual or organization that is not party to a lawsuit but volunteers or is invited to submit a brief to weigh in on a particular issue. Ideally, amici offer the court a perspective not provided by the actual litigants—perhaps a potential ramification or consequence or implication that has been overlooked by the parties. To an extent, amici help prevent unintended consequences.

Such cases were popular fodder in the relatively liberal New York press. Some of the coverage had a "Look what those hicks have done now" tone, and some of it had a "These hicks are coming to get you next!" tone. Either way, I was ready with quotes highlighting the backwardness of the fundamentalists and extolling New York (only half-jokingly) as the last bastion of support for the US Constitution. As a well-educated Jew from a West Virginia steel town, I could wear a lot of colorful hats for the media—sometimes playing up my blue-collar roots, other times playing off the media's misguided assumption that I had been born, raised, and educated on the East Coast.

I saw an opportunity to turn the New York State School Boards Association into an ideas shop, a think tank of sorts. In the past, the organization had opposed anything that might cost property tax dollars—which is to say it opposed pretty much everything. On the other hand, our frequent nemesis, the New York State United Teachers, supported anything that provided educators with salary, benefit, and pension enhancements. In short, there was really no consistently thoughtful and outspoken voice on education *policy*, and I felt the association could become a group with the right ideas on education and the political know-how to achieve its goals.

Soon, the association was putting out position papers on seemingly every issue in the education spectrum: gifted children, bilingual education, special education, early education, and nutrition and fitness, to name a few. But lots of organizations have smart people on board who produce wonderful position papers that simply collect dust. I wanted the association to be not only right but also relevant.

With that goal, I brought in two people whom I thought could get us noticed with the public—the ultimate constituency for any advocacy group—and the legislature. Dan Kinley, an excellent legislative analyst from a politically prominent Albany family (his father was the treasurer of the state Democratic Party in New York), was an expert in "smart bomb" legislation (legislation that appears to apply to everyone but actually applies to only one constituency—e.g., the Kiryas Joel statute).

Bill Pape grew up on Long Island, the son of a well-connected policy wonk, and had worked for a state senator before I hired him as the association's press officer. They worked hand in glove with me. Pape created a newspaper for the association and convinced the legislative aides at the New York State Capitol (who do much of the work for the politicians) that the membership across the state read it religiously. Pretty soon the legislative aides were also reading the newspaper. When the legislature called for clarification on any of the position papers, Kinley and Pape were able to explain the policies in detail. In a short period, the School Boards Association became known as the go-to source on any aspect of education legislation in the state. That's a valuable thing considering that education is not only one of the most perennially newsworthy local topics but also one of the most expensive and legislatively complicated. Reporters wanted to write about it, but few of them had the inside knowledge of the legislative process required to understand how it all fit together. I would drop pithy distillations to the media and Bill Pape or Dan Kinley would fill in the details for the reporters.

As a result of the higher profile of the association, the membership became more involved, more active and interested. By increasing their involvement, we were able to get school board members (who were, after all, elected officials in their own right) to influence their local politicians back home. In a few short years we had managed to turn a "just say no," budget-focused backwater into a forum for talking about the things that most school board members and most parents were really interested in: education policy. Moreover, those who disagreed with us on issues were now on the defensive, forced to respond in the media and engage in public debate. So we were well positioned to take on Mario Cuomo and the New York State Legislature.

When I got back to my office after the confrontation with Cuomo, Jay Worona and I began to discuss legal strategy. We were a good team, because we came from somewhat different perspectives, we respected each other, and we were willing to consider and concede the strengths and weaknesses of opposing positions. A much more observant Jew than I, Worona is also much more sensitive to the reality of anti-Semitic discrimination. And so, where I was prone to see both the crass political maneuvering behind the law and the consequences of extending the principle of the law ad infinitum (fearing Catholic, Baptist, and black- and white-only school districts, not to mention districts for retirees without children to educate), Worona was inclined to see the perverse forms of anti-Semitism that he felt must have forced the Satmar into this situation. The truth, as we both would learn, was somewhere in between. The Satmar were neither as manipulative as I imagined nor as helpless and victimized as Jay saw them.

In any event, though sensitive to what he felt was the likely mistreatment of the Satmar, Worona quickly saw that, as an intellectual matter, the law was a disastrous and unnecessary precedent, one likely to further inflame religious as well as ethnic tensions. His mind was abuzz with legal theories and strategies. For once, instead of just being amici, Worona would be the lead attorney on the case. He was primed and pumped for the challenge, but there was a threshold hurdle to clear: Could we sue?

Contrary to the popular notion that anyone can sue anyone, anytime and anywhere, for anything, in order to bring a lawsuit one must have standing, or *locus standi*. One cannot challenge the constitutionality of a law without first showing that one is or will be harmed by the law. In other words, you must have a stake in the outcome, something to lose. Before Jay finished the short walk back to his own office, he was already having grave doubts about the not-for-profit association's standing.

But one thing was certain: Al Hawk and I, as individual taxpayers, had standing whether the organization did or not. Violations of the Establishment Clause are one of the only constitutional infringements for which both New York State statutory law and the US Supreme Court will allow taxpayer standing. That is, any taxpayer affected by the law in question can challenge it. This contrasts sharply from almost any other constitutional violation or deprivation. At the time, a person couldn't sue the US government (or the New York government, for that matter) just because he believed the government had spent his tax money improperly or unwisely.* However, the state law considered the separation of church and state so important that taxpayer standing was allowed. The benefit of this rule was that Al and I could proceed under our own names, meaning we would have our day in court regardless of whether the School Boards Association could get standing. (Groups or associations or corporations are not granted taxpayer standing; they must demonstrate particularized harm—that is, they must show that the law in question has harmed a member of the group. The fact that the law was supported by the Monroe-Woodbury Central School District, a major dues-paying member of the association, did not help with this point).†

But if I were to sue personally, rather than on behalf of the association, I couldn't do so on the organization's dime. To sidestep that problem, Jay and his extremely able cocounsel, Pilar Sokol, agreed to do all of their work on the KJ case in a volunteer capacity, after hours. As time would go on, Pilar's pivotal role would become more and more apparent.

Next question: Whom do we sue?

---

* This changed with the Supreme Court's 2010 decision in *Citizens United v. Federal Election Commission*, 558 US 310 (2010).

† Officials at Monroe-Woodbury were livid when they heard I intended to sue. From their perspective, creating the Kiryas Joel school district eliminated a perpetual administrative headache for them—and got a troublesome and increasingly powerful voting bloc out of their way. Although we did not set out to sue the school board, its attorney, Lawrence W. Reich, insisted that the Monroe-Woodbury board should be a party to the litigation, arguing that without the involvement of the school board ours was a "lifeless, dispassionate controversy predicated upon abstract principles of law" and claiming that the board had the "greatest political stake and interest in the litigation." See "Memorandum of Law on Behalf of the Board of Education of the Monroe-Woodbury Central School District," 1990, submitted by Reich and attorneys with the Northport, Long Island, law firm of Ingerman, Smith, Greenberg, Gross, Richman, Heidelberger & Reich.

The more Worona looked into the problem, the more difficult that question became. Thinking systematically, he reasoned that the complaint had to allege a violation of the state and federal constitutions—specifically that the law violates the Establishment Clause of the First Amendment of the US Constitution and the Blaine Amendment of the New York State Constitution. As a taxpayer, I definitely had a constitutional right to a government that does not act in support of religion. But who was violating that right? Was it the governor for signing the bill and thus making it law? Was it the governor simply as the head of state in New York? Was it the state comptroller for spending the state's money? Was it the legislature for appropriating the funds? Was it the commissioner of education or the department of education for executing the law? Was it the Village of Kiryas Joel for asking for the law? Was it the new school district of Kiryas Joel for existing?

As Worona was tackling the thorny legal aspects of this question, I had to take into account the equally weighty political aspects involved. I wanted to avoid a case called *Grumet v. Cuomo* if possible. Also, I didn't think it would be wise (either for myself or the association) to take a position that made Cuomo the enemy. Win or lose, we were going to have to work again with any or all of the possible defendants, and I didn't want to burn any more bridges than necessary. (Ultimately, however, we would have no choice but to name the governor and other state officials as defendants).

The next step was for Worona to write a complaint and brief demonstrating how the law violated the New York State and US Constitutions. There were two options: we could allege either that the Satmar were actually using taxpayer money to support their religion in an unconstitutional way, *or* we could allege that the law itself violated our rights by supporting the Satmar religion. I much preferred the second approach, which is known as a facial challenge to the law. It was clean and simple. We would argue that the state violated the Constitution merely by enacting the statute; whether or not the Satmar implemented it in an unconstitutional manner made no difference.* (This was also partially a question of resources and timing. A facial challenge did not involve discovery, or a pretrial demand for documents and other information in the possession of the adversary, which is very expensive.)

Once we had decided to bring a facial challenge to the law, there was the question of venue—that is, where to bring the case. Since a federal right was at stake, we could have begun in a federal district court, but we dismissed the idea. In the first place, we would also be bringing claims relating to the New York State Constitution's Blaine Amendment, and I reasoned that the federal courts would be reluctant to intrude in state affairs. As far as I was concerned, even if by some remote chance the case failed under the federal Constitution, it was a sure thing under the Blaine Amendment. Further—and this goes to the PR/political side of the battle—I feared it would offend both the judiciary and political branches in New York if we were viewed as mounting an end run to bypass New York's courts. Finally, as a matter of practicality, given the conservative trajectory of the federal courts, I generally preferred to litigate in state court.

Worona and Sokol worked tirelessly on our complaint and brief and put together what I thought was a dazzling and compelling argument. We filed the lawsuit in New York Supreme Court in Albany† and waited for a response from our adversaries, who meanwhile had moved

---

* Consider the analogy of highway speeding. A police officer cannot issue a ticket simply because one drives a car that is capable of going over the speed limit; the officer has to catch the driver going over the speed limit by using a radar gun to measure the speed of the car. Most lawsuits are like that. On the other hand, there are some cars that no one is allowed to drive on the street, such as Formula 1 race cars, which are illegal because lawmakers have decided that these cars are so unsafe that we cannot trust anyone to drive them at any speed on a public road. It was this second analogy that applied to Kiryas Joel. Worona's facial challenge alleged that the Pataki-Lentol law gave so much power, so much support, to the Satmar religion that I shouldn't have to wait until my rights were violated in practice to challenge it.

† In New York, the "supreme court" is a trial court, not an appellate court—the low court rather than the high court.

full steam ahead on forming the new district and had hired staff to operate the school.

I was particularly curious to see who the Satmar would retain to go up against my young, relatively inexperienced attorneys. I had unflinching confidence in Jay and Pilar, but when I found out the name of our adversary, my first reaction was *Oh shit*.

7

WHO IS OUR ADVERSARY?

---

*Our fathers were the first men who had the sense, had the genius, to know
that no church should be allowed to have a sword.*
                    —Robert Ingersoll, the "Great Agnostic" (1833–1899)

WITH AN ADVERSARY like Nathan Lewin, I knew pretty
much how it felt to be David standing in the shadow of Goliath.
Lewin had clerked at the US Supreme Court for Justice John Marshall
Harlan II. He had worked for solicitors general Thurgood Marshall and
Archibald Cox. His clients had included the likes of Richard Nixon,
John Lennon, Jodie Foster, and a number of Jewish organizations that
he had represented on religious liberty issues. He went to and taught
at Harvard. Lewin had argued dozens of cases, both as representative
of the government and as a private practitioner, before the US Supreme
Court. Jay Worona, on the other hand, had set foot in the place just
once, as an observer of another argument in a church-state case concerning student religious clubs in public schools.

As an attorney who is a member of the US Supreme Court bar
and a Jew, I was quite familiar with Nat Lewin's legacy and, frankly,

viewed him as a professional icon. He was smart, colorful, and incredibly resourceful—the indisputable dean of Orthodox Jewish attorneys.

Lewin was born to a prominent Polish family in 1936 in the Lodz ghetto. When the Germans invaded Poland in 1939, his parents fled with him through the woods across the border to Vilna, in Lithuania, traveling from there by train for fourteen days to Vladivostok, a city on the east coast of Russia, and then on to Japan by boat. After the war, the Lewins came to New York City and settled on the Upper West Side to pursue the American Dream.

Nat was valedictorian of his class at Yeshiva University in 1957 and went from there to Harvard Law School, where he earned excellent grades and was a member of the *Law Review*, an honor reserved for a small percentage of the best and brightest. He had hoped to work in a law firm during the summer between his second and third years but found that his religious customs precluded that possibility. The Civil Rights Act of 1964 was still six or seven years off, and law firms had every right to refuse employment to someone because of his religion. And who wants a student intern who can't work Saturdays?

After graduating from Harvard, Nat spent a year clerking for Judge Edward Lumbard on the Second Circuit Court of Appeals in Manhattan, a highly respected court one step down the judicial ladder from the US Supreme Court. Lewin then landed a clerkship with Justice Harlan, the dream job of any young lawyer and, frequently, the ticket to professional success. He later used his experience and credentials to obtain a job in the US Justice Department when Robert Kennedy was attorney general. From there, he went to the Office of the Solicitor General, which represents and defends the federal government before the Supreme Court, and argued twelve cases before the highest court in the nation. He later joined the Washington, DC, law firm of Miller, Cassidy, Larroca & Lewin and very quickly established himself as an ingenious lawyer with a penchant for handling religious issues and a knack for pulling rabbits out of his hat.

For example, in the 1970s Lewin was approached by Steven Solarz, a congressman from Brooklyn who was looking for help on a bill that would allow employees of the federal government to work extra hours before or after *yamim tovim* (Jewish high holidays) so they wouldn't have to use up all their vacation time. After Solarz introduced the bill, the Department of Justice decided it was unconstitutional and invited the congressman to a meeting. At the meeting, after the head of the Office of Legal Counsel finished what he had to say, it was Congressman Solarz's turn to speak. He turned the table over to Lewin, who worked his magic.

Lewin told a story from his clerkship with Justice Harlan. Every Friday afternoon, with the Jewish Sabbath approaching, Harlan would send Lewin home by sunset and permit him to work Sunday to make up any lost time.

"Do you think Justice Harlan thought he was violating the Constitution?" Lewin asked the Department of Justice representatives at the meeting. The room went absolutely silent. Shortly thereafter, the Office of Legal Counsel called Congressman Solarz and told him the council had changed its position and would support the bill.

In the 1980s Nat argued a US Supreme Court case involving Simcha Goldman, who worked for an Air Force hospital that would not allow him to wear his yarmulke. Nat lost at the Supreme Court by the narrowest of margins, 5–4—and then, abracadabra, he got Congress to pass legislation specifically allowing yarmulkes in the military.

Lewin was also the author of New York's original *get* law. In the early 1980s the Rabbi Moshe Sherer of Agudath Israel—an umbrella association of Conservative Jewish organizations—called a meeting of Jewish leaders to brainstorm about the increasing problem of husbands who left their wives without giving them a *get*. A *get* is a Jewish divorce and can be granted only by the husband. A woman who does not obtain a *get* is not barred from a civil remarriage, but under the traditional Jewish law (the *halakhah*) the woman cannot remarry within the faith, and any children from a second marriage are presumptively bastards, who in turn are forbidden from marrying other Jews. New York courts had dealt with the issue for decades. After the meeting convened by Rabbi Sherer, legislation was proposed to address the problem. Once the measure was drafted and submitted, the rabbi got a call from Governor Cuomo's office with some bad news: the bill was unconstitutional and the governor would not sign it. Sherer had no choice but to call in the big gun—Nathan Lewin. Lewin literally rewrote the bill, called it the "removal of barriers to remarriage" act, and got Cuomo to sign it on a wink and a nod. Nobody was under any illusion that this act was doing anything but providing an accommodation to Jewish women.

By 1989 Lewin was one of the most sought-after First Amendment and general appellate litigation lawyers in the country. An elite cadre of associates worked on his cases. Prominent political figures in Washington and Tel Aviv sought his advice, and his fees were among the highest in the country. Lewin was probably commanding more money for a couple hours of work than I could pay Jay Worona for a week. He could easily afford to take on low- or no-profit causes of interest to him, especially those involving the Jewish community, and he readily took the Kiryas Joel case when contacted by Abe Wieder.

As a patriot of Israel and a non-Hasidic Jew, Lewin was far from sympathetic with many of the practices and ideas of the Satmar. Nevertheless, he had long since devoted himself to defending Jews of all kinds. In addition, he was immediately interested in Wieder's case for his own reasons.

Lewin felt that the Supreme Court had gone too far in separating church and state, to the extent that it was infringing on citizens' rights by forcing them to choose between religious exercise and indispensable government services. The solution, in his mind, was for the government, in certain carefully monitored instances, to accommodate the needs of religious sects when providing services. Lewin often argued that education was among those indispensable government services, and that the court had made it extremely difficult for some very religious people to take advantage of that service.

So this was our adversary, a man who was resourceful enough to find his way around the US Constitution to get the result he wanted, an attorney well known to and highly respected by the judiciary, a lawyer so seasoned that he would hardly need to introduce himself when he walked into court.

Regardless, I was confident Jay Worona would prevail.

Jay's brief began with a twenty-five-page attack on the Satmar's practical capacity to run any government facility in a constitutional manner, let alone something as sensitive as a school district. The Satmar, according to his brief, "make social isolation a goal of the community. To avoid undesirable acculturation, the Satmar separate themselves, and especially their children, from the outside community whose 'hostile' or 'impure' influences are deemed to pose a direct threat to their culture and insular existence." Worona accused the Satmar of running a totalitarian theocracy: "The Rebbe oversees almost every aspect of Hasidic life. For example, it has been reported that he gives Hasidic boys their first haircut, oversees education, and approves marriage agreements. Before Hasidim enter the work world, they must get approval from the Rebbe."

The idea was clearly to paint a picture of the Satmar as incapable of supporting secular institutions. It was necessary for Worona to prove that the Pataki-Lentol law was nothing more than religious segregation, and to do that he had to show that the religious and municipal authority in Kiryas Joel were indistinguishable.

Perhaps the most damaging area of Worona's brief described the story of Joseph Waldman and his dissident faction within Kiryas Joel.

When Grand Rebbe Joel Teitelbaum died in 1979, he was survived only by his wife, Alte Feiga, the *rebbetzin*.* His three daughters had

---

* The *rebbetzin* is wife of the rabbi and, in a community like Kiryas Joel where the rabbi is revered, she enjoys a special status. Often, the *rebbetzin* is a spiritual counselor to the congregation, especially the women.

predeceased him, and he had no sons. Upon Joel's death, his nephew, Moses Teitelbaum, succeeded him as grand rebbe. The *rebbetzin* did not like Moses, and more important, many of the key people who had been connected to Joel were shut out of his new leadership. A small dissident group, Bnei Yoel, soon formed around the *rebbetzin*; its most vocal member was Joseph Waldman, a Satmar whose family had served the household of Grand Rebbe Joel as bodyguards and personal assistants. Waldman and his group proclaimed Moses's succession invalid, and the dispute in the community grew so heated that it literally came to fisticuffs.

The creation of the village school district had called for the election of seven school board members. The Grand Rebbe Moses anointed seven candidates—one for each spot. The dissidents ran Joseph Waldman as an eighth candidate. The rebbe considered it intolerable for anyone to run for an office—public or otherwise—without his permission, so he not only ordered Waldman expelled from the main temple (Congregation Yetev Lev) but also had all six of Waldman's children kicked out of the private schools they attended. Jay laid it all out in his brief, adding:

> Furthermore, hundreds of Rebbe Moses's followers rioted in front of [Joe Waldman's] residence, throwing rocks at his house, screaming "Shegitz Aroas," which loosely translates into "infidel, non-Jew," and demanding that he leave the area. These incidents were reported to have occurred immediately following a speech by Rebbe Moses at Congregation Yetev Lev in Kiryas Joel. In the speech, the Rebbe stated that the person who ran for the school board and went against the Satmar leadership would die a disgraceful death. [When Waldman sought relief in court for these actions] he was condemned by the Satmar leadership as having "sinned by seeking help from a secular court."

In short, Worona's brief asked how a government could be permitted to not only subsidize a community that treats people this way over religious disputes but also *endorse* these values by allowing them to run a semiautonomous branch of the state government. To me, that was a key point.

Tolerance is a good thing, and there is no question at all that the Constitution, common sense, and fundamental fairness require tolerance of the Satmar lifestyle *as long as it doesn't interfere with the lifestyles of others.* But how could the government justify subsidizing a community that relegated women to second-class citizenship, that offered its benefits only to members of a specific congregation, let alone a specific religion? It was obvious at the time that the debate was surely not limited to a tiny community in rural/suburban New York State. It was about government funding and support being given to a group known to have inhibited the rights of those with whom it disagreed.

At the other end of the political spectrum and in other parts of the country, similar questions were being asked about the extension of equal rights and official dignity to gay people, people with disabilities, and immigrants. "Politically correct" vocabulary was lampooned, and not just because many of the terms were awkward and silly. The popular perception of public schools continued to plummet, and the right wing became increasingly wary of the official dignity that modern curricula conferred on the art, literature, and history of formerly marginalized groups. Conservatives clamored for tuition vouchers for parochial and other private schools, on the theory that the government ought to create a competitive market for education so that individuals could remove their children and themselves from government programs with which they disagreed (and channel government funding to set up programs with which they agreed).

Forbidding the use of government funding to support specific religious views is at the heart of the First Amendment. So consider the embarrassment when some of these schools subsidized by government vouchers turn out to be celebrating repudiation of accepted scientific principles and findings (e.g., antievolutionists) or ethnocentric, racist, and/or sexist lifestyles. Even disregarding the oversight the government would have to engage in to prevent the worst abuses, consider the irreparable harm done to the integrity of our political system when children are led to believe that the government endorses certain religious schools of thought. Messages draped in the authority of both patriotism and religion are not easily questioned by even the most independent-minded students.

And, anyway, do we as a nation really desire a public market system for education? Shouldn't the school system promote agreed-upon values and standards? Had the consensus on such standards and agreed-upon values broken down by the late 1980s, or had previously minor areas of contention become deal breakers to certain groups? Had the populace shifted, or was it an issue of small groups pushing the margins?

Huge elements of the larger American polity were already in conflict over issues of even smaller weight. By the end of the 1990s the question of whether there was a "war on Christmas" would be dignified with commentary in popular cable network broadcasts. And yet there is a serious side to such manufactured controversies. People are distracted by whether the thing in front of the city hall is called a holiday tree or a Christmas tree. It is easier to deal with an issue like that, with little impact on real life, than to worry about how the districts are being gerrymandered in the county or what children are learning in the classroom. At the national and state levels, there is no doubt that keeping the public distracted about the latest minor perceived value issue (even though these issues may be very valid in their own right) helps obscure the way that significant money is being used in our national and state capitols to convince legislators to enact things they know are wrong, and indeed may be unconstitutional, such as the Kiryas Joel legislation.

After characterizing Kiryas Joel (accurately and fairly) as a place where the religious authorities and the municipal authorities were indistinguishable, Worona's brief went on to lay out the legal standard. On that argument, Jay relied on the 1971 US Supreme Court precedent in *Lemon v. Kurtzman.*

Lemon arose from a dispute over whether state funds could be used to help parochial schools pay their teachers. Back in the late 1960s, when more and more people were sending their kids to public schools and the public schools were diminishing the demand for parochial schools, Pennsylvania and some other states passed laws allowing the state government to reimburse private schools for the cost of teachers' salaries, textbooks, and other materials. This happened only in areas where the vast majority of private schools were Catholic, so such laws essentially caused state taxpayers to finance religious education for a specific group.

In *Lemon*, the Supreme Court held the law unconstitutional as a violation of the Establishment Clause of the First Amendment. The case is important for two reasons. First, it is a definitive, bipartisan, cross ideological statement against such practices. The majority opinion was written by Chief Justice Warren Burger (a Nixon appointee) and was joined by justices Hugo Black and William O. Douglas (who were appointed by Franklin Roosevelt), John Marshall Harlan and Potter Stewart (Eisenhower appointees), Thurgood Marshall (Johnson), and Harry Blackmun (Nixon).

Second, Burger's opinion created its three-part litmus test, known as the *Lemon* test, to provide the lower courts with a roadmap on when a particular law steps afoul of the Establishment Clause. Burger viewed the test as a tidy distillation of all of the court's previous Establishment Clause rulings. Again, in order for a law (or other government action) to be consistent with the Constitution, it must (1) have a secular legislative purpose, (2) not have a primary effect of either advancing or inhibiting religion, and (3) not result in excessive government entanglement with religion. Failure to satisfy any of the three prongs violates the Constitution. The *Lemon* ruling noted that 95 percent of the Pennsylvania schools benefitting from the law were Catholic, and that the sole beneficiaries of the law were Catholic school teachers—clearly unconstitutional under the newly minted test.

Worona's brief argued that the creation of the Kiryas Joel Village School District violated all three prongs of the *Lemon* test, as well as the Equal Protection Clause of the Fourteenth Amendment and the Blaine Amendment to the New York Constitution.

Lewin was fairly confident he could get around the *Lemon* test; he was less confident, though, that the New York courts would give him a pass on the Blaine Amendment. Worona had not belabored the Blaine point in his brief, but the American Jewish Congress, in an amicus brief supporting our position, developed that argument in great detail.

Lewin had some concern that a New York court would find the Blaine Amendment stricter than the Establishment Clause, which could have meant that New York constitutional law would trump federal law and the Supreme Court could not interfere by hearing the case (the New York courts had a reputation for using the state constitution to inhibit federal scrutiny). But he felt there was a good chance that the case would be evaluated purely on the merits of the US Constitution and the First Amendment, and he liked his odds.

As a frequent participant in Supreme Court proceedings and careful observer of the court, Lewin had sensed that the court had become increasingly uncomfortable with *Lemon*. Several post-*Lemon* members of the court, including Chief Justice William Rehnquist and Justices Antonin Scalia and Sandra Day O'Connor, had intimated uneasiness with the rule. The court's Establishment Clause jurisprudence had been all over the map since Rehnquist became chief justice in 1986 and the court began its rightward march.

There was a tiny, but by no means negligible, chance that if Lewin could steer this case through the New York tribunals without those courts killing the school district on state constitutional law grounds, the Supreme Court of the United States would take the case and reverse *Lemon*. The key would be avoiding a decision based only on state law (and thereby precluding Supreme Court review). With Rehnquist and three other Reagan appointees on the bench, and Justices Blackmun, Marshall, Byron White, and William Brennan aging and likely to be replaced by George H. W. Bush appointees, Lewin felt that *Lemon*—a decision that in his mind had long and unfairly stood in the way of federal funding of religious schools throughout the country—was ripe for a takedown.

But first he had to get through New York Supreme Court justice Lawrence E. Kahn, a politically astute, Jewish judge in Albany.

8

HERE COMES THE JUDGE

The interest of the public lies not so much in the continuation of aid to non-public schools as it does in the continued vitality of the Establishment Clause.

—Marburger & Griggs v. Public Funds for Public Schools

WHEN I HEARD that Justice Kahn was assigned the case, I contacted a local legal reporter to get a sense of what kind of judge we were dealing with. I knew Kahn mainly by reputation, and his was solid. I'd heard he was smart, honest, and politically shrewd. And I'd marveled, somewhat curiously, at his ability to render decisions that garnered headlines and often praise in the local media. But I was looking for more behind-the-scenes insight into what we might expect. My media source advised me, "Larry Kahn's got balls. He calls them as he sees them, does what he thinks is right, and doesn't give a damn if he gets reversed. He's not afraid of anybody."

I smiled, because I knew that a judge, especially a Jewish judge, would come under close scrutiny in a case like this, where we were asking a "lowly" state trial judge to tell the governor of New York, a self-fashioned legal scholar, that he had trampled on the US Constitution, and to tell a significant and very powerful segment of the Jewish community that they couldn't run a public school district. But Kahn, I learned, could not be intimidated or bought and had no trouble bucking the powers that be—the very politicians who could make or break his career. In fact, he made a habit of it.

With his Harvard Law and Oxford University credentials, roots in Albany, and powerful ambition, as a young attorney Lawrence Kahn had attempted to ingratiate himself with the local Democratic political machine. After he graduated with distinction from Harvard, Kahn came home to practice law with his older brother, Robert, and to get involved in government. He was quickly brought into the Albany Democratic fold as an adviser to Erastus Corning, a legendary figure who served as Albany mayor for more than four decades and ran the city like the old-fashioned boss he was. It was kind of an odd role for an upper-crust blue blood like Corning, who ran a very ethnic and working-class city.

The Albany machine was one of the most successful political juggernauts in the country and, along with Chicago's Daly machine, one of the last. Republicans had generally dominated upstate politics since the Civil War, but in the 1920s a hardscrabble tavern keeper and cock-fighting promoter named Dan O'Connell decided to "throw the bums out." O'Connell put together a political apparatus built of Irish workmen that would run Albany County for the next fifty years, and he installed Corning as mayor for life. O'Connell was gruff, rough around the edges, blunt, sarcastic, and fond of declaring that "all dogs are nicer than most people."

If O'Connell was the gears and guts of the machine—and he was—Corning, the upstate aristocrat, with his elegance and grace and breeding, was the public face of the clockwork. Corning's great-grandfather, also named Erastus, had founded the New York Central Railroad, which was for decades the largest, most profitable company in the United States. His father was the lieutenant governor during Al Smith's last term as governor of New York.

With Corning and O'Connell at the top, the Albany machine soon became one of the most dominant in the country. Their aim was to control every elected or appointed position connected to the city and county of Albany, and they did it brilliantly, with old-fashioned ward-heeler tactics and by applying an adage that US Speaker of the House Tip O'Neill would coin decades later: "All politics is local."

I remember when I first went to work for Mario Cuomo and bought a house in Albany. The moment I closed on the purchase, the property taxes went up. A lot. That wasn't a big surprise, since the house had not changed hands for more than twenty years and I had paid far more than the previous purchaser had. Neither my wife nor I thought anything of it. Soon afterward, when my registration as a member of the Democratic Party reached the local political office, the neighborhood ward heeler knocked on my door.

"Mr. Grumet," he said, "I just want to tell you that Mayor Corning is *personally* offended that your property taxes have been raised. If you would please sign this petition, I think we can start the process of having your reassessment overturned."

Within a matter of weeks, the taxes indeed were reduced. In fact, I learned that the Albany machine made sure that property taxes of loyal Democrats were *never* reassessed.

One way that the machine was able to maintain such tight control was that Albany, though important because of its role as the capital of the wealthiest state in the union, was a relatively small city, with a population hovering around one hundred thousand people. This allowed the top brass in the machine to take a personal interest in almost every aspect of the city's operations.

For example, when I was the assistant commissioner for special education, I learned that the Albany School District had yet to recognize the existence of even one learning disabled student. It was not

uncommon for school districts to avoid evaluating and classifying special needs children; otherwise the district would be on the hook for the
high cost of serving any special needs students it recognized. Even so,
neither I nor anyone on my staff had ever seen avoidance of responsibility on such an obvious scale. After I wrote a report on this issue
and sent it to the school board, I received a call from Mayor Corning's
office, inviting me to drinks at the Fort Orange Club, the premier private social club in town. Suspecting the mayor was far more interested
in twisting my arm than toasting my astute observation, I instructed
my secretary to decline the invitation. Then I sent the report to the
press—along with the obvious implication that the machine was behind
the failures. The day after the story broke, I returned home to find that
the large, beautiful, and perfectly healthy maple trees in my front yard
had been chopped down, chipped, and carted away by the city.

Another story has it that when Queen Juliana of the Netherlands
visited Albany in 1959 (in honor of the anniversary of the Dutch founding of the city), Governor Nelson Rockefeller was so embarrassed by
the sorry state of Albany, which at the time consisted of little more
than sprawling neighborhoods of crumbling Victorian homes, that
he resolved to sweep away some of the worst slums and replace them
with a series of towers of the most up-to-date design—something to put
Albany on the architectural map (it was eventually named the Nelson
Rockefeller Empire State Plaza). A problem was that the State of New
York cannot float bonds to finance projects without a citizen referen-
dum—but it *can* authorize counties and municipalities to float bonds.
In order to get around this problem, the governor wanted Albany
County to finance his complex.* Mayor Corning agreed to the deal

* Mayor Corning and Governor Rockefeller were such larger-than-life figures, simultaneously in public office in Albany, that a perpetual clash of egos was inevitable. Local
  lore holds that the titans battled over everything, including their respective legacies, as
  evidenced by their construction projects. Rockefeller built the Empire State Plaza, a huge,
  modern state office and cultural complex in the center of downtown Albany. However,
  while no one refers to the Nelson A. Rockefeller Empire State Plaza by his name—it is

on the condition that instead of self-insuring the complex (as the state normally did with its buildings), the state would purchase insurance from Albany Associates, a small firm owned by Erastus Corning.*

Justice Lawrence Kahn, bright and connected but not beholden to anyone, grew up in the O'Connell-Corning political culture. He paid his dues, for a while, but quickly grew impatient when repeatedly told he would have to wait his turn for his professional and political aspiration: a judgeship. Kahn wasn't owed anything—*yet*. And, crucially, he didn't owe anything—*yet*. That gave him some freedom.

When a spot on the New York Supreme Court bench in Albany became available, Kahn was denied the party's endorsement, which went to Thomas Whalen (who would later replace Corning as the mayor's chosen successor). It was not unusual for the party to support a favorite son; rather, it was quite expected. What was unusual was for someone to challenge the party, and Kahn did just that, bucking the machine and running not only without its blessings but in opposition to O'Connell and Corning. Very few others had exhibited the same chutzpah, and their days in politics were over instantly and irrevocably. Kahn not only survived but thrived, for the same reason anyone prevails against a bully: he would not be intimidated. Even though Kahn lost the race against Whalen, he came alarmingly close. The machine knew he was potential trouble. The next time a supreme court seat opened, Kahn, by then a Republican, had the support of both major parties. And a supreme court judgeship in Albany is a plum.

---

simply the Empire State Plaza or South Mall to locals—the largest building on the campus (and the tallest skyscraper in the state outside of Manhattan) is universally known as the Corning Tower.

* Corning was a fascinating and historic figure, and I barely touch on his incredible political career and life. Anyone intrigued by this man and interested in learning more would do well to check out a wonderful biography of the mayor by Paul Grondahl, an outstanding *Albany Times Union* journalist: *Mayor Corning: Albany Icon, Albany Enigma* (Albany: Washington Park Press, 1997).

The Albany supreme court bench has no more power than the supreme court in Buffalo or Brooklyn, but because Albany is the capital, the local judges routinely preside over suits against the state. State legislators in Albany and the machine bosses of the capital have always gone out of their way to nominate well-trained lawyers of distinction who could garner cross-endorsement. Politicians in New York have never been beneath treating judgeships as so many chips in a grand poker game. But when it comes to the Albany courts, a compromise in favor of quality seems to have been worked out in a fortuitous way: since neither party wanted to spend money on a judicial campaign (there's little patronage; supreme court judges usually have only two staffers, a secretary and a law clerk), they tended to cross-endorse each other's candidate. This resulted in a system of checks and balances; neither party would support the other party's candidate if he (and in those days, it was *he)* was a rank political hack or incompetent.

So I was confident that we had a judge who had the brains and the courage to do the right thing. But I also knew that in a case like ours, doing what's right is not as simple as it sounds. In our attack on the law itself, Kahn would be legally required to consider what is known as the equities of the issue. In the case of Kiryas Joel, the equities were particularly important, as the education of children with disabilities was at stake. I anticipated that if the judge believed that disabled children would otherwise be left without service, he could easily decide that fairness required a ruling in favor of KJ. As independent and honest as Kahn was, he didn't want to pick up the paper some morning to read, JUSTICE KAHN TO DISABLED JEWISH KIDS: DROP DEAD!

Though I recognized that Kahn was under political pressure and, I suspected, subconscious personal pressure, I hoped that he would be able to separate himself from the implicit force of the governor as well as his own basic humanity and decide the case purely on the law. But I wasn't going to take any chances.

I fully understood sound-bite politics, and I realized that I needed to appeal to the public's ethos, pathos, and logos—as well as to an observant Jewish judge who would have to run for office sooner or later and didn't need his own community rallying against him. As important as an entertaining quote or gossipy lead might be, I recognized the day-to-day need of government reporters: translation. The heavy reticulation of bureaucratese had become incomprehensible to the average specialist, let alone the average citizen.

As head of the New York State School Boards Association, I was in a position to translate education policy to outsiders, and reporters came to depend on me and my staff. Education is one of the few local issues that is always big news, as it's controversial and interesting and it affects every community, every voter. At the same time that education is a vital topic of local news, it is also maddeningly complicated. The labor issues in education are byzantine and the funding issues so complex* that understanding them requires much specialized knowledge.

Communications director Bill Pape and I formed a translation tag team, a clearinghouse of news. I would turn education policy into sound bites that identified who was benefitting and who was being punished, then Pape would follow up and give reporters information that supported our conclusions. Very quickly, the media came to realize that we could be relied upon for the quick quote *and* in-depth analysis—and, crucially, that our information was accurate and credible. In a nutshell, we became the go-to sources on education policy, and not just in regard to Kiryas Joel. That status would yield important dividends as the KJ case made its way through the courts. With our credibility established on education policy, reporters were open to my

---

* In New York most public school funding, as previously noted, is raised locally through property taxes, but those funds are almost doubled by money from the state and federal governments. Federal money is disbursed through the states, not directly to school districts. Although this is a convenient system for the federal government, since it can distribute money to the fifty states rather than the thousands of school districts, it interposes political maneuvering at the state level. In addition to the complicating factor of multiple funding sources, there are multiple funding *targets*, because much of the state and federal money is earmarked for specific programs. The complexity of the process means that legislators can make inscrutable changes with drastic effects without the public understanding how or why the change was made.

other, more speculative comments about the whole range of public policy and political issues of the day. The relationships I had nurtured with the press would prove exceptionally valuable, enabling me to offer a credible viewpoint, which so heavily influenced the legislature.

The media was our best weapon in the legislature, because legislators are often afraid of the power of the press. Power is built on control of information. When the media presence is thin, as it is at most state capitols these days, the few reporters just take the press releases straight from the issuing agency. I was fortunate that during this period Albany still had reporters like John Caher of the *Albany Times Union* and Billy House of Gannett News Service who were willing to go behind the governor's press releases and cultivate sources throughout and beyond the government—people who were willing to say something other than what the top brass wanted them to say. People like me.

Our public relations effort was focused on two key messages. One, we wanted to show that despite the claims of our opponents, there were perfectly legal and legitimate ways for the governor to ensure that the children of Kiryas Joel would receive all of the special education services they needed, deserved, and were entitled to. We publicized all of the many ways that the children of Kiryas Joel could be well served in the event that Justice Kahn ruled the school district unconstitutional, providing the justice with a way to clear his conscience. The kids could be placed in a community school run by Monroe-Woodbury but located in Kiryas Joel. They could be served in a local program operated by the Orange County Board of Cooperative Education Services. The parents could send their children to a private school for the disabled approved for public funding. Or the children's needs could be addressed in a neighboring school district. Any of these options would lead to essentially the same outcome as the unconstitutional legislation: the Satmar kids with special needs would receive quality services without experiencing the kinds of painful culture clashes they had at the Monroe-Woodbury public school.

Two, we wanted to show that the Pataki-Lentol plan could lead to a host of sectarian school districts all over the state. We argued that the leaders of Kiryas Joel had rejected all alternative solutions because they wanted to *totally* control the placement of children *and* grasp the millions of dollars in public funds that would flow to their village educational programs, both public and private. We also pointed out that in a public school system, even private school students (such as those at the Kiryas Joel yeshivas) are eligible to receive state and federal funds for certain limited purposes, such as transportation and bilingual education, and that if the yeshivas remained under the Monroe-Woodbury umbrella, control over that funding would remain with Monroe-Woodbury, not Kiryas Joel. For those reasons, we argued, the village leaders were dead set against any checks and balances that threatened their power and control of public money. I suggested that the kids of Kiryas Joel were unwitting pawns and that this legislation had the potential to someday lead to educational ghettos.

Our strategy worked. Articles and editorials ran in the *New York Times, Newsday,* the *Albany Times Union,* the *Middletown Times-Herald-Record,* the twenty-two Gannett papers, and the *Buffalo News*—all supportive of our position. We had given Kahn political cover through the media. Now we needed to win the legal battle.

The morning of the oral arguments, Jay Worona left the School Boards Association's office, walking downhill toward the courts. The route took him between Mario Cuomo's office on the second floor of the state capitol building on one side of Washington Avenue and the classically colonnaded New York State Education Department on the other. Jay said he had the strangest sense that those two enormous buildings were closing in to pulverize him, but at the last minute spit him down the hill another block to the Albany County Court House and the chambers of the Honorable Lawrence E. Kahn. Opposing counsel Nat Lewin was already in the courtroom, his persona and legend creating an intimidating aura for us, but not for the judge. Justice Kahn immediately started firing a barrage of questions: What would happen if he ruled in favor of our side? How would the children be served? Does the court really have the authority to strike down a law that hasn't even been tested? How do we know the district can't operate in a constitutional manner? Shouldn't the court defer to the lawmaking authority of the legislature until and unless its work is proven to violate the Constitution? When will the bickering between Kiryas Joel and Monroe cease to plague the courts?

Worona and Pilar Sokol did their best to field Kahn's pressing questions while Lewin urged the judge to defer to the legislature and give the law a chance to prove its vitality and constitutional validity. All the attorneys were outstanding, and I was immensely proud of my two young lawyers and the way they stood up to a legend like Lewin. Whatever happened, I was confident that our arguments were presented loudly and clearly, and that we were leaving Kahn with the legal tools he needed to rule our way.

But Kahn had a decision to make. He instructed his law clerk, Michael Stafford, to begin preparing a decision based on the arguments. That is typical. Judges routinely use their clerks as sounding boards and often give them first crack at a decision, even without debating the case. Sometimes, the clerk and the judge share an opinion, sometimes they are at odds, sometimes the clerk prevails on the judge to view the case differently, and sometimes the judge's initial reaction wins the day. At times the judge and clerk discuss the case before the clerk takes a crack at a decision; at other times they don't, because the judge wants a fresh view and doesn't want to influence his or her underling. But while it is a collaborative process, at the end of the day the decision is the judge's and it's his or her name that goes on it. The only instruction Kahn gave Stafford before sending him off to draft an opinion was this: ignore, for the time being, the state constitutional argument and, for the moment, stick with the US Constitution.

I can only speculate as to why Kahn wanted to rule on the federal Constitution, where our claim was not nearly as strong, and ignore the state constitution, where I had thought we couldn't possibly lose. My guess is that a number of factors, legal and political, played into Kahn's decision. I suspect he knew the case had the potential to go to the US Supreme Court if he decided on federal constitutional grounds and he wanted to give the justices an opportunity to reconsider or refine the *Lemon* test if they were so inclined.

At around the same time, the New York State Court of Appeals—the state's highest court—was itself debating whether, when it had the option, it should rule only on the state constitution or only on the federal Constitution, or both. A state-only ruling would preclude federal review, leaving the court's work beyond the scope of the Supreme Court and denying the Supreme Court an opportunity to make an important pronouncement on constitutional law. Ruling only on the US Constitution meant foregoing an opportunity to stake independent state constitutional grounds.

To no one's surprise, Stafford's first draft would have denied both sides' motions for summary judgment, or an immediate decision that essentially adopts all of the arguments of one side of the dispute. But Stafford's draft went further: it would have ordered a trial to determine if the school district was being run properly. This decision, in effect, would be a denial of our facial challenge, which argued that the law was improper regardless of how it was implemented.

Kahn didn't agree with his clerk's take, but it helped gel the issues for him and helped him decide the course he would take, if only because he thought Stafford got it wrong. The Constitution is not a wait-and-see document. The point of the *Lemon* test, which Kahn was bound to follow as long as he was committed to ignoring the state constitution to get to the federal Constitution, was to evaluate the conduct of the government when it made the law—not the application of the law. Kahn decided to draft the opinion himself.

The relationship between the judicial and the political branches bears mention here. It is a delicate balance. While the third branch of the government has the *judicial* power to decide disputes, it also has the *political* power to void the acts of other branches of government. But judges are usually careful, when potentially intruding in political matters, to act only against the *means* by which the legislative or executive branch executed the policy, rather than the *policy* itself (since setting policy is a prerogative of the political branches). When a judge renders a law void, he or she will usually try to do it in a manner that makes it possible to achieve whatever legislative goal is at hand. In other words, when courts find they have to strike down a law, they usually try to do so in a way to salvage the goal of the law if not the method. Most judges would rather say, "You can't do what you're trying to do this way," rather than, "You can't do it at all."

In Kiryas Joel, Kahn wanted to send a message that it was constitutionally unacceptable to serve Satmar children with special needs by giving a school district to a religious community. But he may also have wanted to leave room for the legislature to serve those kids in some other way, and ensure that he didn't paint lawmakers into a corner.

Meanwhile, Kahn was starting to get pressure from his own community—some in favor of the legislation, some opposed. He put enormous effort into crafting a legally sound, balanced decision and, on January 22, 1992, issued a succinctly articulate opinion finding that the establishment of the Kiryas Joel Village School District violated all three prongs of the *Lemon* test.

> First, it has a sectarian rather than a secular purpose. There is no doubt that the legislation was an attempt by the executive and Legislature to accommodate the sectarian wishes of the citizens of Kiryas Joel by taking the extraordinary measures of creating a governmental unit to meet their parochial needs.
>
> The statute rather than serving a legitimate governmental end, was enacted to meet exclusive religious needs and has the effect of

advancing, protecting and fostering the religious beliefs of the inhabitants of the school district.

Kahn went on to state that the "residents of the Village of Kiryas
Joel have unequivocally refused and rejected any attempts to provide
for the education of handicapped pupils from the village at a neutral
site previously offered by the Monroe-Woodbury School District" and
described the village and its coterminous school district as "an enclave
of segregated individuals who share common religious beliefs which
shape the social, political and familial mores of their lives from cradle
to grave. . . . The legislation is an attempt to camouflage, with secular
garments, a religious community as a public school district."

The justice continued:

> The intent of the Legislature and executive to be responsive to the
> citizens of Kiryas Joel is laudatory and reflects the political process
> straining to meet the parochial needs of a religious group. However,
> their action violates the First Amendment which prohibits legis-
> lation which promotes the establishment of religion. The Satmar
> Hasidic sect enjoys religious freedom as guaranteed by the very First
> Amendment that they are now seeking to circumvent. This short
> range accomplishment could in the long run, jeopardize the very
> religious freedom that they now enjoy.
>
> The strength of our democracy is that a multitude of religious,
> ethnic and racial groups can live side by side with respect for each
> other. The uniqueness of religious values as observed by the Satmar
> sect is especially to be admired as nonconformity becomes increas-
> ingly more difficult to sustain, however, laws cannot be enacted to
> advance and endorse such parochial needs in violation of our deep-
> rooted principle of separation of Church and State.

Wow! I viewed the decision as a stunning victory and lauded Kahn's
ruling as legally and politically astute. Kahn had adroitly spelled out all

the issues, making a wonderful record for appeal—which we all knew
was inevitable. The Albany reporter I had asked about Kahn months
before was right: Kahn had balls, and he wasn't afraid of anyone—not
even his own community.

Predictably, the judge's decision was not well received in the village of Kiryas Joel. Abe Wieder was livid. The Satmar had prevailed
on their political "friends" to establish the district because they didn't
want to rely on the courts, and now they were stuck in a legal battle.
They had brought in the best lawyer money could buy. They had spent
vast sums setting up the one and only public school in the Kiryas Joel
Village School District for a handful of special needs pupils. They had
gone to court and by luck of the draw got a Jewish judge. Wieder's
reputation in the village (and more important, with the grand rebbe
himself) was now at stake as he discussed appealing the decision with
attorney Nat Lewin.

Meanwhile, he had to break the bad news to Steve Benardo, the
expert in special education and school administration whom the village
had recruited to run the school.

9

ESTABLISHMENT

_____

The First Amendment's purpose was to create a complete and permanent separation of the spheres of religious activity and civil authority by comprehensively forbidding every form of public aid or support for religion.
—Justice Tom C. Clark, *Everson v. Board of Education*

IHAD ENCOUNTERED STEVE Benardo years earlier and taken an immediate liking to him. His passion, intellect, and fierce commitment to children with disabilities seemed at odds with his unassuming, pleasant appearance and demeanor. Our paths, and swords, would cross many times in the ensuing years, but I had and have nothing but respect for Steve. I learned quickly that behind the nondescript eyeglasses and bushy mustache was a formidable adversary and first-rate intellect.

A Sephardic Jew whose parents emigrated from Spain to New York City, Steve grew up bilingual, with a background combining the idealism of the 1960s with an immigrant work ethic and values. That combination yielded an unwavering commitment to public service. For Steve, there could be no better way to serve the public than through a career in public education, particularly special education. He welcomed the opportunity to help students with disabilities—who in the recent past would have been written off as useless and quite possibly institutionalized—blossom into all they were capable of becoming.

Special education, the most challenging frontier of education at the time, was only beginning to emerge from the dark ages of abuse, punishment, and indifference into an exciting new paradigm based on humanity and rational expectations and motivated by discovering just what could be expected of any given child. Children with disabilities had been abused physically and culturally for so long that it was anyone's guess what they might be able to achieve. The goal now was to assume the children were capable and then deal with the disabling condition. For example, teach blind children Braille or with tape recordings, and they can learn as much as their peers.

But the early 1970s was a time of unparalleled change in public education, change that reflected a variety of demographic, economic, sociological, and political evolutions.

Demographically, we had the desegregation movement, and while the white liberals were fully on board intellectually, they were a lot less enthusiastic with the notion of busing kids from the ghetto into their middle-class neighborhoods—and upset at the thought that their children could be sent to school in the slums. Many of them took their kids and their tax dollars to the suburbs. At the same time, the industrial migration to the South and Southwest took its toll on the Northeast and the revenue stream available to the area's public schools, especially for programs such as special ed.

Also, the teaching field was undergoing its own transformation. Long dominated by underpaid women who viewed themselves—quite legitimately—as professionals but unfortunately eschewed organized representation, the field was suddenly attracting more bread-winning men receptive to unionization.

It was against this backdrop that Tom Hobart and Al Shanker joined forces to turn the fledgling New York State United Teachers union into one of the most powerful political and lobbying forces in the state. When funds became available for public education, NYSUT did its best to steer the money into teacher salaries and pensions rather than innovative programs for kids. Still, legislation enacted both nationally and in New York State in the mid-1970s required all school districts to offer parentally approved, individualized programs for kids with special needs in the least restrictive environment possible, regardless of the cost. Service was required, and due process mandated.

That was the entrée Steve Benardo needed.

Benardo was instantly smitten with the notion of publicly funded special education; it excited his innate sense of fairness, humanity, and justice, and also his need for new intellectual challenges. But he wanted to run a program, not teach under a protocol imposed by someone else. So he enrolled in a doctoral curriculum in educational administration and emerged as one of the few bilingual special education experts in the country. Steve's first job after earning his doctorate was as a special education adviser to the Bronx representative on the New York City school board.

In those days, the city still had an appointed school board whose function was largely limited to "oversight" of the chancellor, the executive of the system. It was an unwieldy system, with the borough presidents (of the Bronx, Brooklyn, Manhattan, Queens, and Staten Island) each appointing one member, while the mayor appointed two.

By the time Benardo got his first job there, much of the Bronx—long the dream destination of New York's rising middle class—had descended into urban blight. A borough that was once bucolic, almost quaint, with its wide parkways and avenues, the city's largest park system, a world-famous zoo and botanical garden, splendid housing, and convenient access to the business centers of Manhattan, was now pockmarked with dilapidated and abandoned buildings and plagued by rampant crime and perpetual economic strife. Its school system reflected the borough's poverty and abandon. Benardo inherited a system in financial peril where many students lacked fundamental English skills and even basic written language skills in their native tongue, had little support at home, and came from families with little or no understanding of how to care for members with disabilities. Concerned simply with survival, such families had neither the means nor the motivation to demand programming for their children.

Frank J. Macchiarola, the chancellor, was struggling to maintain a school system in a city barely equipped to serve "mainstream" kids, let alone disabled children costing three times as much to educate. He persistently shortchanged children with special needs via extreme understaffing and a game his counterparts all over the country were playing: refusing to acknowledge that a child was in need of special services and letting the parents sue if they didn't like it. Meanwhile, as tens of thousands of children awaited their evaluations, the money that should have been dedicated to them was diverted to "normal" kids. Indeed, for several years, New York City had a seemingly permanent list of more than fourteen thousand children who were thought to be severely disabled and who were waiting for evaluations.

At the time, I was the state education department's assistant commissioner in charge of the Office of Children with Handicapping Conditions, tasked with ensuring that people like Macchiarola complied with the law. But he was used to getting his way and didn't at all appreciate the notion of some bureaucrat from Albany trying to tell him how to run his schools. Not surprisingly, we ended up in court, and Macchiarola sent Benardo as a witness. Steve knew we were right, legally and morally, but Macchiarola ordered him to "tell the judge that it doesn't matter how many of those kids are waiting in line because nothing's playing at the movies." Steve did exactly as instructed, and I'm pretty sure I saw steam come out of the ears of US district judge Eugene Nickerson, a onetime candidate for the US Senate and governor who really found his niche in the judiciary and became an outstanding federal judge.*

Nickerson, whose own child was receiving special needs services, just glared at Benardo—Macchiarola's sacrificial lamb—before cutting him off in midstream. "Well, you tell Frank Macchiarola that I'm going to send him to jail." Steve was greatly relieved that it wasn't *he* who was going to jail. Ultimately, the city was held in contempt, and a special master was appointed to oversee implementation of the court order to evaluate and serve the children.

By coincidence, I was quickly developing a close friendship with George Shebitz, the chancellor's counsel who, like Steve Benardo, knew the boss was wrong. In his testimony, the chancellor said he couldn't reduce the backlog because he was unable to find qualified special educators to perform the services. I subsequently testified that twenty-five of my highly qualified staffers had applied for city jobs and were turned down, and submitted staff affidavits. Macchiarola was so frustrated that he sent Shebitz to communicate with me, and we promptly discovered a common bond.

Shebitz and I both had law degrees and master's degrees in government administration. We both totally bought into the philosophy of integration. We both worshipped Thomas Jefferson. We both believed to our core in society's responsibility to assist the most vulnerable, and agreed there are few who are more vulnerable than children with disabling conditions. Benardo had grown equally close to Shebitz, so ours was an unlikely trio; we were officially on different sides of this dispute, but privately we all agreed that Macchiarola was dead wrong. Steve later became the first superintendent for special education in the Bronx—a critically important position—and indeed became a pioneer and renowned expert in bilingual special ed. George became a

---

* Nickerson, a descendant of President John Adams, was appointed to the federal bench in 1977 by President Jimmy Carter. As a judge, he had a reputation for keeping lawyers on a short leash and had little patience for courtroom antics. He died in 2002.

successful education attorney, serving school districts throughout the state and specializing in the rights of children with disabilities.

About eight years after Benardo and Shebitz had left the chancellor's office, Steve received an out-of-the-blue call from George, who said he needed some help with a special education problem. "First, I would've gone anywhere for George, but, second, special educators have a kind of community code—if somebody calls you and asks for help, you just do it. It's part of the game," Benardo recalls. For a lot of good reasons, special educators had developed an us-against-the-world mentality, and without hesitation or further inquiry he went over to George's office. There he was surprised to find himself in a room full of Hasidic Jews, who promptly cornered him and began talking about their busing fight with the Monroe-Woodbury district, a segue into a discussion of the Pataki-Lentol bill that Cuomo had just signed. One of the oddities of the legislation was that the Satmar were required to prove to the state department of education that they could actually operate a school district. They asked Steve to write up something to satisfy State Ed.

"To tell you the truth, I thought this would be an easy task," Steve remembers. "I thought I would just take a few hours to help out my friend George. How hard could it be? I mean, I knew the law backwards and forwards. I was running the whole freaking Bronx! I had a three-thousand-person staff. I knew what I was doing. The first thing I did was call the [superintendent] of Lancaster, Pennsylvania, to find out how he handled the Amish."

Benardo soon discovered that the issue with the Amish was in many ways unrelated to the Satmar Hasidim. After all, the Amish fought to be left alone and to be free of force-fed government services; Kiryas Joel, on the other hand, wanted the government's services and subsidies and amenities—on their terms and in conformance with their religious mandates. So Benardo drove up to Albany to do a little research.

"When you've gone to school as much as I have, you think there's a book for everything. I thought I'd go up to State Ed and check out the book on how to start a school district."

Steve remembers venturing into the pillared porticos of the state department of education building, where he eventually found an office that seemed right, the Office of Private School Organizational Structures. An employee there informed him that there hadn't been a new school district created in New York State in many decades.

Benardo spent the next five months working on the project every single night after he left his job as Bronx superintendent. He drove up to Kiryas Joel each night after work, talking to people in the village to get a full grasp of their needs and concerns. He began going up in the daytimes, burning through every vacation day he had accumulated over twenty-one years.

"When they first asked me to do this, they asked what I wanted to be paid," Steve says. "At the time, my kid wanted to go to summer camp and it cost $3,000, so I said $3,000, which made sense to me. I had no idea what consultants got paid. I had no idea what the scope of this was going to turn out to be. I was just helping out George."

Finally, the day came for Benardo to present the proposal to State Ed. At the meeting were Manny Axelrod, superintendent of the Orange County Board of Cooperative Education Services (a peculiarly New York institution that originally provided regional programs for vocational training and later also special education), and Dr. Hannah Flegenheimer, the state division director for special education. Hannah had been my chief aide during my days at State Ed when we were defunding private schools that accepted public funding to serve students with disabilities but did not serve them well. We moved thousands of children with disabilities into less restrictive settings in the public schools. Indeed, Hannah had provided the staffing when I was working with Judge Nickerson to force New York City schools to evaluate and serve all of their disabled children. I admire her courage, integrity, and intelligence more than almost any public servant I have ever met. Hannah arrived at the meeting with an attorney and was clearly intent on holding Steve's feet to the fire.

Steve had brought with him the school board of this soon-to-be public school district, whose members were selected to serve by the grand rebbe himself. Not only did none of them appear to speak much English, but none of them had ever been in a public school, let alone attended one. George Shebitz came with Benardo as the KJ district's attorney.

Benardo submitted a massive tome that described everything about the district, which, at that point, had no building or staff. Flegenheimer demanded to know if boys and girls would be segregated according to religious traditions, and whether they could take gym together. She was promptly expelled from the room. After a two-hour discussion, without Hannah and her apparently jaw-dropping inquiry, Manny Axelrod took out a small mallet, whacked the table, and declared the birth of the Kiryas Joel Village School District. "By the way," he asked, "who's the superintendent?" Without a word in advance to Steve, George Shebitz said the board wanted Benardo to take the job.

Steve was stunned, and more than a little annoyed that George would be so presumptuous as to assume he would give up a huge job in the Bronx to assume the responsibilities of the first superintendent of the first new school district established in New York in a generation. But once they were out of earshot of Axelrod, Shebitz convinced Benardo that Abe Wieder would make it well worth his while, and that running the new school district of Kiryas Joel would be more rewarding than anything he would leave undone in the Bronx.

Steve decided to take up the challenge. He immediately impressed the KJ community, both with his bureaucratic expertise in garnering state funding and his ability to build an impressive program. He also became one of the highest-paid superintendents in the state, though he served one of the smallest districts.

When Benardo started assembling the KJ district in 1990, Monroe-Woodbury was providing $181,000 worth of services to the community, holding classes in two temporary classrooms. Steve went to State Ed and got $1.2 million overnight. Still, finances were tough the first year, and the district survived largely on IOUs. The second year, Steve applied for and received significant state and federal funding. So in short order he established a brand-new, adequately funded school district that served the needs of the KJ children far better than Monroe-Woodbury ever had, and actually better than the community had dared to hope. Furthermore, the village residents were relieved of the responsibility of paying the high property taxes that were levied by Monroe-Woodbury. This is what you'd call a win-win-win for the KJ community, and the credit goes to Steve Benardo.

At first the district just took in the village's special needs kids aged five through twenty-one, but it soon expanded to pre-K and early childhood education and began accepting Satmar children with disabilities from other communities as well. Being a part of the child's (and family's) life from early years to adulthood allowed Kiryas Joel to provide an extraordinary continuum of services. As issues arose in a child's development (or in a parent's adjustment to realistic goals for his child), Steve could easily fine-tune programming based on input from teachers and therapists who had interacted with the child at a range of different ages. In a few short years, the student body had grown from the original group of thirteen children to several hundred.

"It's exactly what one would want to develop. If you had a blank page and somebody told you to forget the rules, forget the regulations, forget any of those concerns, and just create a school for special education students, I really believe it would look like our school," Steve says.

Irrespective of culture, parents of special ed students have a variety of anxieties about their children—concerns ranging from denial of the condition to obsession over it. One way Benardo fought those anxieties was to install a two-way mirror in a classroom so that parents could observe the services without interfering. He also recognized that denial was a natural reaction of parents and that most parents could move past it if they weren't forced to confront the disability head-on, if they could ease into it on their own terms. So he had a separate entrance and a separate area for the parents of preschool and younger kids so that they didn't have to see older kids, allowing them to hold onto, for the moment, the belief that their kids would "grow out of it." That way parents could come to grips with their own child's potential and limits, accepting the hard and sometimes cold facts gradually and in their own time. It was an important innovation, and a very creative solution to an old problem in special education.

Benardo was also able to put together a well-qualified staff, most of whom were Orthodox Jews. Every single staff member spoke at least two languages, mostly Yiddish and English, with a smattering of Hebrew, Spanish, and Russian. Everyone on the professional staff had at least a master's degree, and most had doctoral degrees. Many of them were intrigued by the opportunity to make a real difference at the ground level.

As the district prospered and the children thrived, the community dug its heels in more than ever. Although my association's public relations campaign had suggested a number of ways in which the village could achieve exactly the same results, with the same staff, in a way that didn't desecrate the Constitution, the Kiryas Joel leaders weren't hearing it. There was little chance they were going to backtrack, and no chance they were going to give up what had become a treasure chest of state and federal aid,* at least not without a real fight.

When Justice Kahn's decision came down, Steve viewed it as a momentary distraction, knowing that the district would appeal, as of course it did, and that the status quo would be maintained while the

---

* In addition to aid for the children whose special needs they were serving, the district was also getting millions of dollars in transportation aid for the nondisabled students in the private yeshivas, as well as control over who drove the buses (see chapter 2). Those extra benefits materialized solely because of the existence of a "public" school district.

case worked its way through the courts. The next fight would be in the appellate division of the state supreme court, a tribunal composed entirely of gubernatorial appointees, some of whom dreamed of getting promoted to the top rung of the judicial ladder. And there I was, asking these judges to tell the governor that the law he signed was unconstitutional.

10

REVIEWING THE DECISION

The prospect of church and state litigating in court about what does or does not have religious meaning touches the very core of the constitutional guarantee against religious establishment, and it cannot be dismissed by saying it will happen only once.
          —Justice Potter Stewart, *New York v. Cathedral Academy*

JUSTICE KAHN'S DECISION sent shock waves throughout the educational establishment and religious communities, and suddenly an issue that I always knew was a big deal started garnering intense interest. The Satmar, of course, worried that Kahn's decision would stand, forcing them to close down. But like myself, many others (including a number of Jewish organizations) were deeply concerned that if Kahn were to be reversed, the Establishment Clause would suffer a vicious blow that could dramatically weaken the Jeffersonian wall of separation between church and state. We all knew the stakes were high, and we all knew the case could eventually go to the Supreme Court.

In the New York court system, there are two levels of appellate courts. The first level is the appellate division of the state supreme court, which is composed of elected trial judges (like Kahn) who have

helpful as the case continued its journey through the courts. Casey also spent a considerable amount of time refuting Levine's dissent. While it concerned me somewhat that the dissent was longer than the majority opinion, and that the majority was so intent on responding to Levine, I was glad that the majority had thoroughly addressed the issues in the dissent.

From the majority standpoint, the legislation violated the *Lemon* test,* especially the prong that bars legislation in which the primary or principal effect is to advance religion. The majority saw the district's argument (*it just happens that this secular school district's boundaries coincide with the boundaries of a religions enclave*) as the sham that it was:

> Regardless of whether the public school operated by the Village District is a neutral site, and regardless of how scrupulous the district is in maintaining the secular nature of the educational services, we are of the view that the symbolic union between church and State effected by the creation of a school district coterminous with a religious enclave to provide within that enclave educational services that were already available elsewhere is significantly likely to be perceived by adherents of the Satmar Hasidim as an endorsement, and by nonadherents as a disapproval of their religious beliefs.
>
> We emphasize that it is not the location of the public school in the religious community and the provision of public educational services to sectarian students that we find offensive to the Establishment Clause. The impermissible effect is the symbolic impact of creating a new school district coterminous with a religious community to provide educational services that were already available in an effort to resolve a dispute between the religious community and the school district within which the community was formerly located,

---

* Again, under *Lemon v. Kurtzman*, 403 US 602 (1971), a statute must have a secular purpose, its primary effect must be one that neither promotes nor inhibits religion, and it must not foster "an excessive government entanglement with religion."

a dispute based upon the language, lifestyle and environment of the community's children created by the religious tenets, practices and beliefs of the community.

Levine saw it differently—much differently. In his view, the needs of the Satmar children were not necessarily based on religion; rather, he argued, they were culturally based. Levine would have given "the Satmar Hasidim their day in court to establish that the statute can be and has been implemented in a way that sufficiently separates the Village District's provision of special education services for their disabled children from their precepts and practices to avoid conflict with the Establishment Clause." He argued that absent direct proof that the district was a religious operation, the court should assume that it is not, despite the fact that our argument centered on the adoption rather than the implementation of law.

> The ultimate ground for the majority's invalidation of [the law] . . . is its conclusion that the primary or principal effect of the legislation is to advance religion. I disagree. . . . I believe that this Court should not be looking for ulterior motives. . . . As repeatedly stated, the motive for the Satmar parents' refusal to accept the special educational services for their handicapped children offered by the Monroe-Woodbury District was not religious, but was to protect the children from the psychological and emotional trauma caused by exposure to integrated classes outside the Village that were inadequately addressed by the professional staff of the Monroe-Woodbury District.

Levine added:

> While I am not able to discern with complete confidence why the majority rejects the . . . religious-neutral explanation by the Satmar

for their refusal to accept the special educational services of the Monroe-Woodbury District, the majority's rationale seems to be based on either one of two propositions. The first of these is that the Satmar's explanation is disingenuous, i.e., that segregated education of even its handicapped children is in fact at the core of the Satmar sect's religious beliefs. . . . Alternatively, the majority's decision may be read as concluding that the [Satmar's] professed explanation for rejecting the Monroe-Woodbury District's offer of services is . . . religion based because the Satmar's cloistered lifestyle and cultural outlook are derived from their religious beliefs. This . . . has grave constitutional implications. . . . In effect, the majority is saying that the State may not respond to a bona fide *secular interest* of the Satmar Hasidim, i.e., the psychological and emotional vulnerabilities of their handicapped children, because the culture bringing about the insecurities of these youngsters was "molded" by Satmar religious precepts. In a real sense, then, the majority is holding that merely because of some link between their religion and a legitimate secular need, the Satmar are disqualified from receiving from the State the purely secular services to meet that secular need. The case law simply does not support such a rigidly impenetrable wall between church and State.

In response, Justice Casey cited "uncontradicted evidence of a direct link between the language, lifestyle and environment of the community's children and the religious tenets, practices and beliefs of the community. . . . The dissent's suggestion that the creation of a new school district was the appropriate remedy to address the Satmar parents' claim that the services offered by the Monroe-Woodbury District were inappropriate for the special needs of their children is less than compelling."

Levine's dissent, skillfully and articulately distinguishing between cultural and religious accommodation, gave us some real problems, because it offered the New York Court of Appeals a plausible way to duck the case. If the court of appeals wanted to avoid overturning the Pataki-Lentol law without endorsing it, the judges could take the path suggested by Levine. I had to admit that Levine had made a plausible and principled argument—although I still believed our argument was more plausible and equally principled. Fortunately, there was no Supreme Court authority on the question.

And the question, going to the heart of the Establishment Clause, was probably outside the purview of the state courts. From a tactical standpoint, Levine perhaps undermined his own dissent. Worona and Lewin had introduced competing experts testifying on the question of theocracy in the village, and the judge's argument would have been better served by choosing sides between the experts rather than attempting to divine a Supreme Court–approved method of disentangling religion from culture in a few highly tangential cases about Christmas trees or menorahs.

Meanwhile, the further the case went up the judicial ladder, the more attention it garnered. The divided opinion of the appellate division captured the interest of Establishment Clause scholars across the country, several of whom filed amicus briefs. When courts, especially high courts, are faced with important decisions about policy, they often welcome these "friend of the court" briefs, which tend to be written by lawyers and academics who have deep experience on the issues before the court. Not infrequently, academics who happen to have written articles touching on issues before the court will send these to the court as well. If a court cites information from the article, it's considered a great honor in academic circles.

Most of these amici relied on the *Lemon* test, despite the fact that at least four of the nine Supreme Court justices and maybe even a majority had implied that *Lemon* had run its course and outlived its usefulness.

Marc Stern of the American Jewish Congress (AJC) had a different approach. One of the nation's most venerable Jewish organizations, conflicts in the public schools is to create religiously identifiable school districts."

Next, Stern wanted to refocus the court on the broad political and constitutional principles behind the *Lemon* test and the Establishment Clause itself. The *Lemon* test, Stern argued, was devised to help the court sort out the marginal cases, like whether there can be a prayer during a college graduation or whether the Ten Commandments can be displayed at a school. But the Kiryas Joel situation was not a side issue; it was a direct affront to the Establishment Clause, as it represented an actual granting of government authority to the leaders of a religious group. Stern argued that the court should just knock the Kiryas Joel school district out as a direct establishment and, therefore, contrary to the First Amendment. His brief concluded with a clarion call for the New York Court of Appeals to hold back the tide of resegregation in America:

> The original idea of a common school is under broad attack from many sources. There are constant proposals for schools for specific racial and ethnic groups, sometimes for one sex or the other. Here the legislature has created a school district for members of one religion only. The time and place to stop this disturbing trend is now. Whatever else the Kiryas Joel School District may be, it is not a common school. Its existence is inconsistent with our Constitutional system, and cannot stand.

Jay Worona's brief, strategically conceptualized to complement Stern's amici, described in detail how the New York State Legislature and the governor had violated each prong of the *Lemon* test. First, the legislature had no nonreligious purpose for creating a Hasidic school district; indeed the governor's message upon signing the bill referenced only an accommodation to religion. Second, the only identifiable purpose of the legislation was to advance and endorse the Satmar religion and to place the imprimatur of the state upon the grand rebbe's theocracy. And third, the existence of the school district would require extensive monitoring and thus entanglement between the government and religion.

We knew that the *Lemon* test argument, while sound, was a bit dicey, because of a 5–4 decision on school prayer the US Supreme Court had handed down on June 24, 1992 (after Kahn's original decision, but six months before the appellate division's ruling). *Lee v. Weisman* was the first major school prayer case decided by the Rehnquist court. The case itself was about a somewhat marginal question—whether a rabbi could offer a nonsectarian prayer before a public school graduation. But it was a litmus test of whether the addition of Clarence Thomas to the Supreme Court would result in a rollback of the rules governing school prayers. In *Weisman*, Justice Anthony Kennedy broke with the conservative wing and established what today is known as the coercion test—that is, whether the act of government has the effect of coercing participation in a religious exercise:

> The school district's supervision and control of a high school graduation ceremony places subtle and indirect public and peer pressure on attending students to stand as a group or maintain respectful silence during the invocation and benediction. A reasonable dissenter of high school age could believe that standing or remaining silent signified her own participation in, or approval of, the group exercise, rather than her respect for it. And the State may not place the student dissenter in the dilemma of participating or protesting. Since adolescents are often susceptible to peer pressure, especially in matters of social convention, the State may no more use social pressure to enforce Orthodoxy than it may use direct means. The embarrassment and intrusion of the religious exercise cannot be refuted by arguing that the prayers are of a *de minimis* character, since that is an affront to the Rabbi and those for whom the prayers

that prevented the Satmar from receiving government services without impinging on the free exercise of Satmar beliefs. "For reasons that are secular and not religious, the Satmar handicapped children are unable to leave Kiryas Joel and attend the heterogeneous special education classes provided by Monroe-Woodbury," they insisted in their legal brief.

I viewed this argument as a mistake in legal, logical, and political terms, because it hinged on an absurdity. The Satmar's argument struck me as the equivalent of a white supremacist community arguing that their white children in Little Rock would be so traumatized by having to go to school with black kids that the state should provide a segregated public school environment for them.

Now that the case was headed to the court of appeals, we redoubled our efforts to draw media interest. Frankly, we wanted as much attention as we could get, and we hoped that such interest would resonate with the judges of the court of appeals and dissuade them, if they were so inclined, from ducking the issue as Levine had. We framed the case as a major confrontation between the governor and the Constitution and between the board of regents and the governor, with potentially profound implications for the religious rights of the average citizen. Our effort was highly successful, and we garnered the attention of the *New York Times*, the *Albany Times Union*, the Gannett chain, the Associated Press, *Newsday*—in short, all of the most influential and broad-based newspapers in the state. Those papers ran numerous stories about the conflict, many of them editorializing on the matter and suggesting that Kiryas Joel's school district threatened the entire premise of the melting pot and could lead to serious revivals of separatist tendencies in the schools.

But we knew, of course, that it wasn't the press we ultimately had to persuade but seven of the sharpest legal minds in the state: the judges of the rightly renowned New York State Court of Appeals.

11

DOES IT PASS THE TEST?

I have sought to shape not just a good court but an excellent one, a court of strong and intelligent jurists who bring competence and commitment to every case and dispense justice based on reason, logic and the accumulated experience reflected in the law.

—Governor Mario Cuomo

LIKE NO OTHER governor before or since, Mario Cuomo had a respect for the New York State Court of Appeals that bordered on reverence.

As a young lawyer, Cuomo had clerked for a court of appeals judge, Adrian Burke, and often described the two years he spent at the court as among the most rewarding and formative of his career. Before leaving office, he would appoint the entire court, all seven judges, putting in place an incredibly balanced panel of three Democrats, three Republicans, and one independent. He named the first black judge ever appointed to a full term on the court (Fritz W. Alexander II), the first woman to serve on the court and the first woman chief judge (both Judith S. Kaye), and the court's first Hispanic judge (Carmen

Beauchamp Ciparick).* Cuomo stunned the political establishment
when he selected, for his very first appointment, an upstate, law-and-
order Republican (Richard D. Simons). Before Judith Kaye, he even
appointed a Republican as chief judge (Sol Wachtler).†

Cuomo agonized over those appointments, studying the decisions
of nominees who had prior judicial experience and examining the professional and personal records of those who did not. It was often specu-
lated that Cuomo would have preferred, and was perhaps better suited
for, the courthouse than the executive mansion, speculation fueled in
part by a story he often shared of his mother. According to Cuomo, on
election night 1982, when he became the first Italian American elected
to a full term as governor of New York, the governor-elect turned to his
immigrant mother, Immaculata Cuomo, put his arm around her, and
said, "Mama, what do you think now?" She responded, "Is not bad. But
when you gonna be judge?"‡

When Kiryas Joel got up to the New York Court of Appeals for argument on April 29, 1993, there were six judges on the court, all of them

---

* For a thorough analysis of Mario Cuomo's appointments to the court of appeals, see Ben-
jamin Pomerance's insightful article "When Dad Reached Across the Aisle: How Mario
Cuomo Created a Bipartisan Court of Appeals," *Albany Law Review* 77 (2013/2014): 185,
www.albanylawreview.org/Articles/Vol77_1/77.1.0185-Pomerance.pdf.
† Critics suggest, with some justification, that Cuomo gets more than his share of credit
for appointing three Republican judges and promoting Wachtler to chief judge. He chose
Simons and, later, Howard Levine only after his first choices didn't pan out. And many
skeptics have asserted that the promotion of the politically ambitious Wachtler to chief
judge was based on the governor's political calculus more than the jurist's legal acumen.
Wachtler was a potential rival for governor. By making him chief judge, the reasoning
goes, Cuomo neutralized a serious threat to his reelection. Cuomo may well have had
political and other considerations in mind when he made the appointments, but the
people he appointed were outstanding judges. I do not think the governor would have
sacrificed quality for expediency, at least when it came to court of appeals appointments.
‡ Cuomo told this story on many occasions, including November 21, 2007, when he
received the Federal Bar Council's Emory Buckner Medal for outstanding public service and delivered his "Our Lady of the Law" speech. The full text is archived at *2parse*
(blog), July 5, 2009, http://2parse.com/?page_id=3322.

appointed by Cuomo.* I was unconcerned that those judges—Chief Judge Kaye and judges Simons, George Bundy Smith, Stewart F. Hancock Jr., Joseph W. Bellacosa, and Vito J. Titone—were all Cuomo appointees, and I felt confident that they would decide the case on the merits rather than any allegiance to the governor. They were too smart and had too much integrity to engage in such crass political calculation. But I *was* concerned that the court would follow the lead of Howard Levine, the dissenter in the state supreme court case, who would finally join the appellate court a few months later. I knew the high court greatly respected his judgment.[†]

The argument before the court of appeals lasted for nearly an hour—a relatively long session. Our three adversaries—Nat Lewin for Kiryas Joel, Lawrence Reich for the Monroe-Woodbury Central School District, and Assistant Attorney General Julie Mereson for the state—argued first, and in my view, got nowhere. They basically insisted that the legislation creating the Kiryas Joel school district was necessary for cultural, not religious, reasons. Under questioning from Chief Judge Kaye, Lewin was boxed in and had to admit that if the district was created specifically to cater to the interests of a religious sect, it could not stand.

Lewin: "If this were a religious gerrymander, I think we would be in a very difficult position, and maybe an untenable position. If what happened was there was a drawing of lines . . . to deliberately take into account a religious community and try to single it out—"

But the chief judge cut him off and came back with a rhetorical question for which he had no good answer. "In practical effect, isn't that what's happened?"

Reich and Mereson followed, relying on the same logic as Lewin. "There are many areas of the state where by choice or chance or

---

* There was one vacancy that Cuomo would fill in August 1993 with the appointment of Howard Levine.

† When Levine was on the appellate division, a law clerk at the court of appeals told me it always made the clerks' jobs easier when an opinion or dissent came up that was written by Levine. "All we had to do was follow Levine and we knew we couldn't go wrong."

freedom of association virtually all of the individuals are of a common religious background, and we would suggest that the mere fact that people choose to associate within a particular community does not render their actions unconstitutional when they take civil, secular action," Reich argued. "The desire for separation is the desire to be free of acculturation, rather than a religiously based precept of the Satmar. . . . We believe that under *Lemon*, this passes constitutional muster. . . . There is absolutely nothing in the record . . . to indicate that the Kiryas Joel school is under the direction or control of a religious denomination or that religious tenets are taught at the school."

Mereson insisted that the legislation was religiously neutral. "Once you recognize that these were secular concerns that prevented these parents from sending their children to the Monroe-Woodbury schools, you will see that the political process did its work, that it was neutral, that it was trying to break an impasse," Mereson told the court. "It was a neutral action that did not favor religion. There was not a single accommodation to religious tenets of the Hasidic sect."

The chance for us to make our case finally came about forty minutes into the argument, and Jay Worona dove right in with a fervor unmatched by his rivals and, I thought, appreciated by the court. From the gallery, where I was seated, Jay appeared more energetic, more passionate, and better prepared than his opponents.

"Throughout the arguments you have heard today, we've talked about everything that is happening in the school district being secular in nature. *That is not the issue of this case!*" Jay argued forcefully. "The issue of this case was, why was this school district established? . . . The point we need to look at is why this particular district was established in the first place."

Chief Judge Kaye attempted to corner Jay: "Mr. Worona, if a religious group moved into an area, dominated an area in terms of population and in terms of election to the school board, would that board then be unconstitutionally constituted?" But Jay, without hesitation, put that question to rest—"No, Your Honor"—and went on to argue that the surreptitious creation of Kiryas Joel was a political "sham," unconstitutionally orchestrated, not a cultural happenstance.

"The parents of Kiryas Joel presently sent their nonhandicapped children to parochial schools, and they pay money to do that," Jay told the court. "And certainly if they wish to exercise their religious rights for their special education students, they should have the same responsibilities. To do otherwise would violate the Establishment Clause and place the state in a position where no longer heterogeneity and pluralism would be the purposes of public education, but indeed homogeneity."

Kaye pushed the issue. "These children . . . are unquestionably entitled to services from the state," the chief judge stated. "Is there in your view no way they can receive them other than to enter the premises of the Monroe-Woodbury public school?"

Again, Jay was ready and did not miss a beat. He seemed to have anticipated the question. "I am glad you asked that question," he responded. "My answer is, yes, they could be entitled to a neutral site, if indeed there were secular reasons, like safety. . . . [The US Supreme Court has not said] that you can isolate a parochial school and its students solely for the purpose of isolating them."

The decision came down on July 6, 1993, about six weeks after oral argument, and we prevailed in a 4–2 ruling with three different writings. Judge George Bundy Smith, writing for the majority, was joined by Chief Judge Kaye and Judges Simons and Hancock in declaring the Pataki-Lentol bill unconstitutional under the second prong of the *Lemon* test, which says a challenged act of government, to survive Establishment Clause scrutiny, must have a "principal or primary effect . . . that neither advances nor inhibits religion." I was delighted with the decision but disappointed that the court, like the appellate division, relied only on the second prong of *Lemon*. It did not rule on the other prongs of *Lemon* or, more significantly, on the New York State

Constitution. In essence, Judge Smith took the path of least resistance (which he may have had to do to forge an opinion at least three judges would sign onto):

> Because special services are already available to the handicapped children of Kiryas Joel, the primary effect of chapter 748 is not to provide those services, but to yield to the demands of a religious community whose separatist tenets create a tension between the needs of its handicapped children and the need to adhere to certain religious practices. Regardless of any beneficent purpose behind the legislation, the primary effect of such an extensive effort to accommodate the desire to insulate the Satmar Hasidic students inescapably conveys a message of governmental endorsement of religion. . . .
>
> Our conclusion does not, as the dissent declares, "drap[e] a drastic, new disability over the shoulders of young pupils solely on account of the religious beliefs of their community," nor does it "penalize and encumber religious uniqueness." Special services are made available to the Satmar student within the Monroe-Woodbury School District. Our decision does not impose any additional burdens on the students within Kiryas Joel; it simply determines that the Legislature may not treat the Satmar community as separate, distinct and entitled to special accommodation.

Chief Judge Kaye and Judge Hancock wrote separate opinions agreeing with Judge Smith. I found Kaye's particularly enlightening, as well as revealing. At the time, she was in her first year as chief judge, and I thought that the wisdom she evinced in this case, and her skill in so artfully and articulately expressing her viewpoint, was a predictor of a great chief judge. The next fifteen years, and Kaye's historic tenure as chief judge, proved me right, and then some.

Here, Kaye suggested that the establishment of the Kiryas Joel Village School District was nothing less than an attempt by the government to segregate the populace according to religion. While she agreed that the legislation failed the *Lemon* test, she wouldn't have even bothered to apply the test, because it could never even meet the strict scrutiny test.

Strict scrutiny refers to the test the Supreme Court applies when Congress (or a state government) attempts to infringe on a fundamental right—such as freedom of speech, freedom of exercise, freedom of association, due process rights, and rights of equal protection. The basic idea is that the Supreme Court will allow the government to step on some fundamental rights if the government can show that it has a compelling need and that it has chosen the least offensive method of satisfying that need.

Explaining her decision to apply strict scrutiny to the law, Kaye wrote, "The State engaged in de jure segregation for the benefit of one religious group. Establishment of a public school district intentionally segregated along religious lines is a classic example of government action that must be 'surveyed meticulously.'" Kaye expressed grave concern over "government-sponsored segregation," and reminded her colleagues of *Brown v. Board of Education*, the landmark decision that brought state-sanctioned racial separation to its knees. She argued that the case "must not be assessed in a vacuum but measured against history," insisting that the law was a grotesque overresponse to the problem facing the legislature: the education of a small number of disabled children in a little village.

Kaye did not dispute that the allegedly "intractable problem" of providing special education services to the children of Kiryas Joel "presented a compelling, secular government interest." But she said the legislative response went far beyond what was necessary to resolve the problem, delegating incredible clout to a new school district and trampling the Constitution in the process. In a footnote, Kaye observed the many powers the legislature had bestowed on the religious leaders of Kiryas Joel:

The board of education of a union free school district, in addition to having in all respects the superintendence, management, and control of the educational affairs of the district, is given numerous more specific duties and powers. Thus it is empowered and duty-bound to adopt bylaws and rules for its government as proper in the discharge of its duties; establish rules and regulations concerning the order and discipline of the schools; provide fuel, furniture, apparatus, and other necessaries for the use of the schools; prescribe courses of study; regulate the admission of pupils and their transfer between classes or departments; provide milk, transportation, and medical inspection of schoolchildren; provide home-teaching to special classes for handicapped and delinquent children; provide, maintain, and operate, under prescribed circumstances, cafeteria or restaurant service and other accommodations for teachers and other employees, pupils, and the elderly; and prescribe, and, when authorized, furnish, textbooks to be used in the schools. It is also authorized to purchase property and construct school buildings and facilities thereon; take and hold possession of school property; lease premises, and lease-purchase instructional equipment, for school purposes; sell and exchange school property; insure school property; sue to recover damages, and offer monetary rewards for information leading to the arrest and convictions of persons, for vandalism of such property; provide, where authorized, for lighting, janitorial care, and supervision of highway underpasses; alter former school-houses for use as public libraries; and explore, develop, and produce natural gas for district purposes. It is authorized to appoint teachers and librarians and to raise by tax on the property of the district any moneys required to pay the salaries of teachers employed, and also to appoint committees to visit schools and departments under its supervision and report on their condition. Likewise the board is empowered to discharge district debts or their obligations. It has prescribed powers and duties with respect to self-insurance by the district, accident insurance of pupils, insurance against personal injuries incurred by school volunteers, and group insurance and workers' compensation coverage of teachers and other employees' salaries sums to be paid to specified credit unions. Finally, the board possesses all the powers, and is subject to all the duties, of trustees of common school districts, and has all the immunities and privileges enjoyed by the trustees of academies in this state.

At first glance, Kaye's point about overbreadth and the footnoted catalog of unnecessary powers might seem like so many dry legal complaints, but such is not the case. In fact, with this argument Kaye opened up a second and more fundamental front of criticism, directed not so much at the Satmar but at the legislature. To declare the Pataki-Lentol law an attempt at segregation was to defend a vision of American society that flourished during the civil rights era but had roots stretching back at least as far as the "melting pot" dreams expressed at the turn of the nineteenth century (the term itself was popularized by the Jewish American Israel Zingwill in his 1908 play *The Melting Pot*).

But when Judge Kaye condemned the law for its staggering overreach, it was a defense not of a melting-pot social vision but of a Madisonian political vision that lies at the very heart of American political science. A little over two hundred years after James Madison wrote the tenth in the series of essays that made up the *Federalist* papers, Kaye challenged the court of appeals to check a legislature that had finally learned to evade the lessons of *Federalist* 10.

Madison's essay remains famous for its argument that a republican form of government will frustrate the ability of factions to control the state because the different alignment of each representative's personal interests will make factional juntas impossible. As Madison put it, "In the first place, it is to be remarked that, however small the republic may be, the representatives must be raised to a certain number, in order to guard against the cabals of a few; and that, however large it may be, they must be limited to a certain number, in order to guard against the confusion of a multitude." Madison was correct to note that the public was best protected when power is shared among enough lawmakers to make graft very difficult, but he underestimated the power of discrete insular minorities to hijack or at least frustrate the legislature—as the financial industry has proved on the national level during the last twenty-five years.

Kaye's catalog of unnecessary powers further demonstrated how the system had failed. The culprit—and it would not have surprised James Madison—was a legislative system that concentrated all the power in the hands of a few party bosses. Because only a few people control the New York State Legislature, only a few people even know what the government is doing. There's no incentive for civic-minded watchdogs to enter the legislature, because they'd be stonewalled by the leadership. What's more, because the leadership controls the party campaign funds, they can make sure only team players get reelected. This is especially true in the assembly, where the Democrats' hold is so substantial that the leadership can afford to ignore and isolate uncooperative fellow Democrats without a risk to their majority. Thus, it was easy for a party boss like Anthony Genovese to slip the gift of a school district into an agenda, confident that very few of his colleagues would notice, and that even fewer would recognize the significance of the move.

Judge Stewart Hancock also wrote a separate concurrence. The judge, a descendant of John Hancock, wrote primarily to address the first prong of the *Lemon* test (that the challenged government act must not have a religious purpose). While agreeing with his colleagues that since the legislation was so obviously contrary to the second prong there was no reason to address the first, Hancock went on to analyze the situation under the "purpose" test. And, under that test, Hancock said, the legislation failed miserably and obviously. He astutely observed that for all the chatter about the emotional and psychological trauma of the children, there is not a word "in the statute or its legislative history suggesting that the enactment of [the law] was anything other than the well-meaning desire to comply with the religious requirement of keeping the Satmar children separate from other children."

> Was the purpose of this accommodation anything other than religious? Unquestionably, the accommodation was to meet a requirement peculiar to the residents of Kiryas Joel—that their children be permitted to associate only with children of the Hasidic sect. . . . Realistically, can the legislative creation of the Kiryas Joel School District to make special additional education services available in order to obviate the religious objections of its residents have a purpose other than religious? As a matter of common sense—given the wording of the statute, its apparent intent and the absence of any reference to other than a religious purpose in the legislative history—the answer must be no.

Judge Joseph Bellacosa, a former Roman Catholic seminarian who initially planned to become a priest, wrote the sole dissent, arguing that the legislature's "Solomon-like" approach was geared not to the religious needs of the sect but to the secular and cultural demands of the community. Bellacosa, with Judge Vito Titone, agreed with Justice Levine that the statute was presumptively constitutional and that the legitimate needs of the children were not inevitably based in religion. "The judicial nullification of the democratic prerogatives and solution for this intractable town wide controversy is not justified. Instead, it seems to spring from a reflexive veneration of a symbolic metaphor that sacrifices concededly necessary special education services of a small group of handicapped pupils. A real wall of separation thus arises and solidifies to a mythic height and density."

Exactly 1,923 years prior to the July 6, 1993, decision by the New York Court of Appeals, on the seventeenth day of the summer month of Tammuz, the Roman legions breached the walls of Jerusalem with the intent to destroy the second temple and more or less put an end to the expensive state of disorder in one of their moderately important colonies. Was this factoid totally irrelevant? It may seem so to most people, but not to the Satmar, who have trained themselves to view all events in terms of mystical correlation to their own history. When Abe Wieder, president of the KJ school board, spoke to the *New York Times*, the first thing he did was draw attention to the anniversary, almost accusing the court of deliberately choosing the date, and saying, "This gives us another reason to mourn."

The comments expressed by Malka Silberstein, whose daughter Sheindle was being educated by the KJ school district, were more realistic and less paranoid. She and Breindy Weiss, another mother of a child with disabilities, told the *Times* of how much progress their children had made at Steve Benardo's school. Weiss's daughter had a severe hearing deficiency, a common ailment among the Satmar. "We have a plan for her future," she said. "Without this school, I don't know how we can do it."

Silberstein told of her struggle with the public school in Monroe. "It became impossible," she said. "The law calls for these children to be in the least restrictive environment, but Sheindle was in the most restrictive. She wasn't part of her sibling community and she wasn't part of the public school community."

Of course, the court of appeals' point wasn't that the state shouldn't educate these children; the point was that the state couldn't subsidize and endorse religious segregation.

Meanwhile, reporters gathered outside my office. Echoing Marc Stern of the American Jewish Congress, I told the *New York Times* reporter, "If this case went the other way, you would have many religious groups trying to set up their own schools at public expense to try to purvey their views." I added that the law "might have been the end of separation of church and state as we know it." On the program that Steve Benardo had set up in Kiryas Joel, I said, "The fact that they have not chosen [to teach religion] is not important—they can start tomorrow morning." When asked privately about Mario Cuomo's call for the court of appeals to stay its decision until the Supreme Court of the United States could review the decision, I said, "It doesn't surprise me at all. I guess since a court handpicked by the governor wouldn't help him sell out the Constitution, he's hoping to find support among Reagan and Nixon appointees." Yes, it was a bit hyperbolic, but it reflected my frustration at the time.

In the weeks following the court of appeals decision, I received congratulatory phone calls, read press coverage of the case, and talked to reporters, all of which shed more sidelights on the decision. For most of that month, I could be found in my office at all hours of the day on the phone with one reporter or another. Despite being just a kid from West Virginia, I had pulled off a huge upset—I had beaten the legally overpowering Cuomo on a constitutional issue in a court made up entirely of the governor's appointees! A more decisive victory would have been hard to imagine.

In my years as an aide to Mario Cuomo, I had developed an awe of his legal and political instincts. Although I continue to maintain Cuomo was wrong about Kiryas Joel, my overall admiration for him remains to this day. We had disagreed before, and those arguments had never threatened our relationship. I hoped with this one we could let bygones be bygones, but the fight over KJ felt different, largely because this one went public. Cuomo was clearly furious with me, and I imagine somewhat embarrassed by his court's decision. The litigation made Cuomo look bad, as I had warned him it would when it all began, and I felt sad that this fight might spell the end of our relationship. Though this potential consequence troubled me, I had done what I thought needed to be done.

It had been a thrilling run, and yet, there were various administrative loose ends created by the decision. Jay Worona would have to prepare an order to have the decision carried out—that is, to shut down the school as it was then configured. We most certainly did not want children in need to be left without special services, and I did not think that would happen, as long as the state and Kiryas Joel acted rationally and within the confines of the ruling. In my mind, the leaders of Kiryas Joel had two obvious options, and I assumed they would pursue both.

First, they could return to the legislature and ask for a law that might pass muster with the New York State Education Department and the courts—one that could be applied universally, without singling out their particular religious group. It was easy enough to spur the legislature into action with the right amount of political muscle, but it was something else entirely to spur it into constructive solutions. The legislature's unwillingness to think about what it was doing had caused the problems in the first place, and I had doubts about the ability of representatives to craft a solution that would be acceptable to Kiryas Joel, the education department, and the courts. In the end it didn't matter, as—in contrast to my expectations—the leaders of Kiryas Joel had no legislative backup plan. They placed all their chips on their second option: the US Supreme Court. And for that game, it looked as if Kiryas Joel was about to be dealt the ultimate wild card. Justice Byron White had retired from the Supreme Court, and the name of his likely replacement was leaked: Mario Matthew Cuomo.

12

WOULD THE
SUPREME COURT CARE?

If the provisions of the Constitution be not upheld when they pinch as well
as when they comfort, they may as well be abandoned.
                                        —Justice George Sutherland, *Home Building and*
                                                            Loan Association v. Blaisdell

STEVE BENARDO WAS in his office one July morning in 1993
when a call came in from George Shebitz.

George began, "Well, Steve, the court of appeals decision just came
down. I have good news and I have bad news. The bad news is, we lost."

"Oh Jesus. What's the hell's the good news?"

"It's a short opinion."

"Oh my God, George. What are you saying? What did *they* say?"

"The district is unconstitutional. I'm sure that Hannah Flegenheimer [from the state education department] is already shutting off
funds. I'm going to fly back [from Toronto] on Sunday, and I've got a

call in to Abe and Nat. I don't think Nat will be able to come back from Israel, but we'll have a conference call."

Benardo's mind wandered as George continued to talk about the decision, the dissent, and the implications of both.

As he reflected on how far Kiryas Joel had come in the few years of its existence, Steve still found it hard to explain how a liberal, intellectual, big-city public school advocate like himself had wound up running this very odd little school district out in the middle of nowhere. In these four years, he had grown a little grayer and a little balder and could begin to see retirement somewhere on the horizon after a lifetime of public service. But he still had his youthful passion, which was fueled by his work with special needs children at Kiryas Joel.

Steve had grown attached to the loyal staff who had stuck by him through all the litigation and uncertainty about the future; not a single staffer had jumped ship after Kahn's decision or the appellate division ruling, even though after each ruling the education department cut off funding for the school until it was forced to restore it while the case continued.

Perhaps most important to Steve, he felt the community needed him, or someone like him. He had built a career on his belief in the importance and value of special education. In Benardo's mind, Kiryas Joel's special needs children were not going to be served without the Kiryas Joel public school. It didn't matter to Steve whether the kids weren't served because of Satmar parents or the Satmar religion or the failed leadership at the Monroe public school. He didn't care who or what was to blame. He cared that an entire community of children with disabilities depended on him and his staff. If they didn't educate these children, who would?

Additionally, even though the unique characteristics of a Satmar Hasidic community could be overwhelming or frustrating, Steve enjoyed the intellectual challenge of managing these issues, and he

WOULD THE SUPREME COURT CARE?

developed a kind of wry pride in successfully navigating his district through such fussy details as reconciling the holiday needs of the Satmar and the mostly Christian bus drivers. As perhaps the highest ranking non-Satmar to work in the village, he relished his fly-on-the-wall status in the community and his role as a sort of cultural translator to the occasional bewildered visitor.

Benardo likes to tell a story of one Election Day, when he arrived a little earlier than usual to oversee the setup of the polling booths at the school, the place where all the residents cast their votes. On the narrow sidewalk in front of the school stood a young Latino woman with a notebook and tape recorder. She was wearing an early-'90s lavender skirt suit and expensive-looking high-heeled shoes, and stood out like the proverbial sore thumb in a community where no woman would even dream of wearing such attire. Draped across her shoulders was a sash reading, LOS ANGELES TIMES.

She looked confused.

Steve approached her with his usual Bronx-accented, in-your-face friendly aggression. "Hey, lady, ya need some help?"

"Oh, thank God *someone* speaks English here! I can't get anyone to answer my questions!"

The woman, a reporter for the *LA Times*, explained that the paper had chosen districts for random exit polling, and she was assigned to interview voters in Kiryas Joel as part of a nationwide effort to predict the election. Benardo grinned and stifled a laugh.

"Lady, ya better call your office, because you're going to skew the whole poll if you keep this up. Welcome to Kiryas Joel, the mother of all outliers! I can tell you what the vote in the district is right now: five thousand to four. They make four people vote the other way so they know the machines work."

But the reporter said the paper was committed to its random selection.

"Suit yourself." Steve shrugged, heading back to his office.

At noon, the reporter was still there, frustrated and distraught. She had been assigned to ask voters a list of questions but had made little progress, as few people seemed to speak English and the ones who did reacted with disgust at her queries. Steve glanced at her questions. It was mainly standard polling and demographic fare, but Steve could understand why the reporter was having trouble.

"She had a list of twenty questions that she had to choose from randomly when creating a voter profile, and the twentieth question was 'Are you a homosexual?' And she said the reaction ranged from spitting to fury that the reporter feared could escalate into violence. So she says innocently, 'Is there another word I can use, other than *faygala*?'"*

Although he couldn't count on such charming non sequiturs every day, Benardo got a kick out of the few that came his way, and he generally enjoyed the quirkiness of Kiryas Joel and his role there. But there were more serious problems too. One of the biggest problems involved the Bnei Yoel dissidents, who had challenged Moses Teitelbaum's succession to the position of grande rebbe.

While the dissidents attacked Moses on dynastic succession grounds, they also attacked his policies. They worried that he was insufficiently pious and was far too willing to make deals of convenience with the secular community. Things had begun to get out of control after Moses, whose base was Williamsburg, appointed his son, Aaron, as the rebbe of Kiryas Joel. Aaron had married a woman from a less virulently anti-Zionist Hasidic sect, and since anti-Zionism had been one of the most important intellectual achievements of Rebbe Joel, the dissidents were furious.

The dissidents, of course, were despised by the majority of the community. As Jay Worona had pointed out in our initial brief to the New

---

* *Faygala* is the Yiddish word for male homosexual. It literally translates to "little bird." In Kiryas Joel, asking someone if they are a *faygala* would be unspeakably insulting.

York Supreme Court, if identified they feared beating, stoning, and vandalism by reckless youth or, really, anyone hoping to gain favor with Moses. On more than one occasion riots broke out in Williamsburg and Kiryas Joel. In one case, a cheering crowd of Moses's supporters stopped a car driven by dissidents, dragged the occupants from the car, and set the vehicle on fire. Not unlike the Puritan communities of Massachusetts that preceded them, the Satmar were facing factional disputes, with each group vying to be seen as the most pious, the most faithful.

As the most vocal dissident in Kiryas Joel, Joseph Waldman was a constant thorn in Steve Benardo's side. Among Waldman's complaints against Moses and Aaron was their acceptance of Benardo and Abe Wieder's school district for the disabled. Waldman knew very well that US law required teaching the students in a secular environment, which meant that the children with disabilities were not receiving an authentic Hasidic education. He accused the leaders of selling out the sect's religious values for school and bus money.

The problems with Waldman had begun with the very first school board election, when he expressed his opposition to the existence of the school district by running against Moses's anointed slate of candidates. Though he was expelled from the community's main congregation, his children were expelled from school, and the rebbe's followers rioted in front of his home, Waldman persisted in his candidacy.* He lost —but not by as much as he was "supposed to."

The closer-than-expected margin was an embarrassment to Grand Rebbe Moses. As Benardo recalls, "Kiryas Joel is interesting in the sense that people can't express their anger or disappointment with the leaders publicly, can't really criticize the leadership publicly at all. So they tend to look for private ways to do it, and, I think, voting for Waldman

---

* A few years later, after Waldman again challenged the Kiryas Joel leadership, his car was firebombed in his driveway the night before his daughter's wedding. No one was ever arrested.

that year was a way to stick it to the leaders. I don't know how much of the vote was for Waldman and how much was against Wieder and the rebbe."

Waldman responded by hiring Michael Sussman, a prominent civil rights trial attorney in the region, to bring a lawsuit against the rebbe, embarking on his own personal quest to destroy the school district. Sussman had made his mark as an attorney for the NAACP in the 1970s and '80s, especially in a landmark Yonkers desegregation case that resulted in a court order forcing the city to build integrated housing in order to combat persistent de facto segregation of the schools in Westchester County.

Waldman made every effort to publicize his lawsuit and embarrass the rebbe. He constantly harassed village and school district officials and challenged every decision in the press. He repeatedly offered to assist our litigation efforts, because he thought the existence of the district violated Talmudic principles and felt this was as important as our view that it violated constitutional principles. Indeed, he called us day after day with new gossip and allegations.

When he wasn't trying to close down the school district, Waldman was trying to get his kids into it. After they were kicked out of the village's private schools, Waldman told Benardo he was sending them to his school. It was simply a ploy to get inside to take pictures. He was hoping to find something to prove the school was teaching such un-Hasidic secular topics as English (in which case he would take the photos to the dissidents), or something to prove the school was teaching religious topics (in which case he would go to us or the government). Benardo had Waldman escorted off the premises— which worked just long enough for Steve to figure out a way to shut down Waldman's admissions efforts. It suddenly occurred to him to ask for the immunization records for Waldman's kids, knowing that Waldman opposed immunization and suspecting that civil authorities were ignoring such requirements in KJ's private schools. When

Waldman refused, it gave him an excuse to back down without feeling as if Benardo had "won."

When Benardo hung up the phone that morning in July 1993, it really hit home what the New York State Court of Appeals had done and what its decision potentially meant. For three years, he had refused to seriously consider the precarious situation of the district. He knew the work product was outstanding, knew that the children deserved the services they were getting, couldn't believe that anyone would really want to shut it down, and thought the legal argument was counterintuitive and unintelligible. How could his school be closed for violating the First Amendment when the school itself wasn't operated in an unconstitutional manner? Yet to Steve, that's what the court of appeals seemed to say. (In fact, neither the court of appeals nor I had any interest in the school curriculum itself. To me, it was the law creating the district, not the operation of the school, that was an affront to the Constitution).

The community got the bad news, in detail, the following Monday when Nat Lewin held a conference call in which he advised village and school leaders that the only option remaining was the US Supreme Court, and that the statistical chance the high court would hear the case was about one in twelve thousand. But Lewin knew, as I knew, that the raw statistics were misleading at best. A few short lines in the majority opinion gave Kiryas Joel hope that the justices in Washington would hear its appeal.

In the opinion, Judge Smith wrote:

> The Appellate Division affirmed . . . on both State and Federal constitutional grounds, although its discussion, like [Justice Kahn's] was limited to the Establishment Clause. . . . In these circumstances, *we do not reach the State constitutional issue*, which is based on a

provision significantly different from the Establishment Clause, both in text and history and we modify the Appellate Division order accordingly.

By ruling only on federal grounds, the court of appeals had laid the matter at the doorstep of the Supreme Court. If it had wanted to keep the case away from the justices in Washington, the New York court could have based its decision solely on the state constitution, precluding review by the Supreme Court. By not doing that, it virtually invited the Supreme Court to take the case.

The Supreme Court will not review a state high court decision that rests on state law, unless the constitutionality of the state law is in question. In other words, if the court of appeals had said that the Pataki-Lentol law violated the New York constitution, then the Satmar would have had no appeal to the Supreme Court, because the Supreme Court does not have the power to overturn a state's high court in matters of state constitutional law. The state obviously has to recognize all of the rights in the US Constitution, but if it chooses to offer more in its own constitution, and those rights don't violate the federal standards, the Supreme Court cannot touch it. Why had both Smith and Kaye avoided ruling on the state constitution? Why had they both ignored the Blaine Amendment?

Lewin could only speculate, but he knew that other courts had done the same thing. For example, the famous Supreme Court case dealing with education of the Amish, *Wisconsin v. Yoder*, reached the Supreme Court because the high court in Wisconsin had declined to base its ruling on Wisconsin law.* All that mattered to Lewin now was that they had a chance of a hearing in Washington. Perhaps the court

---

* In *Wisconsin v. Yoder*, 406 US 205 (1972), the Supreme Court found that Amish children could not be subjected to compulsory education past eighth grade because the parents' religious freedom rights outweighed the state's interest in educating children.

of appeals, by deciding the case on the basis of US Constitution, had wanted it to end up in the Supreme Court anyway.

Except for the small percentage of cases that the Supreme Court is constitutionally required to hear (as when two states sue each other), the court largely picks and choose its cases. Typically, the court looks to hear cases that divided the lower courts so it can settle the law once and for all. Sometimes, even though lower courts apply a rule with acceptable uniformity, the Supreme Court may grow dissatisfied with its own rule and take a case just to alter or abandon its own precedent. That was the situation that Kiryas Joel faced. There was little doubt that the court of appeals had correctly applied *Lemon*, so the only reason for the court to hear the case would be to reconsider the *Lemon* test. Lewin suspected the court might be willing to do just that, but getting any case before the Supreme Court is a monumental, and usually unsuccessful, task.

To get before the Supreme Court, Kiryas Joel needed to go through a difficult process called *certiorari*. As part of the process, judicial clerks plow through piles and piles of petitions, weeding out the vast majority and searching for the needle-in-a-haystack petition that presents an issue or question worthy of Supreme Court analysis. If the clerks find something they like, a case still needs the support of four justices before a matter is accepted. The process normally takes months. Kiryas Joel, however, didn't have months. The district's only hope was to obtain a stay in the state court decision, which would allow Kiryas Joel to remain operating until the Supreme Court decided whether to hear the case. Lewin warned the community and Benardo that their chances were slim.

Benardo didn't believe it and wouldn't accept it. He simply could not fathom that they were out of options. Yet knowing he had to break the bad news to his employees, he immediately convened an emergency faculty and staff meeting, explained what happened, and promised to do everything he possibly could to find them jobs.

And then he went to see Terry Olivo, Monroe-Woodbury's superintendent.

Terrence Olivo had worked in the Monroe school district for about twenty years, becoming superintendent in the year that the Kiryas Joel school district was formed, when his predecessor, Dan Alexander, died. Olivo had won accolades for shepherding Monroe-Woodbury through the busing wars of the 1980s. He had worked with Steve Benardo on many of the small crises that forever seemed to plague Monroe-Woodbury and Kiryas Joel. In short, they needed each other, as did their respective districts, for reasons both political and financial. So the two districts had cooperated with each other in their lobbying efforts in Albany.

Despite this long history of teamwork, Benardo wasn't sure if he could count on Olivo this time. It was one thing to ask Olivo to throw his district's political weight behind Kiryas Joel's school district, and quite another to ask Monroe-Woodbury to find places for all of Kiryas Joel's teachers and the funds to do so—especially in light of the court of appeals decision.

Steve held to the somewhat old-fashioned faith in face-to-face negotiations, and never made any big decisions over the phone if he could help it. He arrived at Olivo's office around lunchtime a few days after the court of appeals issued its ruling to fill Terry in on the details, and to get a sense of whether his colleague/friend/occasional rival could help. Benardo started his spiel and Olivo cut him off; he knew all about the decision, fully understood its implications, and was already trying to figure out what Monroe-Woodbury could do to help.

It was a big lift, and both superintendents knew it. There were myriad devil-in-the-details problems, including the fact that since Kiryas Joel's teachers were not unionized, their seniority in entering a unionized district would be a sticking point. But both men also thought that where there was a will, there was a way. Steve went back across Route 17 to Kiryas Joel and immediately began working on the administrative

details of the transfer, polishing the résumés of his teachers and hus-
banding the school's remaining funds so he could provide services as
long as possible.

Meanwhile, the Monroe-Woodbury school board and its attorney,
Lawrence Reich, sent a spirited motion to the Supreme Court, urging
it to hear the case:

> We believe that the [New York Court of Appeals] has misconstrued
> and misapplied the decisions of this Court. . . . Even if *Lemon* contin-
> ues to be viable, we nevertheless respectfully suggest that application
> of the various elements of the test necessarily supports the constitu-
> tionality of the disputed statute. It cannot be gainsaid but that even
> individuals having deep personal and religious convictions may also
> have legitimate secular concerns, primary amongst which may be
> their desire to have their children appropriately educated, and that
> the state may legitimately address such concerns provided it does
> so in a manner which does not directly aid or subsidize a religious
> institution. This Court has on numerous prior occasions sustained
> the validity under the second prong of *Lemon* of governmental pro-
> grams which are "wholly neutral in offering educational assistance
> to a class defined without reference to religion." . . . The statute cre-
> ating the Kiryas Joel School District is such a program, because it
> offers secular educational services in a secular milieu to all district
> residents, without regard to religious or non-religious preferences of
> the parents and because such programs directly benefit the students
> themselves and not their religious faith.

Around that time, Benardo got a call.

"Steve, it's Nat Lewin. I'm here with Abe Wieder and he has something to tell you that I think you'll find pretty interesting."

Lewin flipped on his speaker phone and Steve heard Abe's heavy
Yiddish accent: "Ye-es, the Justice Thomas. He has granted a stay."

The Kiryas Joel Village School District would live another day.

When I heard about the stay, I wasn't particularly surprised, or particularly disappointed. I certainly wanted this long battle over, especially since we had won such a resounding victory, and I was eager to help Kiryas Joel solve the underlying problem—the educational needs of the community's children with disabilities—as quickly (and constitutionally) as possible. But the prospect of a case with my name on it going to the US Supreme Court was exhilarating.

As the case worked its way through the courts, politics in Albany had continued to roil, altering the balance of power and changing some of the players. Mel Miller, the Speaker of the Assembly, was convicted of felony fraud charges (all of which were later overturned on appeal) and resigned his seat. A new Speaker, Saul Weprin, replaced him. Mario Cuomo won reelection in 1990 in an apparent—but misleading—landslide. Although he beat his next-closest opponent by more than 15 percent, the Republican and Conservative Parties were divided in 1990 between businessman Pierre Rinfret and NYU professor and conservative wonk Herbert London. So his margin of victory was less than overwhelming, and it became apparent to a few close observers—such as George Pataki—that the incumbent was vulnerable and potentially beatable in 1994, despite the fact that statewide, Democrats enjoyed an immense enrollment advantage.

The Republicans in New York had dominated the Senate for decades. While briefly disrupted in the 1960s by a Supreme Court decision that said federal courts could weigh in on state gerrymandering, the Republicans generally maintained control of the upper chamber. It was not exactly a diverse crowd; even in the early 1990s there was not a single GOP lawmaker in the Senate who was a person of color, and a grand total of one GOP woman: Senator Mary Goodhue. Goodhue had some health issues and had promised Pataki and the Senate

Republican leader, Ralph Marino, that she would not seek reelection in 1992. That would clear the way for Pataki's move from the Democratic-controlled assembly—where, except in rare circumstances, he had no clout—to the Republican-controlled Senate, where he could get something done. Pataki promised Goodhue that he would wait until her retirement before going after her seat, with the implicit agreement that the GOP would support his candidacy. However, it eventually occurred to Marino and the other more powerful Republicans that if Goodhue left, there wouldn't be a single woman in their caucus, and he sent the incumbent a letter urging her to stay on.

Pataki was incensed and decided to take on Goodhue in a primary. His ambition was to run for governor in 1994, and he wanted to do so from the more visible perch of a senator than the relative obscurity of a minority member of the assembly. He was certain Cuomo could be beat and equally convinced he was the one to beat him.

It was a close primary but Pataki won, with the help of his old allies: the Satmar Hasidim.

Jacob Freund, a Satmar rabbi who sat on important governing bodies in Kiryas Joel, was the community's liaison with Pataki. Pataki had earned his trust as an assemblyman, especially in his shepherding of the school bill through the legislature. Although Kiryas Joel did not have many votes in Pataki's Senate district, Freund deputized busloads of Satmar to register supporters in marginal areas in the district, to canvass the district with Pataki paraphernalia, and to organize telephone drives for Pataki. Freund still speaks with pride of the round-the-clock effort he and the Satmar put in during the last week of the primary. He recalls that the Satmar combed the neighborhoods, practically dragging every Orthodox and Conservative Jewish person to the polls. Even hotly contested primaries suffer low turnouts, so the power of the Satmar to get the vote out was a deciding factor.

At the end of the day, the Satmar helped George Pataki, a barely known assemblyman with little backing from the state Republican leaders, become a state senator. Marino was furious at Pataki. For his part, Pataki never forgave Marino for going back on his word, and never forgot that the Satmar helped him when he needed it most. Shunned by the state party leadership, Pataki turned to a Republican outside of Albany—Alfonse D'Amato, New York's incredibly resourceful and Machiavellian US senator—to begin plotting an effort to take over the governor's mansion.

13

THE SUPREME COURT OPENS THE DOOR

Hold on, my friends, to the Constitution and the Republic for which it stands. Miracles do not cluster, and what has happened once in 6,000 years, may not happen again. Hold on to the Constitution, for if the American Constitution should fail, there will be anarchy throughout the world.

—Daniel Webster

O N JULY 22, 1993, Justice Clarence Thomas circulated a memorandum to the seven other sitting Supreme Court justices (there was one vacancy), advising his colleagues that he had temporarily blocked New York from enforcing the order of its highest court and shutting down the Kiryas Joel Village School District.

"Yesterday I entered an interim stay, pending disposition of the stay applications," Thomas wrote. "I now refer the applications to the Conference, together with my vote to grant."

The rest of the memo laid out Thomas's argument for his colleagues to join him in granting the stay. He addressed the four criteria for granting a stay, including the "reasonable probability that four members of this Court will vote to grant Certiorari." Among his arguments for taking the case, the most interesting addressed *Lemon*.

"The Court of Appeals relied exclusively on the *Lemon Test*, which has been subjected to intense criticism both within the Court and without," Thomas wrote, citing an opinion of his colleague on the right wing of the court, Antonin Scalia. "It is not inconceivable to me, that at least four members of the Court will have an interest in using this case as a vehicle for clarifying *Lemon*'s status."

It is a fair bet that Thomas, viewing Kiryas Joel as a "vehicle for clarifying" the *Lemon* test, more likely saw it as a way to eliminate *Lemon*, and suspected (or knew) that at least four judges would be happy to do away with the precedent or water it down to the point that it was meaningless.

Next, he addressed the second criterion, the possibility of reversing the judgment of the lower court. Thomas acknowledged that "given the uncertainty that characterizes this Court's Establishment Clause jurisprudence, it is extremely difficult to predict with any degree of accuracy how a case like this one would be decided." But he added, "In my view, however, there is a significant possibility that the Court will vote to reverse the Court of Appeals' judgment" if the court agreed to hear the case. "In sum, I believe that the issue in this case is close and difficult, and that reasonable minds can differ both as to how that issue should be analyzed and as to whether the Court of Appeals' resolution of the issue was correct."

Aside from another alert to other justices of his intentions, this comment offers an interesting side note on the Supreme Court's behavior. Here we have one of the court's most conservative judges admitting that there was little reason to think that the New York court's opinion defied any Supreme Court precedent. In other words, Thomas was

calling not for the Supreme Court to correct the New York Court of
Appeals but for the court to reconsider its own failure to set a clearer
standard. If a stay and, after that, cert were granted, the court might
be crafting a new framework for applying the Establishment Clause.
The case, in Thomas's opinion, cried out for a different approach from
the court.

Whatever the result, the decision would be most influenced by
the centrist Justice Sandra Day O'Connor and the slightly right-of-
center Justice Anthony Kennedy. Thomas, almost certainly, had already
formed an opinion, but most likely framed it as a "close and difficult"
case over which "reasonable minds can differ" as a way to project an
air of collegiality to the fence-sitting colleagues he hoped to win over.

A stay required five votes and certiorari required four, so if Thomas
could find five votes for the stay, he could feel pretty confident about
getting four for cert. As a bonus, he would also have identified the
justices he might be able to work with to form a majority willing to
reconsider *Lemon*.

The most senior justice in 1993 was Harry Blackmun, a Nixon
appointee best known for his opinion in *Roe v. Wade*, the landmark
1973 abortion decision. Blackmun began his Supreme Court career
as a reliable conservative before drifting steadily to the left during the
1970s and '80s. He had remained a staunch defender of *Lemon* and
rather quickly determined, in agreement with his clerk, to vote against
the stay.

Blackmun was a compulsive organizer and note taker who directed
that his papers should be revealed a mere five years after his death
(in comparison, recently retired Justice David Souter has directed his
papers to be closed until the fiftieth anniversary of his death). Thanks
to the early release of his notes (Blackmun died in 1999), we now have
a pretty good idea of just what went on in the court's consideration of
Board of Education of Kiryas Joel Village School District v. Grumet. In
fact, as the votes on Thomas's memo came in, Blackmun kept track of

them on the cover page of his personal copy. He jotted down plus and minus signs; next to the plus signs, he added the initials for the justices in favor of the stay, and next to the minus signs, he added those against. A plus sign appears next to the name of Justice Antonin Scalia.

Scalia, a Reagan appointee, is well known for his aggressive and sometimes caustic rhetoric. When deciding how to apply the Constitution to cases, he is an outspoken advocate of the so-called originalist approach, which searches for a sense of what the Constitution meant to "reasonable" people at the time it was ratified in the late eighteenth century and then attempts to apply it to modern problems. He has been a successful evangelist for this approach, which I and other liberal observers condemn on several fronts.

First, deciding what a reasonable person would have thought two hundred years ago is an impossible proposition. We can't simply go with what we might imagine the founders intended, especially in an Establishment Clause case, because, as we have seen, Jefferson and Madison had very different ideas on what the First Amendment meant. Second, it would be even more difficult to assume what they might have thought about a public education system, which did not yet exist. Third, the "originalist" approach seems to ignore the fact that America had a Civil War and a subsequent series of constitutional amendments that greatly changed the meaning of the Constitution, modifying the powers of the various units of government and of the Bill of Rights, not to mention the rights of entire new classes of minority groupings of citizens.

Still, originalism has attracted a cadre of very principled supporters (as well as the less principled who viewed the theory as a way to undermine the activism and liberalism of the Warren court in the 1950s and '60s). Scalia and Thomas embraced similar but by no means identical approaches, often rooted in originalism, and they frequently voted together.

The next two responses noted by Blackmun were votes against

granting the stay. The first was from John Paul Stevens and the second from David Souter.

Stevens, a Ford appointee, came to the court as a highly respected antitrust lawyer who was catapulted to national prominence after leading an investigation into corruption on the Illinois Supreme Court. Although appointed by a Republican, Stevens had often voted to preserve the legacy of the liberal Warren court, and by the time he retired in 2010, he was solidly on the left side of the bench. Although generally a judicial conservative, Stevens held an expansive view of the Fourteenth Amendment and the Establishment Clause, and both positions would have made him inclined to deny Kiryas Joel's petition for a stay. Also, he was not at all likely to look favorably upon granting cert to a case from a state high court that was almost unquestionably decided correctly under existing precedent.

David Souter, appointed by the first President Bush in 1990, had surprised many conservative politicians in 1992 by writing forcefully in favor of a constitutional protection for abortion rights in *Planned Parenthood v. Casey* (a case that many expected to overturn *Roe v. Wade*) and against prayer in school ceremonies in *Lee v. Weisman* (expected by many to roll back earlier decisions striking down school prayer). Souter detested Washington DC, and when he retired in 2009, those close to him all cited his disgust with the city and with the political environment of the court. When Souter refused to advance a radical conservative agenda, he and Scalia seemed to develop a difficult professional relationship, often trading barbs in their decisions. Now, faced with a case that might be a platform for articulating a narrower view of the Establishment Clause, Souter voted against a stay, probably because he believed that the New York Court of Appeals applied Supreme Court precedent correctly. With this vote, Souter further disappointed political conservatives, who viewed him as a traitor to their cause.

The next vote to come in was that of Justice Anthony Kennedy. Ronald Reagan had turned to the Californian after his first two choices

to succeed Justice Lewis Powell failed.* Because his holdings were char-
acterized by an unusual combination of a mild libertarianism with a
strong defense of the prerogatives of the judiciary as well as an international outlook, he had often surprised both conservatives and liberals,
including his colleagues on the court. Consistent with his somewhat
libertarian "Don't Tread on Me!" perspective, Kennedy tended to draw
the line at coercion—any action by which the government could be
seen as foisting religion on the citizenry. Kennedy voted with Scalia
and Thomas for the stay.† That left two judges, and both their votes were
needed to grant the stay.

Chief Justice William Rehnquist, a Nixon appointee and former
devotee of Senator Barry Goldwater, had made a career out of deference
to the other branches of government. Also, as a clerk for Justice Robert
Jackson in the early 1950s, Rehnquist wrote a notorious memo arguing against court-ordered school desegregation just as the court was
considering the landmark *Brown v. Board of Education* case, actually
defending the "separate but equal" doctrine:

> To the argument made by Thurgood Marshall that a majority may
> not deprive a minority of its constitutional right, the answer must
> be made that while this is sound in theory, in the long run it is the
> majority who will determine what the constitutional rights of the
> minority are. One hundred and fifty years of attempts on the part of
> this Court to protect minority rights of any kind—whether those of
> business, slaveholders, or Jehovah's Witnesses—have been sloughed
> off, and crept silently to rest. If the present Court is unable to profit
> by this example it must be prepared to see its work fade in time, too,

---

* Reagan nominee Robert Bork failed to win confirmation after a legendary battle of
intellectual wit with the Senate. Another nominee, Douglas Ginsberg, withdrew from
consideration after acknowledging he had used marijuana.
† We viewed Kennedy's quick vote for the stay, and later his vote for certiorari, ominously. I
was concerned that he might be inclined to overrule the *Lemon* test with one that simply
asked if the government was coercing religious participation.

as embodying only the sentiments of a transient majority of nine men. I realize that it is an unpopular and unhumanitarian position, for which I have been excoriated by "liberal" colleagues, but I think *Plessy v. Ferguson* was right and should be re-affirmed.

Rehnquist was a solid vote for activist state governments, loath to invalidate any state law on constitutional grounds and seemingly regretting the Fourteenth Amendment, which required the states to recognize the federal constitutional protections afforded their citizenry. It did not in the least surprise me that Rehnquist voted for the stay.

With Rehnquist's vote it was clear that Thomas had the four votes necessary to grant certiorari. Justice Sandra Day O'Connor, seeing the writing on the wall, cast the fifth vote for the stay: "I am inclined to think the New York Court of Appeals reached the correct result in this case. I am not inclined to grant certiorari, however inasmuch as four other Justices appear to believe that certiorari should be granted, I will provide the fifth vote to enter a stay pending disposition by the conference."

O'Connor's note was illustrative. On the one hand, the note was an act of collegiality: the justice cast the swing vote, ensuring that her colleagues would have an opportunity to grant cert if they were so inclined. But she also signaled to the other conservative justices that she was disinclined to overturn the New York Court of Appeals on Kiryas Joel. Perhaps more than any justice, O'Connor championed the notion of an independent judiciary. She was well known for writing very narrow opinions that were so case-specific that it was difficult to predict what her decision would be in future cases. Along the top of the original memo from Clarence Thomas, Justice Blackmun added O'Connor as the fifth vote, but he marked her name with double underlining, perhaps as a reminder that her vote would likely be available to affirm the New York Court of Appeals.

Another vote to overturn the court of appeals probably wouldn't come from retired justice Byron White's replacement. Democrat Bill

Clinton was in the White House, and it was unlikely he would appoint Clarence Thomas's ideological soul mate. But the situation was complicated by the fact that Governor Mario Cuomo was widely thought to be the president's first choice for the position.

A number of published theories have discussed what went on, but reportedly Cuomo was offered White's seat twice; he refused it, then accepted it, and finally refused it for good. (Cuomo, with his perpetual indecision on a run for president, had earned the nickname Hamlet on the Hudson). In 2012 the former president confirmed that Cuomo declined the nomination. But political pundits have claimed that Clinton and Cuomo never had a particularly good relationship, and one theory holds that the president didn't really want the governor on the Supreme Court. For political reasons, the story goes, Clinton gave him the honor of declining the position and, as a consolation prize, put his son Andrew in his cabinet as HUD secretary. *

A few weeks after the Supreme Court granted the stay, President Clinton nominated Ruth Bader Ginsberg to fill the vacancy. She was the first Jewish woman on the Supreme Court and an architect of a brilliant legal campaign to extend the Equal Protection Clause in the Fourteenth Amendment to women. It was a short time before the stay would lead to certiorari and at least six months before the Supreme Court would hear the case, but with each step that the Village of Kiryas Joel took toward the Supreme Court, we found ourselves sucked into national movements of such scope and force that everyone would soon forget that the case had started with Sheindle Silberstein in a reindeer costume.

---

* Many believe that the person Clinton really wanted on the high court was New York chief judge Judith S. Kaye, who had written the brilliant concurrence in the Kiryas Joel case. Kaye, who had earlier been courted by the Clinton administration to become the nation's first female attorney general, preferred her role as the leader of the greatest state court in the nation. See Steven C. Krane, "Judith Smith Kaye," Historical Society of the New York Courts official website, accessed September 18, 2015, www.nycourts.gov/history /legal-history-new-york/luminaries-court-appeals/kaye-judith.html.

Nobody could predict how it would come out, although we all knew the implications for the Establishment Clause were profound. Four of the justices—Rehnquist, Thomas, Scalia, and Kennedy—seemed receptive to permitting government involvement in religion, as long as people did not feel coerced. Four others—Blackmun, Stevens, Souter, and O'Connor—seemed to prefer a stricter standard. And nobody knew where Ginsberg stood on the Establishment Clause.

The week that the court's decision on certiorari came down, Linda Greenhouse, who covered the Supreme Court for the *New York Times* for almost thirty years, wrote in the Sunday, December 5, 1993, edition that *Board of Education of Kiryas Joel Village School District v. Grumet* "has the makings of a potentially great Supreme Court case precisely because the issue it raises cuts across all the established categories and goes to the heart of the matter—to what extent may the secular state accommodate the needs of a religious population?" Greenhouse, whose Supreme Court coverage was so influential that some senior judges blamed her for the leftward movement of several Republican appointees, went on to suggest that the Supreme Court had indeed taken the case in order to rewrite *Lemon*, but that it remained questionable whether five justices could agree on a new test.

Like many observers, Greenhouse noted that the case would force the court to clarify the relationship between the Free Exercise and the Establishment Clauses of the First Amendment. In a world where more and more vital services are provided by the government (education, health care, infrastructure, etc.), conflicts between certain approaches to these two clauses are inevitable: the Satmar claimed that if the state would educate their kids with disabilities only in the ordinary public school, then it was denying their right to free exercise of religion because the Satmar would be forced to disobey religious beliefs in order to receive the benefit of publicly funded education.

The doctrine that bridges the gap between the Free Exercise Clause and the Establishment Clause is known as "accommodation." Under this doctrine, the government may accommodate religious beliefs if those beliefs are burdened by state action. For example, if a law against narcotics prevents a Native American tribe from using peyote, a plant known for its psychoactive properties, in its spiritual rituals, the government may be able to exempt the tribe from the law for limited purposes. *Wisconsin v. Yoder*, the Supreme Court ruling that the Amish should not be forced to attend public school after the eighth grade, was an accommodation case: the government lifted a burden that a state had imposed on religion. Kiryas Joel, however, presented a much different take on the issue. The leaders of Kiryas Joel were not asking the court to relieve them of a state-imposed burden, such as the requirement to attend school. They wanted their own public school, funded with public money, to run on their own terms.

At the same time that commentators acknowledged the thorny issue of the relationship between the Free Exercise and the Establishment Clauses, Greenhouse and others blamed the Supreme Court for making a mess out of an already complicated area. Greenhouse called the court's doctrines "barely coherent, making the validity of a public Christmas display, for example, turn on whether the crèche stands alone (unconstitutional) or is accompanied by candy canes and reindeer (constitutional)." Marc Stern, the lawyer for the American Jewish Congress, explained the court's failure to come up with a coherent framework as a failure to agree on how to reach an answer rather than a failure to agree on the answer. "The problem isn't the solution—a lot of times the solution is visceral, something is clearly not appropriate—the problem is in how you get there, and the court just hasn't been able to agree on that."

When an issue as fundamental to American notions of government as the First Amendment is being reassessed by the Supreme Court, many influential policy groups insist on having a say. Shortly after the court granted cert, Worona and I were contacted by attorneys from numerous organizations eager to provide amicus briefs. They included the American Civil Liberties Union, the American Jewish Congress, Americans United for Separation of Church and State, the National School Boards Association, the General Council on Finance and Administration of the United Methodist Church, the National Council of Churches of Christ in the USA, the National Coalition for Public Education and Religious Liberty, the Council on Religious Freedom, the New York Committee for Public Education and Religious Liberty, the New York State United Teachers, and many others.* These were some of the most prominent and respected education and religious liberty organizations in the nation, and they were staffed by attorneys who had been trained at the nation's most respected law schools and who had worked for some of the nation's most respected judges. Some of them were important academics in their own right.

The case was scheduled to be heard in March 1994. Several months earlier, I was hearing regularly from the amici who supported us, expressing concern over whether my young attorney, who had never argued a case in front of the Supreme Court, was up to the task and fearing that a relatively inexperienced counselor might inadvertently nudge the Supreme Court in the wrong direction. I also had a sense that attorneys for some of the organizations thought they, not Jay Worona, should be arguing the case. It was a delicate task to maintain both private and public support for Worona while also keeping up positive relations with the amici, all of whom I wanted to keep in our camp to demonstrate the broad academic/religious/civil rights issues at stake. But there was no way anyone other than Jay Worona was arguing this case. For one thing, he knew the case better than anyone. For another,

---

* Other organizations submitted amicus briefs supporting Kiryas Joel's position, including the National Jewish Commission on Law and Public Affairs, the United States Catholic Conference, the Institute for Religion and Polity, Agudath Israel of America, and several others.

I continued to have complete confidence in Jay. He had shown an unri-
valed mastery of legal principle as well as tactics.

Personally, I was of course thrilled, not just to have my name on a
case before the US Supreme Court but also to be granted an opportunity to speak to a wider public audience about an issue that I thought
was the most important I would confront in my professional life. I
loved the news interviews, loved having my views in the papers, and
loved getting notes from school board members across the country
attached to front page coverage of the case. My board seemed proud of
me now; they had hired me for my vision of using media attention to
bolster the authority of school boards to speak on issues of education,
and I had delivered. There was positive news and editorial coverage
throughout the country, in virtually every major newspaper chain and
on television as well: *60 Minutes* was preparing a complete segment to
cover the issues in Kiryas Joel, C-SPAN wanted to do a documentary
on the case, and I was scheduled to appear with Abe Wieder on *Larry
King Live*. Of course, I knew the bubble could burst if Jay's head were
handed to him by the Supreme Court, as many of the lawyers feared
and even anticipated. But Jay was my lawyer, and his role as lead counsel was not negotiable.

A number of experts predicted that the conservative wing of the
Supreme Court was going to use the case to weaken, lower, and per-
forate the wall of separation between church and state, maybe even
abandon *Lemon* all together. One theory making the rounds was that
Thomas (and perhaps Scalia too) had zeroed in on Kiryas Joel deliberately, reasoning that justices Kennedy and O'Connor could be led further right by the genuinely heart-wrenching image of these unfortunate
Hasidic children with disabilities deprived of educational opportunity.

Still, I was confident. Perhaps it was self-delusion on my part, but
in my heart of hearts, I was certain we would win the publicity battle
as well as the legal battle, and that the court would see, as Chief Judge

Kaye of the New York Court of Appeals had, that the Satmar children could receive all the services to which they were entitled without compromising the US Constitution.

I remember when I called Jay to tell him he was going to argue at the Supreme Court. He was, obviously, elated, but also worried. Very worried.

The court of appeals case had been one of the most closely watched education cases in the nation, and there was no doubt those five years of intense on-the-job training, the long nights, working weekends, and absence of vacation days had been worth it for Jay. He was beginning to feel like the constitutional lawyer he had wanted to be. He had more than justified my faith in his abilities, but Jay was also growing concerned about my exuberance. It wasn't that he took the case more seriously than I—that would have been hard to do—it was simply that he felt more keenly the "responsibility" of handling a Supreme Court case about a major civil right. Also, his lawyerly training to identify the weaknesses of his position and the strength of the opposition made him nervous and skeptical. For me, cert to the Supreme Court simply meant a higher pulpit and a larger audience and, of course, a chance to make an important contribution to the law. For Jay, though, the court's decision to hear the case was ominous.

Perhaps more than any justice in history, Clarence Thomas was known to discount the social value of stability in the law in favor of doctrinal accuracy. In other words, he has little respect for stare decisis, a Latin term for the principle of sticking with old decisions. If Thomas had convinced four other justices to grant a stay and at least three others to grant cert, it must have been to overturn *Lemon*. Or so Worona thought—after all, everyone seemed sure that the Kiryas Joel school district could never survive the *Lemon* test, and everyone seemed sure that the court of appeals had applied the test correctly. Therefore, the only reason for the Supreme Court to hear the case would be to reverse and get rid of *Lemon*. Jay had won three cases by playing by the Supreme Court's rules. But going to the Supreme Court meant that the rules themselves could be changed.

And Jay wasn't so sure he wanted that on his conscience.

14

STRANGE BEDFELLOWS

When the state becomes enmeshed with a given denomination in matters of religious significance, the freedom of religious belief of those who are not adherents of that denomination suffers, even when the governmental purpose underlying the involvement is largely secular. In addition, the freedom of even the adherents of the denomination is limited by the governmental intrusion into sacred matters.

—Justice William Brennan, *Aguilar v. Felton*

WHEN JAY AND I traveled to Washington in January 1994 for a summit with those wishing to join our case as amici curiae, an old cliché popped into my mind: "The enemy of my enemy is my friend."

We were accompanied by Bernard Ashe, the lead attorney for New York State United Teachers (NYSUT) and one of the best education lawyers in the nation, who was interested in joining our cause. Most of the time, we at the New York State School Boards Association were at odds with the union over such issues as teacher discipline, tenure, and merit pay. So ours was an unlikely alliance, and equally odd was the location of our meeting: the headquarters of the National Education

Association (NEA) on Sixteenth Street, a couple of blocks from the White House. NEA had long been a rival of NYSUT and the American Federation of Teachers. Indeed, both organizations had splintered from the NEA. We were meeting, too, with the American Civil Liberties Union (ACLU), which generally supported civil rights but sometimes had a problem with the tension between the Free Speech Clause and the Establishment Clause, and on occasion allied with the conservative American Center for Law and Justice (ACLJ) on such issues. Also represented at the meeting was the American Jewish Congress, which joined in our battle against a school catering solely to Jewish children, and in this matter was aligned with the Baptist Joint Committee for Religious Liberty.

The Supreme Court has been compared to nine scorpions in a bottle, and the atmosphere at the NEA seemingly mirrored that peculiar dynamic—except most of the scorpions seemed intent on devouring Jay Worona. (More on that later.) But the meeting did underscore the diversity of opinions and viewpoints that, dating back to Jefferson and Madison, underpin our perspective of religious freedom and the separation of church and state.

The ACLJ, which was founded in 1990 by the evangelical minister and lawyer Pat Robertson, is a right-wing conservative group established as a counterweight to the ACLU. ACLJ's chief counsel, Jay Alan Sekulow, was a Christian follower of Messianic Judaism.* Sekulow had pioneered the so-called viewpoint discrimination argument in a series of Supreme Court cases concerning state action and religion, claiming that anytime the government restricts religious practice or the presence of religious activity (by, for example, banning school prayer or banning Hare Krishnas from airports), it violates the right to free speech. This view had some traction with the right wing of the court, and gave us

---

* Messianic Jews accept Jesus as the Messiah and trace the roots of the movement to the twelve apostles—who, like Jesus, were Jewish.

some concern—especially if the ACLU were to adopt it in our case. In my mind, the viewpoint discrimination theory was a severe threat to the Establishment Clause.

With the viewpoint discrimination premise, the court could conceivably read the Establishment Clause literally and pare it down to cover only those instances where the government actually "established" an official religion. The conservatives, who would prefer more religious influence (so long as it's a religion they approve of), were enamored with Sekulow's theory. And it resonated with the free speech absolutists on the left, those who think that anything that potentially restricts speech leads us down a slippery ramp to suppression of speech. We hoped the ACLU would stick with us, and Worona and the other amici persuaded the group that Kiryas Joel represented a dangerous weakening of the separation of church and state. They successfully headed off an unholy ACLU-ACLJ alliance.

The Baptist Joint Committee for Religious Liberty brought another interesting perspective. With their long commitment to separation of church and state, a viewpoint rooted in New Testament theology, the Baptists were an important ally. Baptists, like other "nonconformists," had suffered generations of discrimination in Europe. They were very concerned with protecting their rights and freedoms in the United States, and of course it was in Thomas Jefferson's letter to the Baptists in Danbury, Connecticut, where Jefferson first pledged to erect a wall of separation between church and state. The Baptists were our natural allies.

But . . .

In the 1970s, when the Republican party was reinventing itself to appeal to fundamentalist voters in the South and Midwest, a conservative faction in the Southern Baptist Convention (SBC)—which was and remains by far the most important governing body of American Baptists—began a takeover of the SBC. These conservative Baptists were in favor of forsaking the age-old Baptist commitment to church-state separation for a political alliance with the surging Republicans. Meanwhile, the Baptist Joint Committee, which represented Baptists in Washington and had been filing briefs in support of separatist views for decades, was also targeted by the SBC junta. The SBC felt that Republican-controlled governments at the national and the state levels would support fundamentalist social policies if the separation of church and state were weakened, but the Baptist Joint Committee, traditionally the legal arm of the Baptist movement, held firm in favor of separation of church and state.

From 1979 (when the splinter group first successfully elected the president of the SBC) until the early 1990s, relations between the SBC and the Baptist Joint Committee deteriorated steadily. The Baptist Joint Committee refused to abandon the principles of church-state separation in exchange for what it considered a very bad marriage with political conservatives. Even though the conservative faction had been electing presidents of the SBC since 1979, it took ten years to fully consolidate control of the most important committees. In 1991 the conservatives finally succeeded in cutting all funding to the Baptist Joint Committee. Nevertheless, there was a cultural and institutional need to maintain the illusion of Baptist unity, so the SBC and Joint Committee at first avoided appearing in public on opposite sides of an issue. Our case would be among the first, and few, in which the SBC and Baptist Joint Committee appeared on opposite sides.

Interestingly, a similar schism had opened between the American Jewish Congress (AJC), renowned champions of separationist litigation, and Agudath Israel, an organization that ran a large Orthodox Jewish system of yeshivas and very much wanted access to government funding streams for their programs. Agudath Israel filed a brief supporting the Satmar; attorneys Marc Stern and Norman Redlich of the AJC supported our cause and were at our meeting at the NEA headquarters.

Coincidentally, Redlich, a former corporation counsel for New York City, had been one of my professors at New York University Law School in the 1960s, and I had edited a casebook on municipal law for him.

The AJC had been supporting our position through the New York State courts and was one of the best friends of our case because, as the most venerable and influential Jewish civil rights body, the AJC's participation helped shield me from allegations that I was an anti-Semite or a self-hating Jew. Stern recalls that the meeting about the case was typical of most important amici conferences. "Everybody has a stake and everybody wants to show off. It's very hard. On the one hand, having a broad coalition shows that your side isn't just represented by a narrow-minded crank," Stern told me.

On the other hand, more voices inevitably mean more dissension. Since every civil rights group has a different purpose, and often a different political base and constituency, finding common ground can be difficult.

"I was doing a brief once," Stern recalls, "for 120 odd civil rights groups with the late Marvin Frankel* and we were relatively close, but the brief had to be approved by 120 groups. No matter how many drafts we went through, there were always some words or some language or some legal theory we couldn't use. . . . Most of the people who run these organizations are not practicing lawyers and have no idea of the feel of the case or how to present a winning argument. But they have a true sense of what their own political needs are, so I find it really confining. Thankfully, at this point in my career if I say 'The law is X and we can go Y distance with it,' there's a certain amount of deference, but that wasn't always the case."

Our meeting at the NEA was fascinating, with the different organizations ardently pressing *their* agendas while Jay and I tried to keep them focused on *ours*. Some groups saw the case as simply one of a series of attempts by the conservatives on the court to jettison the *Lemon* test in favor of a coercion test. For these groups, preserving *Lemon* was the goal. Others were inspired by Chief Judge Kaye's opinion and wanted to

---

* Marvin E. Frankel was a renowned litigator, federal judge in the Southern District of New York, and scholar who taught at Columbia Law School. He died in 2002.

stress that Kiryas Joel's school district represented a direct affront to the Establishment Clause. Because they saw the KJ district as a precursor to a future of religiously segregated school districts and the end of the Establishment Clause as Americans had come to know it, they favored ignoring *Lemon* and going straight to the language of the Establishment Clause. During the meeting, the various groups managed to divide the important legal and policy arguments among themselves, and it wasn't until Worona left to take a personal phone call that an ulterior motive for the meeting became apparent.

The instant Jay left the room, the meeting abruptly shifted to a discussion of whether this wet-behind-the-ears whippersnapper from Upstate New York was of sufficient experience, stature, and pedigree to take this important case to the US Supreme Court. It was pointed out that he had never argued a case at the Supreme Court. "The First Amendment is at stake, and you can't send a novice against Lewin in a case like this," one of them argued. Lewin had argued a couple of dozen cases in front of the court.

Earlier, Jay and I had detected jealousy and condescension from the Harvard-, Yale-, and Columbia-trained attorneys involved in this dispute in one way or another, but I had no idea that the sentiments were that strong.

I was furious. I angrily reminded everyone in the room that Jay Worona knew this case better than any of them and better than anyone, that he had matched wits and minds with seven of the sharpest legal intellects in the state—the judges of the New York Court of Appeals, who had on many occasions made mincemeat of the Ivy League lawyers—and that he had already won this case three times. As to his age and experience, I noted that Sarah Weddington was twenty-six when she argued and won the iconic *Roe v. Wade.** Not for a nanosecond was Jay's position as lead counsel in any jeopardy. I didn't tell Jay about the attempted coup until much later, because I didn't want to distract

---

* Sarah Weddington, an attorney and former Texas state legislator, is best known for representing the plaintiff in *Roe v. Wade*, 410 US 113 (1973), the Supreme Court's landmark abortion rights case.

him, but he couldn't help but notice the condescending looks and snide comments.

"Basically what I learned was that the intelligentsia in Washington really enjoys listening to themselves talk," Jay recalls. "When they learned that this local yokel from Albany was going to be litigating this very important case, they decided to use the meeting in Washington as an opportunity not to have me tell them what the case was about so they could decide how to write their briefs but to make me feel as small as possible so I would tuck my tail and run away. I discovered that they didn't give a crap about what happened in the Hasidic community or the legislation in Albany but only the issue of the almighty *Lemon* test and their own personal approach to the separation of church and state. It all had a profound effect upon me, because instead of taking a *screw 'em* attitude, which, now that I'm fifty I could take, at thirty-two years old I thought, *Oh my god, what have I got myself into?* and I prayed, *Dear Lord, please don't let me screw up!*"

After averting the coup, I suggested the amici get down to the business of writing their briefs, and I must say their writings were impressive. I was very pleased with the breadth and scope of the arguments, and very confident that the issues were thoroughly laid out for the Supreme Court. Now it was a matter of getting Jay prepped—and we all knew that the best way to do that was to hold a series of dress rehearsals, so to speak. With the help of the National School Boards Association, a series of "moot courts" were set up, two of them at prestigious law schools—New York University and Albany Law School—and a third at the legendary Supreme Court and appellate advocacy law firm of Hogan & Hartson.*

The preparations for the moot courts were extensive, and Jay crammed for months, attempting to anticipate the questions and responses he would get from the pretend judges at the universities and the law firm, who in turn were anticipating the questions and responses

---

* Hogan & Hartson was an international law firm that merged with a London firm in 2010 and became Hogan Lovells.

he would encounter when he actually appeared before the high court. The moot court at Hogan & Hartson was especially instructive.

Worona remembers that the "chief judge" gave him a particularly hard time, showing him the ropes of Supreme Court advocacy and just how penetrating the questions of the conservative justices were likely to be. "He was very helpful, very generous with his time," Jay recalls. "There was an exercise where we would make a mock argument and he would critique what I did, how I delivered the argument. It helped me understand what is and what is not effective oral advocacy."

The mock chief judge would eventually become rather famous in his own right: John Roberts, who had clerked for Justice Rehnquist and would, years after our case was decided, succeed him as the real chief justice of the Supreme Court. Roberts helped prep Jay for the sort of questioning he could expect, especially from his former boss and Scalia.

But even after the best preparation in the world, neither Worona nor any of the amici thought they could win a vote from Chief Justice Rehnquist or his two archconservative allies, Thomas and Scalia. The key to the case, we were certain, would be getting O'Connor and Kennedy. Stevens, because of his separationist record, could be counted on to support our arguments, and Ginsburg, though in some ways an unknown quantity, was proven to have an expansive view of equal protection (perhaps making her sensitive to Kaye's segregation analysis) and was widely expected to favor a strong separation between church and state. However, this would be one of her first cases as a Supreme Court justice, and history is replete with examples of new judges who, once joining the high court, changed their stripes or defied expectations. Justice Blackmun, who may well have been the brains behind *Lemon* (which was signed by his childhood friend Warren Burger), could be counted on to apply the *Lemon* test. By 1993 Justice Souter was known to favor stability in the court's decisions; we and the amici felt confident that Souter could be persuaded to apply *Lemon* or, at least, a test reflective of the goal of *Lemon*. Further, his recent concurring opinion in *Lee v. Weisman** gave us hope, given his analysis of church-state relations in that case. That made four likely votes for our position. The fifth would have to come from Justice O'Connor or Justice Kennedy. From our perspective, the best target was O'Connor.

Although O'Connor's decisions have been criticized by some academics over the years, and it remains debatable whether her way of looking at cases will be influential in the future, there is little question that while on the court, O'Connor was one of the most influential justices in history. In nearly every tight decision from the late 1980s through to the early years of the new century, O'Connor cast the deciding vote.

We suspected O'Connor was receptive to reconsidering and perhaps retooling the *Lemon* test. She was not a strong separationist when it came to church and state, and she was a vocal opponent to the court's decision in *Aguilar v. Felton*, which held that New York City's practice of sending public school teachers into parochial schools to teach disabled children violated the Establishment Clause:

> Common sense suggests a plausible explanation for this unblemished record. New York City's public Title I instructors are professional educators who can and do follow instructions not to inculcate religion in their classes. They are unlikely to be influenced by the sectarian nature of the parochial schools where they teach, not only because they are carefully supervised by public officials, but also because the vast majority of them visit several different schools each week, and are not of the same religion as their parochial students.

---

* *Lee v. Weisman*, 505 US 577 (1992), was the Rehnquist court's first major school prayer case, and it was a blockbuster. By a 5–4 vote, the court shot down, on Establishment Clause grounds, a practice in Providence, Rhode Island, of inviting clergy to deliver benedictions and invocations at public school graduation ceremonies. Essentially, the decision suggested that the constitutionality of any graduation prayer turned on the specific facts of the case.

. . . The actual and perceived effect of the program is precisely the effect intended by Congress: impoverished schoolchildren are being helped to overcome learning deficits, improving their test scores, and receiving a significant boost in their struggle to obtain both a thorough education and the opportunities that flow from it. . . . The risk that public school teachers in parochial classrooms will inculcate religion has been exaggerated. . . .

For these children, the Court's decision is tragic. The Court deprives them of a program that offers a meaningful chance at success in life, and it does so on the untenable theory that public school teachers (most of whom are of different faiths than their students) are likely to start teaching religion merely because they have walked across the threshold of a parochial school. I reject this theory. . . .

Kiryas Joel's attorney George Shebitz thought a plausible outcome of the Supreme Court case might be a reversal of *Aguilar*. Shebitz strongly believed that the Kiryas Joel situation had occurred only because of *Aguilar*, and he felt that O'Connor would solve it with a reversal.

On the other hand, O'Connor generally embraced a Madisonian view of the First Amendment, which might, Worona and Stern thought, lead her to uphold the New York Court of Appeals decision. Since Madison had advocated the view that the government could support religion but, if it chose to do so, must support all religion equally, the attorneys supporting our position thought that O'Connor's vote could be won by focusing on the fact that New York State singled out the Satmar for special treatment.

But that remained to be seen.

15

MAY IT PLEASE THE COURT

---

*Some Framers simply did not share a common understanding of the Estab-
lishment Clause, and, at worst . . . they, like other politicians, could raise
constitutional ideals one day and turn their backs on them the next.*
                    —Justice David Souter, *Lee v. Weisman*

"**O** YEZ! OYEZ! OYEZ!** All persons having business before
        the Honorable, the Supreme Court of the United States, are
admonished to draw near and give their attention, for the court is now
sitting. God save the United States and this Honorable Court."

With those words from the court crier, the argument was underway.

It was March 30, 1994, a sparkling spring day in Washington, and
there we were at the legal citadel. The Supreme Court building rises
from street level in such neoclassical excess that one justice suggested
the judges should arrive riding on the backs of elephants. When the
building was completed in the 1930s, Chief Justice Harlan Friske Stone
found it "almost bombastically pretentious" and "wholly inappropriate." As we approached, I think we all felt a bit intimidated to be standing at the bastion of justice. Jay Worona mounted the steps in awe, a

comparative welterweight entering the ring, praying he wouldn't get pummeled by behemoths. An avid runner, he had jogged past the court building a couple hours earlier, and was startled to see a line of spectators eager to hear the arguments—*his* arguments.

Our opponent, Nat Lewin, was already in the gallery, looking as suave, comfortable, and at ease as one would expect from an attorney who had so regularly argued before the high court. I think Jay and I were both taken aback when retired justice William Brennan, an icon to us, walked into the corridor and warmly greeted Lewin like a long lost friend. At least perceptually, Lewin clearly had a home court advantage. But Jay was too focused on the job at hand to give it much thought.

With the crier's announcement, the nine justices strode through openings in the curtains, filing in by reverse seniority and taking their spots behind the bench. The chief justice gets the center seat, flanked by the associate justices. The most senior sit to the chief's left and right, the most junior at the far ends, and everyone else in between. Chief Justice William Rehnquist quickly glanced at the assemblage in his courtroom, leaned forward slightly, and declared, "We'll hear argument now in Number 93-517, *The Board of Education of Kiryas Joel Village School District Versus Louis Grumet* and two cases consolidated with it for argument. Mr. Lewin?"

Like all good appellate advocates, Lewin cut to the quick: "The statute that is being challenged in this case as inconsistent on its face with the Establishment Clause of the First Amendment involves no governmental participation in the teaching and propagation of religious doctrine and underwrites no public employee to participate directly in religious indoctrination."

The die was cast. In Lewin's view, the fact that the school did not provide religious instruction was paramount. Lewin went on to reason that the village was constitutional, and therefore the school district must be legitimate—an illogical exercise, I thought. He would pin his hopes on persuading the justices to focus on the students with disabilities and the organization of the village instead of on the act of the legislature. Lewin added a quick pitch to Justices Blackmun and Souter, suggesting that the Kiryas Joel district satisfied the reservations both of these justices had expressed previously about church-state entanglements. He got in as much as he could before the interruptions began. And then he was bombarded.

Justice O'Connor lobbed the first grenade. "Were the laws of the State of New York," she asked, "not such that other people similarly situated could form their own special school district? Why did a special law have to be enacted here?"

Lewin explained that all school districts in New York were formed by special acts, but O'Connor was plainly not satisfied with that answer, and she was less than satisfied with his peculiar attempt to equate the creation of a school district to the collection of trash. Under his analogy, if the state collected trash on Saturdays and one community felt that it couldn't, for religious or cultural reasons, take trash out on Saturdays, then the state could make a special provision for that community to put out trash on another day.

"Well, Mr. Lewin," O'Connor responded curtly, "if such a law were to neutrally extend to everybody in New York, so that anybody similarly situated could dispose of their own trash, I think you have a very good analogy. I have a little trouble seeing why the same analysis applies when the law that you're examining is not neutral."

Music to my ears! If Lewin couldn't persuade O'Connor that the law was neutral or get her to focus on the plight of the children, I thought, we had an excellent chance of winning her swing vote.

The next question, from Justice Kennedy, was also encouraging. "Is it fair to say that governmental power was transferred here to a geographic entity based on the religious beliefs and practices of its residents?" he demanded, cutting to the heart of the case.

Lewin immediately attempted to argue, but Kennedy cut him off. "If my characterization that I used in the question were deemed the appropriate characterization, would you lose the case?" It was obviously a theoretical and rhetorical trap, and Lewin attempted to sidestep it by stressing, again, the legitimate creation of the village. Lewin was taking a beating and he knew it, but he got a break from Justice Scalia after noting that the establishment of the Village of Kiryas Joel was rooted in a zoning dispute.

"Well, that may be unconstitutional too, Mr. Lewin," Scalia said sarcastically. "If people for religious reason have larger families we can't have special zoning communities with special zoning rules, either."

Scalia continued, "The argument being made is that if they had large families for some other reason, not a religious reason, you could establish a special community with different zoning laws for that group, but if they have large families for religious reasons, just as this community has certain customs that make it difficult for them to go to another community for their schooling for religious reasons, then it's 'bad.'"

It was exactly the opportunity that Lewin had been looking for, and he hammered the softball that Scalia lobbed over the center of the plate and took the opportunity to portray himself as the savior of the religious freedom provisions of the First Amendment. "Well, our view of course is that that turns the First Amendment on its head!" Lewin said with flourish. "That essentially meant that the free exercise of religion, which is protected by the Constitution, becomes the one impermissible vice that invalidates anything that's done, and we think—"

Souter cut him off in midsentence. "Yes but leaving that argument aside—"

Souter interrupted, dismissing Scalia's point entirely: "I take it that the upshot of the forces that led to the creation of the village was that in fact the village was defined by adherence to this sect. That was the result, I take it?"

Ginsberg jumped in. "Your case I think would be considerably harder if you didn't have the school district that coincided with the preexisting village boundaries," she said.

I was frustrated and wanted to interrupt and remind everyone that villages do not run school districts in New York, and that this was unique.

The remainder of Lewin's argument was fairly uneventful—except for an odd interjection by Chief Justice Rehnquist. Looking uncomfortable, and occasionally standing up and wandering around, Rehnquist, suffering from back pain and other health problems, interjected, "Is this place geographically located up around Rochester?" To this day, I don't know where, if anywhere, the chief justice was going with that question. Lewin seemed equally baffled, partially because he didn't know why in the world it mattered, and partially because he appeared to have no idea where Rochester was (some three hundred miles from Kiryas Joel). With that, his time was up.

Assistant Attorney General Julie Mereson, New York State's lawyer, went next. Mereson began by drawing a distinction between accommodating religion and advancing religion, but was quickly cut off by Scalia.

"Do you see a difference between [accommodating religion and advancing religion]?" Scalia demanded. "By tolerating it and facilitating it, you advance it. I mean, do we have to pretend that there's a difference between the two?" Scalia's comment went to the heart of the *Lemon* test and punctuated his long-held concern that the court had built too high a wall between church and state.

Mereson attempted to explain the distinction, but she was struggling. "I believe there's a great difference between the two," she responded. "There's a red line between the two that sometimes is hard to discern, perhaps."

O'Connor asked, with growing exasperation, "How is this neutral? If the legislature set up just a special school district for this one situation, instead of passing a law to the effect that groups of people or villages or towns can form their own school district by applying neutral criteria?"

Mereson attempted to salvage her case by stressing that the New York State Legislature was simply reacting to a demonstrated need when it created the Kiryas Joel school district. "There was a local problem that did not need a general statute for other groups in the State," she said. "The problem here—"

She got no further before she was cut off.

to formulate an answer when Souter did it for him, seemingly debating with the chief justice as Jay stood between them like a volleyball net.

"But isn't the difference," Souter said, "that there wouldn't be any alternative to having a school district in the Roman Catholic case, where there is an alternative to having this school district in this case?"

Jay was starting to get the feeling that he wasn't so much a net in a volleyball game as a wall in a rather aggressive squash match between Rehnquist and Souter, with each of them smashing the ball off him. The squash game continued with Scalia, Rehnquist, Kennedy, and Ginsburg bouncing questions to each other off Worona. At one point Ginsburg interrupted Kennedy, who shot back, "May I just finish?"

A lesser attorney would have come unglued. But despite the interruptions and peculiar back and forth between the justices, Jay kept his composure and managed to present the gist of his argument forcefully. During the few moments that he was able to come up for air, he struggled to bring the focus back to the New York State Legislature's impermissible establishment of a school district with full governmental powers for the purpose of supporting the religious isolation of a particular sect. It seemed to be to little avail, as the justices were too busy playing cat and mouse with Jay. They certainly did not seem sympathetic to his case (Blackmun noted, "The Justices get so excited!").

"We believe that a political constituency defined along religious lines has in fact been established by the statute," Jay told the court. "The particular community of individuals who are devoutly religious were imbued with governmental powers and functions to allow them not simply to be exempted, as this court has in the past accepted, to privately pursue their religious perspectives, but rather, New York State has offered its arm to these individuals to be able to run a school district with full governmental [power]."

At one point O'Connor suggested that the legislature's maneuver in creating a one-village school district, instead of enacting a law that would apply equally to any community, could "set a dangerous precedent." Kennedy opined that "the rationale for the district was religious, pure and simple." Scalia questioned why, if the accommodation to Kiryas Joel wasn't legal, it isn't unconstitutional for Congress to go out of session on Good Friday or Passover or Easter or Rosh Hashanah. Jay provided the self-evident answer: "Because we're not imbuing any particular governmental functions on any particular religious person to carry out those . . . his religion."

At last, after not even an hour of arguments, the court adjourned and the parties found themselves once again on the marble steps of the Supreme Court building among a phalanx of reporters and a bank of microphones. Some fifty print journalists were there, along with C-SPAN (which was producing a two-hour documentary on the case) and all the major networks.

Abe Wieder—the mayor of Kiryas Joel, head of the Talmudic Academy, and president of the Kiryas Joel Village School Board—approached the media with a glowing smile, flanked by Steve Benardo, George Shebitz, Malka Silberstein, and about ten other Satmar. All of them were ecstatic, interpreting the interrogative tornado that rained down on Jay as proof positive of their victory. But the reporters were more objective, asking questions that in some ways were as probing and insightful as those of the justices.

"How can this not be a religious accommodation?" "What would you say if an Arab community asked for the same thing?" "How do you distinguish between cultural and religious differences?" "Wouldn't it be better to teach tolerance to children?" And finally, "Did anybody win election to the school board without endorsement by the rabbi?"

With that last question, Joseph Waldman, the dissident whose six children had been expelled from the private schools when he challenged rabbinical dictates and tried to run for the public school board without the rabbi's blessings, began shouting "No! No!" He pushed his way up to the center of the podium just as Benardo was trying to introduce Malka Silberstein so that she could tell the story about her daughter Sheindle and the reindeer costume.

Waldman elbowed his way to the microphones, knocking National Public Radio correspondent Nina Totenberg out of the way. "The village is an absolute theocracy and the public school district is run by the rebbe!"

Eventually, Malka Silberstein was able to have her say, but before long Waldman was back in front of the microphones yelling about the theocracy in Kiryas Joel. He was basically right but came off negatively. As much as the media, particularly the TV media, appreciates a juicy quote, the best of them—like the best judges—prefer a reasoned articulation of the facts over a pyrotechnic performance. So the contrast was clear when, after Waldman ran out of breath, Rabbi David Saperstein, a leader of the Reform Jewish community, arrived at the podium along with Barry Lynn, the executive director of Americans United for the Separation of Church and State, and Brent Walker, the general counsel of the Baptist Joint Committee.

Saperstein cogently explained that his and other prominent civil rights and religious groups had become involved with the case because the interests of all Americans were at stake. He expressed concern that the Supreme Court might use the case to overturn or dilute *Lemon* and impair both the Jeffersonian and Madisonian rationale for separating church and state. The rabbi also noted that the justices had not asked a single question about the *Lemon* test during the entire oral argument. He felt this was an indication that the court did not intend to overturn the famous precedent, a very astute observation.

Barry Lynn added, "I really believe that if this school district is allowed to stand that we will see religious apartheid in America. Clearly, what happened here is that the New York State Legislature in the last hours of the last night of the legislative session in 1989 decided to give in to the demands of a group which believed that separatism is a religious tenet and an important one. They have every right to believe that, but they do not have the right to ask the taxpayers to support their religious belief system."

He then explained articulately why many Jewish organizations supported us in this case: "Many of the Jewish groups in this country understand that American Jews have benefited tremendously from church-state separation, that it has protected their children from Christian bias in the public schools."

Lynn left the reporters with the following question: "Why is the president of the principal synagogue of this community also the [mayor] and also the head of the school board if not to demonstrate very clearly that there is no difference between the religious purposes of the community and what occurs in this specially created school district?"

Before much longer, the press conference was over, the news broadcasts had been prepared, and the articles had been written. I found the press coverage fascinating and considered it particularly interesting that the myriad different reporters came away with varied impressions and observations.

For example, Ana Puga of the *Boston Globe* summarized the case as follows:

> The central question in the case is how far the state can go in accommodating a particular religious group without violating the separation of church and state. At issue is the Satmar Hasidic Jewish community's use of about $6 million in public funds to educate some two hundred disabled children in its own school. Supporters of the community argued that to educate those children in a public school outside their district—where they would mix with children who do not share their culture and customs—would cause "emotional and psychological trauma." But because the Satmar community lacked the funds to establish a private school for the disabled, it instead

persuaded the New York State Legislature in 1989 to create a public school district that includes only their village, thus making public funds available.

Law columnist William H. Freivogel wrote in a column published in the *St. Louis Post-Dispatch* that the court seemed "befuddled" by the case and at times "seemed to wear blinders," adding that the case took a turn toward the "absurd" with Rehnquist's Rochester question. His take:

> Theirs is a story of religious persecution that is suggestive of the small-town New England theocracies that inspired Hawthorne's fiction and the First Amendment's separation between church and state. If the Supreme Court upholds the Kiryas Joel district, it may open the way for more state aid to religious schools. One wonders whether that would lead to fights within state legislatures over control of scarce resources. Finally, one wonders whether the Supreme Court can get the separation between church and state right—when the separation between law and reality is stark and the lady justice wears a blindfold.

I was quoted extensively in an article that appeared in the March 31, 1994, edition of the *Bond Buyer*, as follows:

> If we lose, and the high court upholds the state's legislative creation of the separate school district, New York and any state could set up school districts with public funding and public taxing authorities to meet religious precepts. People in the parochial school movement have been talking about [government] vouchers to help families pay for some costs of sending children to parochial schools. That's small stuff compared to this. . . . Almost 3 million children attend public schools in New York State, and another 800,000 to 900,000

children attend parochial schools. . . . Why couldn't [the latter] suddenly become public school districts (under a ruling favorable to the Kiryas Joel Village District)? That's what this is all about.

Lyle Denniston, in an article published in the *Chicago Sun-Times* under the headline COURT WARY OF JEWISH VILLAGE SCHOOL, wrote:

> A one-hour hearing on what may turn out to be a decisive case on government aid to religion disclosed distinctly negative reactions to the community's position among most of the moderate justices, who are likely to control the outcome. Only conservative justice Antonin Scalia offered full-scale support for the community's plea. The hearing provided no hint that the community would get its strongest wish: to have the Supreme Court cast aside the strict constitutional formula it has been using for 23 years that generally bars most forms of official support for religious groups. There were also no reliable clues about how the newest justice, Ruth Bader Ginsburg, views that formula.

Interestingly, the same article published the same day but in the *Houston Chronicle* garnered this headline: JEWISH VILLAGE GETTING SUPREME NEGATIVE VIBES; JUSTICES SHOW LITTLE SUPPORT IN HEARING.

In the *Los Angeles Times*, David G. Savage wrote that the justices "sounded as though they wanted to avoid a broad pronouncement in either direction." Linda Greenhouse of the *New York Times* came to the same conclusion: "While the Court could use this case . . . as a vehicle to reexamine its approach to the establishment clause, the Justices appeared absorbed in the details of the case and did not seem eager to make new law."

Joan Biskupic of the *Washington Post* thought that the court, rather than reconfiguring *Lemon*, might use the case to overturn its 1985 decision in *Aguilar v. Felton*. (The court later did indeed overturn *Aguilar*, albeit not in the Kiryas Joel case.)*

In *Newsday*, Timothy M. Phelps observed:

> Although Lewin seemed in danger of losing Kennedy's and O'Connor's votes, which could be fatal since three other justices have taken strong secular stands in the past, he may have picked up some unexpected support from Justice Ruth Bader Ginsburg. . . . Ginsberg, who joined the court this term, has been described as a likely advocate of strict separation of church and state.

USA Today covered the case three ways. A story by its ace Supreme Court reporter, Tony Mauro (who later went on to a stellar career with ALM Media, owner of the highly respected *New York Law Journal* and various sister publications), noted that the justices "were unusually blunt in their questioning, foreshadowing sharp divisions." An editorial called on the court to stand with the New York Court of Appeals and reject a policy "that the nation's founders wisely banned." And a rebuttal by a Roman Catholic nun argued, "It doesn't hurt to be accommodating."

Nat Lewin and I faced off on *ABC World News Tonight* a few hours after the arguments. I argued, "The reason the legislature enacted the statute, if you look at the legislative history, was to solve a religious problem so that people can live within their religious customs. It was done for religious reasons and it violates the Constitution." Lewin countered, "It's a creation of a school district for a village in which

---

* *Aguilar v. Felton*, 473 US 402 (1985), which said that New York City could not send public school teachers into parochial schools, was overturned a few years later in *Agostini v. Felton*, 521 US 203 (1997). With O'Connor writing for the majority, the court held that the Establishment Clause is not offended when public school teachers instruct at religious schools, as long as the material is secular and neutral and there is no "excessive entanglement" between government and religion.

there are people who are devoutly religious. That's all it is. It's not a creation of a district for religious reasons."

Rabbi Saperstein appeared on the *MacNeil/Lehrer NewsHour* and again laid out the case and the implications articulately: "There are thousands of school districts in this country that are predominantly white, but the government cannot create a single one with the intent of having it be white or any other color or any religion. It is a fact that the state intentionally set up a school district along religious lines. That is in violation of separation of church and state. And if this school district is allowed to prevail, then every group, religious group, that is a minority in any particular school district, Catholic, Methodist, Hindu, or anything else, can demand their own school district."

Although I thought we had clearly prevailed in the public relations battle, with the media pretty solidly agreeing with us, I obviously knew that it was the justices and not the scribes whose opinions mattered. I was cautiously optimistic. Lewin and Wieder, on the other hand, were so supremely confident that they chartered a jet flight back to Kiryas Joel in order to tell the grand rebbe the good news. There was dancing in the streets of the village that night, a community-wide celebration.

But the celebration was premature, as the Supreme Court had not yet spoken.

16

JUDICIAL DELIBERATIONS

We are not final because we are infallible, we are infallible only because we are final.

—Justice Robert Jackson, *Brown v. Allen*

ON FRIDAY APRIL 1, 1994, the justices gathered in their conference room, a dark, wood-paneled space with a red carpet, an ostentatious chandelier, and an enormous table. Presidential portraits adorned the walls, and an anachronistic fireplace of carved black stone occupied one wall. Customarily, the justices greet each other with a warm handshake, and then, the niceties dispensed with, sit down in order of seniority and proceed to tear each other to shreds.

Chief Justice Rehnquist went first. He opined that Kiryas Joel's school district passed the *Lemon* test, so the court needn't even bother with any discussion of overruling *Lemon*. In the chief's view, the law did nothing to advance religion and drew an analogy to the Utah Territory established by the Mormons.

Justice Blackmun promptly disagreed, arguing that the Kiryas Joel law unquestionably advanced the Satmar religion and therefore undeniably violated *Lemon*.

In contrast to the chief and Blackmun, Justice Stevens, the only other remaining appointee from the 1970s, mused aloud about the case, calling it "unusual" and saying that the "reasons for the accommodation bother me." He explained his discomfort by saying that it seemed to him that the accommodation had little to do with the trauma the children experienced in the public school but a lot to do with the parents' need to prevent the children from learning about American culture. He indicated that he would vote for our position.

Stevens's reservations were interesting but, on the whole, the opinions of the first three justices to speak were not surprising. Justice O'Connor was next, and she likely held the key. Everyone who followed the case closely was intensely curious about not only where O'Connor would go but how she would get there.

Not unexpectedly, O'Connor immediately invoked her old nemesis, *Aguilar v. Felton*. It would be several more years before O'Connor had the votes to overrule *Aguilar*, but she was clearly intent on planting the seeds with our case. She seemed to suggest, with some justification, that Kiryas Joel was a problem of the court's making. But at the same time, she echoed the comments she made in the courtroom, criticizing the Pataki-Lentol bill and indicating that she would vote to strike down the law. "Appearances are important," she said.

The emphasis on appearances was classic Sandra Day O'Connor, the politician. Maybe there was a colorable argument that the Satmar district did not violate the Constitution—either because the establishment of the village itself was not challenged or because of the distinction between cultural and religious issues—but in her political view, the court could not be seen to countenance blatant religious gerrymandering.

Scalia, the next in seniority, barely let Justice O'Connor finish before he called her concerns "absurd." "Religious toleration is one of the glories of the United States!" he declared, stating an obvious point that was not in dispute. This sort of outburst was typical of Scalia. It was also typical of his disdain for other approaches and the nonchalance with which he could alienate others on the court.

Scalia went on to tell Stevens that he didn't see any reason to separate the children from the parents, as if that were the issue at all. Knowing that without O'Connor, he had very little hope of saving the Kiryas Joel school district, he expressed disgust at his colleagues' inability to turn their Establishment Clause decisions into a workable theory (the liberals and moderates frequently agreed as to the outcome of a religion case but could never agree on the reason for the outcome). This was telling, Scalia thought, and suggested that the outcome was arrived at by means other than constitutional interpretation. "This court," he huffed at his colleagues in the room, "has a new theology for every new religion case. I look forward to dissent."

Scalia's suspicions were confirmed when Justice Kennedy, who was next in seniority, spoke. Kennedy agreed with some of what O'Connor had said, but he was convinced that "this is a religious gerrymander." He thought the text of the statute, which identifies the Village of Kiryas Joel rather than the Satmar religion, was "an attempt to get around the Establishment Clause."

Having lost Kennedy's vote, Kiryas Joel was clearly looking at some kind of a loss. Now those in the minority were faced with cutting their losses and attempting to make the majority decision as narrow as possible. In appellate jurisprudence, that is often when things get most interesting. As long as a justice is in the majority on the final decision, she or he has a voice in how the court arrives at that result. And if a judge isn't thrilled with the final result but can live with it, staying with the majority gives the jurist an opportunity to water down the decision. But once a judge is in dissent, he or she really has no voice in the case and is essentially writing for posterity. That is often the role of Scalia.

As Scalia had accurately, if bluntly, reminded his colleagues, his ideological foes on the court had never been able to come up with more than an ad hoc approach to the Establishment Clause. Each time the court took a religion case, the ostensible reason was to clarify its position. And each time, a majority of justices failed to articulate a coherent solution. Marc Stern of the American Jewish Congress suggests, and I agree, that "all the lower courts—both state and federal—consider the First Amendment to be the special province of the Supreme Court. These cases are always interesting and engaging, unlike the more tedious securities or income tax or evidence cases. The justices look forward to them, they exercise their prodigious intellectual powers on them, and it's really an opportunity for virtuoso performances. So, not surprisingly, they all find different, idiosyncratic ways of arriving at their decisions on religion cases, and especially in Establishment Clause cases."

After Justice Souter indicated he was on our side, the attention turned to Justice Thomas, who of course had been responsible for the case reaching the court in the first place. Thomas took particular exception with Justice Stevens's suggestion that the need for the Kiryas Joel school sprang not from the children's trauma but from the parents' fear of American culture. He spoke of his own experience growing up black in a white society and of the trauma he had suffered in high school just because he was different. Thomas agreed with Scalia that it made no difference whether the parents were protecting their children or their culture.

According to Blackmun's notes, the vote in conference was 5–3 in our favor, with only the newly confirmed Ruth Bader Ginsburg remaining. But even after the justices conferred, her opinion was not clear. Blackmun's notes suggest Ginsberg was inclined to support our position but had not made up her mind.

Regardless, at this point in the case it was a foregone conclusion that the court would rule in favor of our arguments (although we would not know the outcome for several months). The easy part was now over, but the difficult part remained. The majority would have to find enough common ground to offer useful guidelines for the lower courts. One thing was certain: there would be a blistering dissent coming from the pen of Justice Scalia, and the majority would need to put together something robust to deflect his barbs. Since it appeared that the chief justice would be in the minority with Scalia and Thomas, it fell to Justice Blackmun, the most senior judge in the majority, to assign the opinion. Later in the afternoon on April 1, 1994, the day the court met to discuss the Kiryas Joel case, Justice Blackmun sent the following note to Rehnquist: "Dear Chief: I shall try my hand at an opinion for the Court in these cases."

But either Blackmun found that he couldn't write an opinion that would garner the necessary five votes or something else convinced him to pass the assignment to Justice Souter. In fact, it appears that the day before the court heard the arguments from Worona and Lewin, Blackmun had reached a decision he had been toying with for some time: he was ready to retire. By Monday, April 4, rumors had spread, and on April 6 it was official. Justice Blackmun, the author of *Roe v. Wade* and the last signer of *Lemon v. Kurtzman* still on the court, was retiring. Justice Souter let it be known that he would like to write the decision. By the middle of June, he had a draft opinion.

Souter's draft began as two sections. The first section articulated the majority's view of the important facts, and the second presented the court's argument and explanation of its holding. Souter's argument was straightforward. He wrote that the New York State Legislature had failed the Constitution in two ways. First, it had fused religious and civic power by drawing the school district to include only Satmar, when the legislature knew or should have known that it was handing over civic and governmental power to a community where the religious and civic functions were already combined. Second, the legislature had failed to provide this extraordinary benefit in a neutral way, so that it might be available to all communities regardless of religion.

Echoing O'Connor's point in conference that "appearances matter," Souter expressed concern about "the significant symbolic benefit to religion associated with the mere appearance of a joint exercise of legislative authority by Church and State."

The initial opinion acknowledged that the situation in Kiryas Joel was more subtle than an explicit delegation of power to a religious leader but also held that the Supreme Court intended to look behind the express language of the law in order to consider its purpose and effects. "Authority over public schools," Souter wrote, "belongs to the State, and cannot be delegated to a local school district defined by the State in order to grant political control to a religious group."

He continued:

> It is true that religious people (or groups of religious people) cannot be denied to exercise the rights of citizens simply because of their religious affiliations or commitments. [But] where "fusion [of religious and civic power]" is in issue, the difference lies in the distinction between a government's purposeful delegation on the basis of religion and a delegation on principles neutral to religion, to individuals whose religious identities are incidental to their receipt of civic authority.

The most important initial response was from Justice O'Connor on June 16. She wrote, "Dear David: I agree with much of your well-crafted opinion. My one disagreement is that I don't see this case as involving a fusion of governmental and religious functions." She went on to ask Souter to divide his part 2 so that she could join all of the opinion except the part that mentioned "fusion." The note ended with a brief appeal: "I hope you can see your way clear to making the changes."

Souter responded quickly: "Dear Sandra: Thanks for your letter of earlier today and for your readiness to make a Court as far as you are able to go. I am recirculating the opinion divided as you suggested and with what I hope will be satisfactory revisions. . . . I hope the changes will enable you to join to the degree your letter mentions."

This little exchange offers an inside glimpse into the dynamics of the court. It shows the sincerity with which the justices (sometimes) work to find common ground and also the practical methods by which majority opinions are crafted.

Very different was the scathing dissent circulated by Scalia. In a fulminating opinion, he accused Souter of a "breathtaking" attempt to "steamroll the difference between civil authority held by a church and civil authority held by members of a church," and called his arguments "facile," saying that his case "could scarcely be weaker." Scalia well knew Souter's aversion to injecting personal rhetoric into court opinions and did his best to irritate his opponent by attacking Souter by name at every opportunity. Setting up a straw version of Souter's argument, Scalia wrote, "To be sure, when there is no special treatment there is no possibility of religious favoritism; but it is not logical to suggest that when there *is* special treatment there is *proof* of religious favoritism." Building up to a rhetorical crescendo of vitriol aimed at the straw Souter, Scalia accused the court of creating a "novel Establishment Clause principle to the effect that no secular objective may be pursued by a means that might also be used for religious favoritism if some other means is available." Scalia took particularly sharp aim at the failure of the traditionalists on the court to articulate a workable formula for the Establishment Clause, opening with a direct attack on his colleagues:

> The Court today finds that the Powers That Be, up in Albany, have conspired to effect an establishment of the Satmar Hasidim. I do not know who would be more surprised at this discovery: the Founders of our nation or Grand Rebbe Joel Teitelbaum, founder of the Satmar. The Grand Rebbe would be astounded to learn that after escaping brutal persecution and coming to America with the modest hope of religious toleration for their ascetic form of Judaism, the Satmar had become so powerful, so closely allied with mammon,

as to have become an "establishment" of the Empire State. And the Founding Fathers would be astonished to find that the Establishment Clause—which they designed "to insure that no one powerful sect or combination of sects could use political or governmental power to punish dissenters"—has been employed to prohibit characteristically and admirably American accommodation of the religious practices (or more precisely, cultural peculiarities) of a tiny minority sect. I, however, am *not* surprised. Once this Court has abandoned text and history as guides, nothing prevents it from calling religious toleration the establishment of religion.

Souter, for his part, was ready with an equally characteristic response. In three sober paragraphs, in language as needling as Scalia's, Souter cast the dissenter as "the gladiator making a last stand against the lions. Justice Scalia's dissent is certainly the work of a gladiator, but he thrusts at lions of his own imagining." Souter went on to deny all of the alleged outrages Scalia had accused the majority of, and then took aim at what he saw as Scalia's artificial and radical approach with verbiage that would figure prominently in the court's final decision.

17

SUPREMELY DECIDED

We do not disable a religiously homogenous group from exercising political power conferred on it without regard to religion. . . . Nor do we impugn the motives of the New York Legislature, which no doubt intended to accommodate the Satmar community without violating the Establishment Clause; we simply refuse to ignore that the method it chose is one that aids a particular religious community . . . rather than all groups interested in separate schooling.

—Justice David Souter, *Board of Education of Kiryas Joel Village School District v. Grumet*

BY MID-JUNE, WE were on pins and needles. The session was winding down, and every decision day that came and went without a resolution was eating us alive. Jay and I desperately wished we could call the Supreme Court and ask when our case would be decided, but we knew, first, that was exceedingly poor form, and, second, they wouldn't tell us anyhow. Then, on the morning of June 27, 1994, Jay got a call from the court, and almost simultaneously I got a call from a local reporter advising that the Associated Press had just moved an alert that we had won 6–3. I was elated, wired, exhausted, and immensely curious: as important as it was to prevail, it was just as important in the long run for the court to embrace the reasoning we had advanced and uphold the separation of church and state.

In short order, our fax machine sprang to life and slowly started spitting out the decision, all sixty-five pages, at a painfully slow pace. The first page surprised me: Justice Souter had written for the majority. We had thought that if we won, Stevens or O'Connor would write the decision. No matter. As the fax machine grunted out the document, Jay and I huddled together, reading each page as it arrived. The synopsis of the first few pages gave us the gist: since the legislation applied to only one community in the state and clearly catered to the Satmar, it violated the Constitution by favoring one religion (and not making the same accommodation to other religious groups). The court said the legislature had delegated governmental authority to a group defined by its religion, resulting in an unacceptable "fusion" of church and state. The first pages also told us that Blackmun, Stevens, and Ginsburg signed on to Souter's opinion; that Kennedy and O'Connor agreed with the result and part of the reasoning; and that Scalia wrote a dissent joined by Rehnquist and Thomas. With multiple writings, it took a while to figure out which judge was where on various points of the discussion, but we eventually realized that the court had basically avoided the *Lemon* question, neither endorsing nor repudiating the precedent. All in all, the decision broke down as follows in something of a mixed message.

The four-judge plurality, adopting the Souter opinion, said the legislation "singles out a particular religious sect for special treatment," resulting in unconstitutional favoritism toward a particular religious organization. The justices also took Scalia to task for his typically bombastic dissent.

O'Connor and Kennedy agreed that the Kiryas Joel legislation stepped over the constitutional line. But they offered a more accommodating view, implying (accurately, as future events would prove) that they were amenable to ditching O'Connor's old nemesis *Aguilar v.*

Felton. The dissenters were on board with that sentiment; they would have overruled *Aguilar* then and there, even though the issue wasn't before the court. (I had actually thought they could have used *Kiryas Joel* to reverse *Aguilar.* In retrospect, if they had, it would have prevented years of confusion.)

After outlining the history of the village, the school district, and the various decisions that had bubbled up from the New York courts, and noting Chief Judge Kaye's astute observation that the law was an "unnecessarily broad response to a narrow problem," Souter went on to describe articulately just where the law had run afoul of the Establishment Clause:

> Because the religious community of Kiryas Joel did not receive its new governmental authority simply as one of many communities eligible for equal treatment under a general law, we have no assurance that the next similarly situated group seeking a school district of its own will receive one. . . .
>
> Here, the benefit flows only to a single sect, but aiding this single, small religious group causes no less a constitutional problem than would follow from aiding a sect with more members or religion as a whole, and we are forced to conclude that the State of New York has violated the Establishment Clause. . . .
>
> We do not deny that the Constitution allows the state to accommodate religious needs by alleviating special burdens. Our cases leave no doubt that in commanding neutrality the Religion Clauses do not require the government to be oblivious to impositions that legitimate exercises of state power may place on religious belief and practice. Rather, there is "ample room under the Establishment Clause for benevolent neutrality which will permit religious exercise to exist without sponsorship and without interference." . . . But accommodation is not a principle without limits, and what petitioners seek is an adjustment to the Satmars' religiously grounded

preferences that our cases do not countenance. . . . Petitioners' proposed accommodation singles out a particular religious sect for
special treatment, and whatever the limits of permissible legislative
accommodations may be . . . it is clear that neutrality as among
religions must be honored.

The majority also said there were lots of ways to accomplish the
underlying intent of the law without running into constitutional
hurdles:

There are several alternatives here for providing bilingual and
bicultural special education to Satmar children. Such services can
perfectly well be offered to village children through the Monroe-
Woodbury Central School District. Since the Satmars do not claim
that separatism is religiously mandated, their children may receive
bilingual and bicultural instruction at a public school already run
by the Monroe-Woodbury district. Or if the educationally appropriate offering by Monroe-Woodbury should turn out to be a separate
program of bilingual and bicultural education at a neutral site near
one of the village's parochial schools, this Court has already made
it clear that no Establishment Clause difficulty would inure in such
a scheme, administered in accordance with neutral principles that
would not necessarily confine special treatment to Satmars.

Blackmun wrote separately, "only to note my disagreement with
any suggestion that today's decision signals a departure from the principles described in *Lemon v. Kurtzman*. . . . I remain convinced of the
general validity of the basic principles stated in *Lemon*, which have
guided this Court's Establishment Clause decisions in over 30 cases."

Stevens also wrote a concurrence (shared by Blackmun and Ginsburg), opining that New York, when faced with a legitimate problem,
"responded with a solution that affirmatively supports a religious sect's

interest in segregating itself and preventing its children from associating with their neighbors."

In her concurrence, O'Connor said there is nothing inherently unconstitutional about government accommodating religious interests, as long as it does so equally:

> What makes accommodation permissible, even praiseworthy, is not that the government is making life easier for some particular religious group as such. Rather, it is that the government is accommodating a deeply held belief. Accommodations may thus justify treating those who share this belief differently from those who do not; but they do not justify discriminations based on sect. A state law prohibiting the consumption of alcohol may exempt sacramental wines, but it may not exempt sacramental wine used by Catholics but not by Jews.

O'Connor said New York could solve the problem simply by allowing all villages to operate their own school districts, or by setting forth neutral criteria that a village must satisfy to operate its own school district. It has continued to mystify me that no one at the Supreme Court realized that, in New York, no village has the power or authority to operate a school district. School districts are intended by law to be independent of any other form of local government in the state, except in the five largest cities.

Kennedy suggested the core issue wasn't so much that the legislature had created a school district composed of members of a religious sect but that it permitted the establishment of a village that was gerrymandered to keep all but members of the sect at bay. He said the "Establishment Clause forbids the government to use religion as a line-drawing criterion."

Scalia's dissent was, typically, laced with sarcasm. He began with the same statement in his pre-decision memo ("The Court today finds that the Powers That Be, up in Albany, have conspired to effect an establishment of the Satmar Hasidim . . .") and then continued:

> The Court's decision is astounding. [The law] involves no public aid to private schools and does not mention religion. In order to validate it, the Court casts aside, on the flimsiest of evidence, the strong presumption of validity that attaches to facially neutral laws and invalidates the present accommodation because it does not trust New York to be as accommodating toward other religions (presumably those less powerful than the Satmar Hasidim) in the future. This is unprecedented except that it continues, and takes to new extremes, a recent tendency in the opinions of this Court to turn the Establishment Clause into a repealer of our Nation's tradition of religious toleration.

The majority could not allow that outburst to go unanswered:

> We do not disable a religiously homogenous group from exercising political power conferred on it without regard to religion. . . . Nor do we impugn the motives of the New York Legislature, which no doubt intended to accommodate the Satmar community without violating the Establishment Clause; we simply refuse to ignore that the method it chose is one that aids a particular religious community . . . rather than all groups interested in separate schooling. . . .
>
> Our job, of course, would be easier if the dissent's position had prevailed with the Framers and with this Court over the years. An Establishment Clause diminished to the dimensions acceptable to Justice Scalia could be enforced by a few simple rules, and our docket would never see cases requiring the application of a principle like neutrality toward religion as well as among religious sects. But that would be as blind to history as to precedent, and the difference between Justice Scalia and the Court accordingly turns on the Court's recognition that the Establishment Clause does comprehend

such a principle and obligates courts to exercise the judgment necessary to apply it.

As I finished reading the final sentences of the opinion and paused to ponder the fact that I had been part of a case that upheld the Establishment Clause, I was overwhelmed and humbled. But there was little time for reflection—that would come in the days and years that followed. There were calls to make and calls to return.

I called my wife, Barbara, who was teaching a class at Sage College, my daughter Lisa, who was studying at Yale Law School, and my daughter Debbie, who was a graduate student at NYU. I called New York's commissioner of education to offer my help in placing the kids. I called the members of my board who had been so supportive, like Judy Katz, Al Hawk, and Georgine Hyde. We all agreed we had to talk to the press immediately, and had to stress the importance of the separation of church and state. We did not want to lose the main issue in the drama of the disabled children (who we knew could, and most certainly would, continue to receive the services they required), and we felt it essential to keep the focus on the importance of never allowing a governmental unit to be formed for religious purposes.

Meanwhile, we wondered how Governor Cuomo would react, and I personally thought about how angry he would be. As I have said, although I was one hundred percent certain Cuomo was wrong on this matter, I still had enormous respect for his intellect and integrity, and hoped that with this battle behind us we could resume our friendship and let bygones be bygones. On the other hand, I knew well how thin-skinned the governor was, how competitive he was, and how vindictive he could be. I pretty much expected that our relationship would remain strained for the immediate future, perhaps permanently, and anticipated that Cuomo would exact a measure of retribution by shortchanging me and the New York State School Boards Association whenever possible.

What I didn't foresee was that Cuomo would attempt to execute an end run against the US Supreme Court.

met certain criteria. So far, so good. But only one of New York's 1,546 municipalities could meet the criteria: Kiryas Joel.*

There was no attempt to hide the purpose in any of the legislative history. In fact, a spokeswoman for the Speaker of the Assembly, Sheldon Silver,† publicly stated, "The trick for negotiators [was] to craft legislation so Kiryas Joel would be virtually the only village to take advantage of the opportunity to create a district."

I publicly lambasted the new law as the "son of sham," and I told the *New York Times* that I was "personally disappointed in the utter disrespect and disregard the Governor and Legislature have for the Supreme Court." To me, the law was all too reminiscent of the efforts of southern governors and legislatures to evade *Brown v. Board of Education*—the landmark decision barring racial segregation in public education—by enacting new laws to perpetuate their separatist way of life.

The media, appropriately, tore the governor and legislature apart. The *Times* agreed with me in a strongly worded editorial: "The swift election-year move, which could allow more disgruntled school consumers to create their own districts, suggests more concern for politics than law. . . . When public money is used to educate children, it should be used to integrate students of diverse backgrounds—not to conspire in religious and cultural isolation."

An editorial in the Gannett papers called the new legislation "an insult to the democratic process." The *Buffalo News* added, "State

---

* The five criteria were: (1) the proposed district had to have a total students enrollment of at least two thousand, including private school students; (2) the proposed district had to be entirely contained within another preexisting district; (3) the preexisting district had to maintain at least two thousand students after secession of the new district; (4) the wealth of the new district had to be equal to or greater than the statewide average; (5) there would be no more than a 10 percent change in the wealth of the preexisting district after secession of the new district.

† Silver, who became Speaker of the Assembly in February 1994, was and is an important figure in the Orthodox community and a powerful ally of Kiryas Joel. He was well acquainted with all the major players and, in fact, owned a second home in the town of Monroe.

residents should be questioning why their representatives were spending time figuring ways to cater to a small religious group while being unable to resolve a number of other matters that could have benefitted the state as a whole." And the Associated Press opined, "It looks like the New York Legislature is basically attempting to override and nullify a constitutional decision of the Supreme Court."

The Rochester *Democrat and Chronicle* said:

> With the right motivation, the Governor and state legislature can cast aside their gridlocked indecisiveness with remarkable speed. Why, not even a trifling consideration like a United States Supreme Court ruling can stand in their way. . . . This is in such obvious disregard of the spirit of the court's ruling that we can safely predict success for a lawsuit the state school boards association plans to file. . . . Just what is the motivation? . . . Critics point to the bloc voting habits of the Satmar community. But such cynicism does an injustice to our legislators and governor. They don't come that cheaply.

As the *Democrat and Chronicle* suggested, Jay Worona and I were indeed quietly plotting a legal response to the new law. But in truth I was concerned that my board of directors was getting tired of this, and that the energy it took to fight Kiryas Joel would keep us from other priorities. At a special meeting held at the National School Boards convention in San Francisco, I asked my board to reaffirm their commitment to proceed in the case. By a 14–2 vote, they permitted me to pursue additional litigation.

KJ mayor Abe Wieder immediately attacked me in the media, alleging that I had no other lifetime goal than to pursue helpless children. I responded that if it took my life to keep the Constitution intact from the onslaughts of the legislature, it would be a worthwhile venture.

The lawyers for the Satmar, some of whom had been involved in drafting the first legislation, were disdainful of the second attempt at a legislative solution. They were as surprised as we were that the governor's office had not done a more careful job. Nat Lewin did not defend it. George Shebitz was quite outspoken about his opposition to the proposal. The Satmar responded by hiring an Albany lawyer, George Barber, an assistant district attorney who specialized in criminal appeals and knew little about First Amendment law but a lot about the local political and judicial establishment. The case would be heard by Justice Lawrence E. Kahn, who had issued the initial decision invalidating the first law, and the procedural motions would be argued before another local supreme court justice, Joseph Harris.

In late August 1994 Harris issued a thirty-plus-page opinion, ruling against us on a procedural matter and allowing the school to remain open while the case was pending. Harris seemed more interested in debating and refuting the US Supreme Court decision in the previous case than in the procedural issues that were before him; he suggested that the new law provided a "religious-neutral process" and effectively "cut the Gordian Knot that has long kept government and religion at loggerheads." He described the law as a "peace treaty with the Establishment Clause" and predicted we would lose hands down when the merits were decided by Justice Kahn:

> Chapter 241 doesn't result, at least facially and purposely, in giving Satmar handicapped children anything other than what all handicapped children are entitled to under the Individuals with Disabilities Education Act, and the laws of the State of New York (see, Education Law art 89). Satmar children cannot expect to be treated better than first-class citizens by reason of their religion, but not less than that because of their religion. Government cannot, in contravention of the "free exercise of religion" clause of the First Amendment, require Satmar children, or any other children, to cut off their ear locks and wear blue jeans in order to receive benefits the law affords to all children similarly situated.

I begged to differ and told the press that Harris had apparently "decided that when the legislature dressed a wolf in sheep's clothing, it was a sheep."

Meanwhile, the campaign for governor was on and Cuomo was facing a challenge, coincidentally, by Republican state senator George Pataki, who had authored the first Kiryas Joel law. Pataki was largely unknown statewide, but he had the political and financial backing of the powerful US Senator Alfonse D'Amato, another strong patron of government aid to the Satmar. As later events would prove, Cuomo grossly underestimated the Pataki-D'Amato plan to replace him in the governor's mansion. Nevertheless, Cuomo still appreciated the political reality of the Satmar voting bloc. In a midsummer campaign rally in Kiryas Joel, apparently timed to coincide with the forthcoming Harris decision, Cuomo promised that if the second law was declared unconstitutional, he would introduce a third, and if that went down, push through a fourth. "If government can't deal with the problem of children who need special education, then what good is government?" he said.

A reporter who had covered Cuomo's campaign rally in Kiryas Joel gave a tape of the governor's remarks to *60 Minutes*, the most popular show on television at the time. Ed Bradley, a famed journalist and a cohost on the show, contacted my press aide, Bill Pape, and asked if he could interview me concerning the litigation. Bill and I went over to Bradley's office in New York City, and I was filmed while watching—for the first time—a tape of Cuomo's speech. I was shocked to hear the governor insist that he would find a way to give Kiryas Joel its own school district, no matter what the courts said, and no matter how often they said it. Bradley asked if I knew Cuomo. I indicated that he had been a mentor and I considered him to be a constitutional scholar. In response to a question from Bradley, I indicated that I had not seen the tape before, and my first reaction was to compare it to the attempts by southern governors to circumvent the *Brown* decision during my youth.

The interview was taped in late summer but did not air until the first Sunday in November, two days before the election. Prior to that weekend, Cuomo had a decent lead in the polls. However, in a major upset, Cuomo lost and Pataki was governor-elect.

Pataki had been in office only a few months when, as Justice Harris predicted, Justice Kahn ruled against us. Kahn's decision was a huge surprise and disappointment, since his initial opinion, vindicated by the appellate division, the state court of appeals, and the US Supreme Court, had been so prescient. But in this round, Kahn found that the possibility that another community might someday meet the criteria and create its own school district was enough to get the second law over the constitutional hurdle. In other words, Kahn felt that as long as it was technically possible for another community to do what Kiryas Joel did, the Constitution was satisfied.

The local media was shocked by Kahn's decision as well. The *Albany Times Union*, often a great fan of Kahn and his rulings, took him to task for this one, describing the state's end run as "a sneaky way to do what the First Amendment so plainly says a legislature cannot do."

Obviously, we disagreed strenuously with Kahn and appealed to the appellate division, third department, which reversed Kahn 4–1. Justice Thomas Mercure, who had been with us the first time around, wrote the opinion:

> In determining whether the current law is a mere subterfuge, we may probe beneath its veneer of neutrality and consider the purpose for its enactment. . . . As already noted, defendants as much as concede that the current law was enacted to fulfill the purpose underlying the prior law, i.e., to solve the unique problem associated with providing special education services to handicapped children in the Village. Even absent a concession, the Legislature's and Governor's expressions of intent to aid the Satmars, the timing of the legislation and

the content of its companion legislation, which continued the Kiryas Joel Village School District pending reconstitution, permit no serious question on the issue.

As for the practical effect of the law, it should suffice to note that the current law brings about precisely the same result as the prior law, the creation of a special school district for the Village of Kiryas Joel and no other municipality in the State.

Only Justice Edward Spain dissented:

The passage of the current law in the wake of *Kiryas Joel I* is only an indication that a specific problem required a constitutionally permissible solution. This does not signify a governmental endorsement of Satmar religious precepts; rather, the Legislature merely addressed a gap in the law that failed to provide for an exceptional community circumstance, and which became apparent as the problem of educating the special needs children of the Village unfolded.

We headed back to the New York Court of Appeals.

The high court quickly and unanimously overturned the law in a decision by Judge Carmen Beauchamp Ciparick and joined by all of her colleagues—including Judge Howard Levine, who had written the powerfully troubling dissent against us in the first case when he was with the appellate division. They recognized what I thought was self-evident: that the state was "singling out the Village of Kiryas Joel for special treatment and thereby demonstrating impermissible governmental endorsement of this religious community," and consequently violating the second prong of the *Lemon* test (government action that has a primary effect of advancing or inhibiting religion).

Notwithstanding its purported facial neutrality, we interpret chapter 241 as having the nonneutral effect of allowing the religious

community of Kiryas Joel, but no other group at this time and probably ever, to create its own school district. Chapter 241's conferral
of its special benefit on the *Village of Kiryas Joel* alone, as against
virtually all other groups be they religious or nonreligious, effectively
conveys a message of impermissible governmental endorsement of
the Satmar community of Kiryas Joel.

This time, there was no appeal to the US Supreme Court. But the
high court, on April 15, 1997, decided *Agostini v. Felton*, overturning
its 1985 decision in *Aguilar v. Felton* and holding that public school
teachers could instruct at religious schools as long as the material was
secular and did not result in "excessive entanglement" between government and religion.

That, of course, provided a simple and obvious solution: operate
a school in the village of Kiryas Joel as a private school and send public school teachers, at the expense of the Monroe-Woodbury Central
School District, to provide special education services. But nothing in
this painfully drawn-out process was easy. Going that route would have
stripped the Kiryas Joel school board (and thus the village itself) of its
governance powers, as well as millions of dollars in state and federal
aid. These were, of course, the very issues that went to the heart of our
constitutional challenge.

After the second Kiryas Joel law was defeated in the courts, Assembly Speaker Silver attempted to mediate a compromise to resolve the
problem without further legislation. (I'd assured him that any other
legislative attempts would result in additional litigation.) During an
intensive round of direct negotiations between us and the Satmar, a
number of possible solutions were considered, including a neighborhood school run by the Orange County Board of Cooperative Education
Services (BOCES) and a "special act school district," similar to nineteen
other entities in New York State and based on Father Flanagan's Boys

Town model.* But all negotiations fell apart for various reasons. The state education department objected to some provisions. The BOCES superintendent wanted nothing to do with running the schools. And the Satmar didn't want to yield any of their autonomous control over child placement or program, let alone interrupt in any way the steady stream of millions of tax dollars.

With no compromise in sight and the district under court orders to close, the new Pataki administration developed yet another legislative package to keep the district in existence. The newest proposal, which the administration insisted established broader criteria that could cover dozens of potential new districts, was enacted by the legislature as chapter 390 of the Laws of 1997, three months after the court of appeals invalidated the second statute. Pataki signed the measure the night of August 11, 1997, claiming the new law would allow many existing cities to create their own school districts while permitting a number of villages and towns to do the same. Therefore, he reasoned, the legislation resulted in a law of broad application and not one that simply benefited one religious sect. As the *New York Times* reported, "The sponsors of the latest bill, which surfaced suddenly in the wee hours of the morning as bleary-eyed legislators rushed to conclude the 1997 legislative session, said it was written in a way that avoids the constitutional problem created by the two previous laws. They contended that the new legislation is applicable to other municipalities, not just Kiryas Joel, eliminating any improper favoritism that might have been given its 12,000 Hasidic residents."

However, I believed, as did Dan Kinley, my deputy executive director who previously had been a key legislative and governor's office fiscal analyst, that the new statute covered only one other municipality: Stony

* Monsignor Edward J. Flanagan was an Irish-born Catholic priest who established Boys Town, an orphanage in Nebraska. Boys Town provided a rough blueprint for how the Kiryas Joel children could receive services without violating the Establishment Clause.

Point, a nearby village in Rockland County that was having serious racial issues. Outside experts agreed—with the exception of one hired by Kiryas Joel. During legislative debate, Assemblyman Joe Lentol, one of the bill's main sponsors, was unable to identify any other municipality that would benefit from the legislation. Richard Dollinger, a Democratic senator (and future judge) from Rochester, questioned both the constitutionality of the latest bill and the fact that it was included in a package of hundreds of bills rammed through at the end of session: "The first time I saw this bill was this morning about 20 minutes before we started to vote on it. I read it as quickly as I could, and it became clear to me that we were trying to create a special school district for Kiryas Joel. Of course, the pretense was a bill that we would apply to municipalities across the state. But the reality is that it applies to only one place: Kiryas Joel."

The *New York Times* article quoted me as saying that the governor and the legislature were so "sloppy" or so "thoroughly cynical" that it was obvious "all they wanted to do was buy some more free time."

As in the past, the press was harsh. The *Middletown Times-Herald-Record* wrote, "Kiryas Joel's leaders have once again proven their clout in the state legislature. However, New Yorkers who care about the separation of church and state can be grateful that the Hasidic community's writ doesn't extend to the judicial system. Court after court has rejected the notion. . . . Legislators must be embarrassed by this."

Gannett urged Pataki and the legislature to "show some respect" for the New York Court of Appeals and the US Supreme Court. It accused state lawmakers of pandering to the Satmar, coming up with "new phony laws trying to give constitutional cover to unconstitutional funding." The American Jewish Congress issued a press release stating, "Once again, the New York State Legislature has sacrificed constitutional values and sound educational policy on the altar of political expediency. Today's Kiryas Joel legislation—which provides a new method for Kiryas Joel to [secede] from the parent Monroe-Woodbury school district—will no doubt be invalidated by the courts as were its not-so-different predecessors."

The AJC was right, of course. I again sued and again prevailed at each step up the judicial ladder. New York Supreme Court justice Joseph C. Teresi of Albany shot down the new law immediately, chiding the legislature for its effort to "ignore the rulings from courts at every level." Teresi's decision was upheld 5–0 by the appellate division.

The court of appeals, again in a split decision (4–3), said the latest law was obviously an end run, and noted in a decision by Judge George Bundy Smith that with the US Supreme Court's holding in *Agostini*, reasonable people could put this whole mess to rest in a hurry:

> We conclude with an observation that we hope has not been lost on parties who have been locked in litigation for more than a decade. The genesis of all this legislation and litigation, the seeming insurmountability of *Aguilar v. Felton* no longer exists. It is now possible, compatibly with the Federal Constitution, to do what the parties wanted to do before *Aguilar* stopped them. Given this new opportunity, we strongly suggest that the parties make every effort to reach an accord that will benefit the children, and themselves. This is far preferable to the costly and inevitable prospect of further legal strife.

The three dissenting judges—Joseph W. Bellacosa, Richard C. Wesley, and Howard Levine—noted in an opinion by Bellacosa that "it is not un-American or unconstitutional to refuse to be absorbed into the melting pot" and arguing that the Satmar had only taken advantage of their right to seek redress from the government: "These citizens simply took their place in the long line of supplicants walking and working the corridors of power."

When the Satmar predictably appealed, the Supreme Court refused to hear the case, and one would think that would have been the end. But it wasn't. The Pataki administration and the legislature enacted yet a fourth bill in 1999. This one gave any municipality with between ten thousand and twenty-five thousand residents that is contained within a larger school district the right to petition for its own, separate, state-financed district. By the time this final legislation was submitted, I had accepted the executive directorship of another statewide organization that was not connected with the education of youngsters, and my former board had understandably grown weary of this fight. Having clearly made our point about separation of church and state, and confident in our position that the goal was never to deny services to students with disabilities, the New York State School Boards Association decided not to get involved in another fight. As of this writing, the Kiryas Joel Village Union Free School District, with its grand total of one school providing services to some 250 disabled children from birth to age twenty-one, continues in operation.

EPILOGUE

The day that the country ceases to be free for irreligion, it will cease to be free for religion—except for the sect that can win political power.
—Supreme Court justice Robert Jackson, *Zorach v. Clauson*

TWO DECADES AFTER the Supreme Court decision and despite the doomsday predictions of our opponents, the Kiryas Joel Village School District thrives under a fourth state law that finally enabled the community to secure what it wanted without thoroughly trashing the US Constitution. I still considered the law to be of questionable constitutionality, but the point had been made and, from my perspective, the Establishment Clause had survived a dangerous threat.

Since then, the village of Kiryas Joel has grown enormously (a population of around twenty-two thousand in 2014), spurred by extremely low local taxes and incredible amounts of politically acquired state and federal aid. Its theocratic village leaders still know how to use their clout and are still remarkably adept at controlling and delivering votes—and therefore controlling the political process on select issues.

At the state level, the Satmar continue to get financial aid and grants of power available to no other religious group; both political parties fight over who can do more for them. As the power of this little community has grown, so too has the discord with its neighbors. There is an uneasy truce but constant tension between the residents of Kiryas Joel and the rest of Monroe. The village taxpayers, unlike their municipal brethren in the town, almost never see an increase in their property taxes, relying on federal and state dollars to support their education of children with disabilities. This inevitably causes some resentment with the broader community, where taxes rise steadily and where the residents lack the voting bloc power to control political spending.

Meanwhile, the Satmar continue to purchase large tracts of nearby farmland outside the original village, raising local concerns over their intentions. Consider this July 2015 headline in Capital New York, an online news outlet covering New York State politics: FILINGS SHOW KIRYAS JOEL MONEY FLOWED TO CUOMO AFTER VETO. The article goes on to explain that less than a week after Governor Andrew Cuomo (Mario's son) vetoed a piece of legislation that the leaders of Kiryas Joel feared would restrict their ongoing development, a network of limited liability companies with links to the village suddenly gave the governor $250,000 for his campaign. According to the article, nine separate checks "from vaguely titled L.L.C.s entered Cuomo's campaign account." Coincidence?

At the federal and constitutional level, the high wall separating church and state has eroded, though certainly not collapsed, through a generation of new Supreme Court decisions. *Kiryas Joel* was the last clear statement of support for Jefferson's vision, or even Madison's. In the years since, the religious right has heavily influenced presidential appointments to the Supreme Court, and that influence has manifested in a series of decisions that have, in my mind, undermined the Establishment Clause and the principles we fought for in our long legal battle.

For example, look at the court's landmark 2014 decision in *Burwell v. Hobby Lobby*, where for the first time ever it recognized a for-profit corporation's claim of religious adherence. In a 5–4 decision, the court said that a family-owned business did not have to offer its employees contraceptive insurance coverage if doing so conflicted with the owners' religious principles. Two months earlier, the same 5–4 majority upheld an Upstate New York town's practice of beginning its public sessions with a Christian prayer.

Justice Scalia, who was in the majority in both cases, told an audience at Colorado Christian University in October 2014, "I think the main fight is to dissuade Americans from what the secularists are trying to persuade them to be true: that the separation of church and state means that the government cannot favor religion over nonreligion." Of course, I think that is *exactly* what separation of church and state means. As the two recent cases illustrate, however, Scalia's view seems to prevail at the moment.

This trend is troubling to me, but I also view it as a swinging pendulum. With *Kiryas Joel* as the Establishment Clause fulcrum, from which the two extremes can never quite disconnect, I expect that in time the pendulum will swing back toward the Jeffersonian vision.

Reviewing the legacy of *Kiryas Joel*, I think one of the values of the case emerges from a crystal clear, unambiguous fact pattern that could then be neatly applied to constitutional principles. To me, the basic facts continue to fascinate because they so vividly illustrate two of the wonderful guiding principles of our country and our constitutional culture: that people in this country are free to live their lives as they see fit, no matter how far outside the mainstream they happen to be, *as long as they don't interfere with the rights of others*; and that this remains a country of laws that unite, and protect, all of us from the tyranny of both the majority *and* the minority. What a wonderful tribute to the US Constitution that a minority subculture with traditions, habits, beliefs, and practices that are so different from the prevailing culture can flourish and live their lives as they wish, unfettered by the majority.

Yet the Satmar sought to undermine that framework, and would have succeeded had we not mounted our long challenge. Remember, this is a group of people who demanded to be left alone to follow their own religious and cultural precepts with absolutely no interference by the culture or institutions of the surrounding region and nation. They insisted on isolation in a self-designed ghetto. They have every right to do so, and in that regard they are not unlike some other groups and cultures that wish to remain aloof or separate from the mainstream and Main Street. The melting pot concept does not require that the disparate cultural interests abandon their unique mores. Instead it envisions a stew in which all the various ingredients make the meal all the richer and more robust.

The Satmar do not support that vision of the melting pot, and this is their absolute right. But it illustrates how different they are from, say, the Amish, who avoid the have-their-cake-and-eat-it-too insistence that the society outside of the ghetto walls heavily subsidize their choices. Rather than remaining apart from the political infrastructure of the outside world, the Satmar exploit it whenever possible, skillfully and effectively. Examples abound and are well documented, and it is clear to me, all these years later, that resentment by their neighbors has grown geometrically as Kiryas Joel expands its bases of power.

Consider, for example, what has transpired in East Ramapo, Rockland County, in recent years, a story that was reported in a September 12, 2014, segment of public radio's *This American Life*. When we filed the Kiryas Joel case in 1990, Georgine Hyde, one of the most remarkable human beings I have ever met and a survivor of Hitler's concentration camps, was president of the East Ramapo School Board and had served on the board for three decades; in addition, she was vice president of the board of the New York State School Boards Association. Nobody of any political stripe could possibly question Georgine's commitment or integrity, but she became a casualty of East Ramapo's ultra-Orthodox steamroller.

At the time we filed the suit, only thirteen of the several hundred kids in the school district were actually from Kiryas Joel. The bulk of the children were bused in from East Ramapo, one of the biggest and best school districts in the state, the district where Georgine Hyde presided. Although East Ramapo wasn't a Satmar-only community like Kiryas Joel, there were thousands of Hasidic and ultra-Orthodox families there who had made their way up from New York City. Typically, they were quite organized politically, and they could cripple the local school district whenever they chose to do so by voting down the budget (again, in New York, school district budgets are generally subject to public vote). But they had declined to do so as long as public school authorities looked the other way and did not enforce state education laws in their yeshivas. In other words, the rules that generally apply to public *and* private schools, such as ensuring that students receive an education well grounded in reading and math and other core subjects, did not apply to the yeshivas.

That informal deal allowed the two sides to coexist in relative peace for a number of years. However, as school taxes went up and the ultra-Orthodox residents grew increasingly irritated that they had to pay taxes for schools they would never send their children to, the religious community began running congregants for the school board. With the bloc and the fact that relatively few people turn out for school board elections, they soon controlled the school board—despite the fact that they had virtually no children in the public school system. They unseated Georgine and the rest of the old guard and cut services drastically in the public schools. They attempted to shift funding to their private schools, closing public school buildings and selling them to the yeshivas for substantially below market value. They began to circumvent state and federal regulations governing placement of children with disabilities, shifting the kids to religious-based settings subsidized with tax monies.

Their justification for these actions was laid out in a letter that

Yehuda Weissmandl, a prominent citizen of the Hasidic community who was later elected president of the school board, wrote to a local newspaper:

> Dear fellow taxpayer in the East Ramapo school district, again and again, I read about how upset you are about the members of the school board, how we bloc-voted them in, how we don't have the interests of the schoolchildren at heart. Well, let's take a closer look at that.
>
> For many years, you took our tax money, year after year, increase after increase, and you never had a problem with that. But when we finally get together and say, that's enough, that is a problem.
>
> I have a solution. How about giving all of us the option to bow out of the public school system and keep our money in our pockets? You want our money and our silence. Sorry, you cannot have it all your way.

Their gripe—that they were paying taxes for the public school system and getting little or nothing in return—is an argument often made by the elderly and the childless. It's just that those groups are virtually never persuasive, because they simply lack the collective political clout to get their way. The Orthodox voters, on the other hand, had that clout and used it.

A number of their actions were overturned by the state education department, but they tended to reemerge. The local NAACP and ministerial and rabbinical associations asked the state to step in to protect the large minority populations in the public schools, but state officials are often reluctant to stand up to the ultra-Orthodox. Indeed, a number of elected officials in East Ramapo have discussed trying to establish a new religiously based "public" school district.

Meanwhile, in other parts of the state, religious groups have begun to demand public support for their religious needs. For example, in New York City, scores of newly formed churches have been conducting church services in public school buildings. Granted, churches have long been allowed to hold services in public schools temporarily as a result of fires or hurricanes. But the church-planting movement seeks not a place to temporarily worship because of some unforeseen disruption in their normal services but a *permanent, government-sanctioned, and subsidized presence in public schools.* The tactic is currently under challenge in various federal cases.

This type of preferential and grossly unconstitutional behavior is not confined to New York State. The national legal trend at the moment, coming directly from signals sent by the increasingly conservative Supreme Court since *Kiryas Joel,* is to view Establishment Clause disputes from the distorted lens of so-called viewpoint discrimination under the Free Speech Clause of the First Amendment. The notion that a religious viewpoint is like any other speech and equally protected is intriguing and appealing—if one ignores what the Establishment Clause was meant to do (ensure freedom *of* religion and freedom *from* religion). But I suspect that if *Kiryas Joel* were to be decided now, the viewpoint discrimination argument could well carry the day. Still, the decision remains a beacon after all these years, and even the Supreme Court is loath to abandon its precedents. That gives me great comfort.

As I look back, I see that *Kiryas Joel* was a crucial benchmark at a critical juncture. I am certain both Jefferson and Madison would applaud the bottom-line result of the case, and equally certain that they would be gravely troubled by what has occurred since. It is my hope that another lawyer somewhere in our constitutional landscape will have the case, the nerve, and the support to carry the Jefferson-Madison banner to a new generation of American citizens and judges and to preserve our religious freedom, which former president Bill Clinton has referred to as "perhaps the most precious of all American liberties—called by many our 'first freedom.'"* For, as is said, eternal vigilance is indeed the price of liberty.†

---

* On July 12, 1995, President Clinton directed his attorney general and education secretary to annually provide every public school with a statement on "religious expression in public schools." The text of the memo is available at the *New York Times* website, www.nytimes.com/1995/07/13/us/president-s-memorandum-on-religious-expression-in-schools.html.

† The phrase, interestingly, is often attributed to Jefferson, although Jeffersonian scholars find no indication that the founder ever said or wrote these words. More likely those are the words of abolitionist Wendell Phillips, or maybe the Irish attorney John Philpot Curran. No matter. If Jefferson didn't say it or write it, I am abundantly confident he would have endorsed the message.

ACKNOWLEDGMENTS

THIS STORY NEVER would have occurred if the New York State School Boards Association, and leaders such as Judy Katz, Al Hawk, Gordon Purrington, and Georgine Hyde, hadn't had the courage to take on the most powerful politicians in the state. I begin by thanking the association and its leaders for standing by me every step of the way.

This book grew, perhaps oddly, out of discussions I had with George Shebitz, a close friend who, in this case, was my adversary as counsel for the Kiryas Joel school district. Although we were on different sides of the case and had decidedly different opinions on how it should come out, we both realized the constitutional significance of the case and the importance of telling this story. George planted the seed, but much to my regret, he passed away and will never see how his offhand suggestion for a book blossomed into *The Curious Case of Kiryas Joel*.

Still, getting an idea for a book and writing it are two rather different things, and while I owe George credit for getting the ball rolling, I owe an immense debt of gratitude to my friend Justin Jamail. Justin is a brilliant young lawyer, the associate general counsel with the Metropolitan Opera, a graduate of the excellent Fordham Law School, and an insightful poet who did graduate work in fine arts at the University of Massachusetts. Early on, Justin and I together interviewed scores of legislators, county leaders, state officials, reporters, and residents of Orange County who were involved in the story. We conducted interviews that consumed eighty hours of tape, all of which were transcribed with the help of Pat Agard, my executive assistant. Justin also reviewed thousands of pages of litigation material and helped construct the first draft of the manuscript. This book could not have been written without him, and the materials he provided to me and my coauthor, John Caher, were absolutely invaluable. Justin provided John, a veteran legal journalist who was likely the first reporter to grasp the significance of this case, with the meaty substance that we were then able to mold into this book.

Justin and I were blessed with the cooperation of many of the players, beginning with the Kiryas Joel mayor Abraham Wieder, who was also president of the village school board, and including: Steve Benardo, the superintendent of schools at Kiryas Joel; Rabbi Jacob Freund, a key adviser to KJ and to Governor Pataki; and Nat Lewin, the legal legend, who represented the Satmar throughout most of the litigation. Both of the sponsors of the original legislation, George Pataki and Joe Lentol, provided incredible insight into the process, as did former Speaker Mel Miller. One important voice that is missing is that of former governor Mario M. Cuomo, who declined to be interviewed. Although, much to my regret, this case severely strained my relationship with Governor Cuomo, I always respected and in some ways revered him, and at this writing I still feel a loss over his death on New Year's Day 2015.

The local perspective contained in the book was enriched by the hours we spent interviewing area individuals: local activist Ann Krawet; Roxanne Daugherty, chairwoman of the Orange County legislature; Michael Amo, the county legislative representative from Kiryas Joel; State Senator Billy Larkin; Assemblywoman Nancy Calhoun; Monroe diner owner Sotirios "Steve" Lagakos; Monroe-Woodbury school board president Carl Onkin; and superintendent of Monroe-Woodbury Schools, Tony Olivo.

Marc Stern of the American Jewish Committee added great historical perspective, as did Barry Lynn of Americans United for the Separation of Church and State, and Tom Hobart, longtime president of the New York State United Teachers union.

Jay Worona, the David who went up against Goliath at the Supreme Court and won, generously reviewed the manuscript, as did Dan Kinley, the wunderkind legislative analyst who was a crucial asset as the case progressed.

Mike Spain, associate editor of the *Albany Times Union*, was characteristically helpful and patient as he tracked down necessary resource materials. Clearly, Mike's investigative reporting skills remain sound despite his now working in a management position, as he was able to find what we needed even though the materials had been misfiled in a folder labeled Curious Joelle. The fruits of Mike's efforts are the many Skip Dickstein photos that are posted, compliments of the *Times Union*, to our website: CuriousKiryas.com. Also on the website (so kindly created by my friend Ron Lai, an IT expert now working in Australia) are photographs generously provided by the *New York Law Journal* and photographer Rick Kopstein.

Our agent, Janet Rosen of Sheree Bykofsky Associates, believed in this project from the get-go and charitably shared her expertise as we drafted the proposal and sought a publisher. Our publisher, Chicago Review Press, and our editor, Lisa Reardon, proved to be a perfect fit and contributed greatly to this book. Lisa has a wonderful eye, a keen editorial sense, terrific judgment, and an uncanny knack for catching miscues and holes that none of the half dozen people who read the manuscript had noticed. Devon Freeny, the developmental editor at CRP, contributed his sharp eyes and sharp mind and further polished our work.

I would be remiss if I failed to acknowledge the support, encouragement, and endorsement we received from three of the top legal minds in recent New York history: former governor and attorney general Eliot Spitzer, late New York chief judge Judith S. Kaye, and the Honorable Sol Wachtler, Distinguished Professor of Constitutional Law at Touro Law School and former chief judge of the New York State Court of Appeals; as well as two of the nation's premier advocates of religious freedom: Nadine Strossen, the John Marshall Harlan Professor of Law at New York Law School and former president of the American Civil Liberties Union, and Barry Lynn, executive director of Americans United for the Separation of Church and State. Their thoughtful endorsements are posted in their entirety on our website.

Last, and most certainly not least, I thank my family—Barbara, my wife, and my daughters Deborah Lynn and Lisa Fleming Grumet—for their love, affection, support, encouragement, and wise counsel.

One final note: My daughter Lisa, an attorney and director of the Diane Abbey Law Institute for Children and Families at New York Law School, has carried on this family fight. Lisa represented the New York City Board of Education in major litigation (*Bronx Household of Faith v. Board of Education*) to stop another attempt to erode the wall of separation between church and state. In that case, religious groups claimed a right to conduct Sunday church services in public schools. Lisa's argument to the contrary ultimately carried the day when the US Supreme Court refused to hear the religious group's appeal. I thank Lisa for helping to ensure that the vision of Thomas Jefferson and James Madison, a vision so fundamentally essential to our freedom, extends to yet another generation.

CHRONOLOGY

___

1975   Grand Rebbe Joel Teitelbaum leads members of his Satmar Hasidic sect from the Williamsburg section of Brooklyn to the town of Monroe in Upstate New York, designating their community Kiryas Joel, or Village of Joel. The Satmar teach their children in separate schools (Torah study in private yeshivas for the boys and special private academies for the girls to prepare them to become mothers and homemakers in the community), but there is no provision for children with special needs.

1976   New York enacts legislation requiring that children with disabilities receive appropriate schooling at public expense. The Monroe-Woodbury Central School District sends public school teachers into Kiryas Joel to provide special education services.

1977   The community of Kiryas Joel reaches a population of 525, sufficient to declare itself a village under New York law, and does so. A legal entity, the Village of Kiryas Joel, is formed.

1985   The US Supreme Court decides *Aguilar v. Felton*, striking down a program that used federal funds to pay the salaries of teachers providing special education services to children in parochial schools. With this decision, the Monroe-Woodbury school district has no choice but to stop serving the special needs children of Kiryas Joel in a village school and place them in the area's public schools. The situation troubles Satmar parents, who do not want their children exposed to the outside world.

1986   The Village of Kiryas Joel sues the Monroe-Woodbury bus drivers' union to force it to provide male bus drivers to transport boys to their private yeshivas (religious law forbids Satmar from riding with female drivers). When the union wins the suit, boys begin walking to school rather than ride in buses driven by women.

1988   The state's highest court, the New York Court of Appeals, holds that Monroe-Woodbury school district cannot be compelled to teach the village's disabled children at a site separate from other public schools.

1989   Governor Mario Cuomo signs a law creating the Kiryas Joel Village School District, making the Satmar enclave the only village in the state with the power and authority to operate its own public school system.

1990   Steven Benardo, head of the special education program for some thirty thousand students in the Bronx, is hired to set up and run the new school in Kiryas Joel—and opens the school in three months.

Al Hawk and Louis Grumet of the New York State School Boards Association file suit challenging the law.

1992   State supreme court justice Lawrence E. Kahn in Albany rules that the law creating the Kiryas Joel school district is unconstitutional. Kahn calls the legislation "an attempt to camouflage, with secular garments, a religious community as a public school district."

Kahn's ruling is affirmed by the appellate division of the state supreme court, but the midlevel appellate court splits 4–1. The majority expresses concern that the Kiryas Joel district is "likely to be perceived by adherents of the Satmar Hasidim as an endorsement, and by nonadherents as a disapproval, of their individual religious rights." Justice Howard A. Levine of Schenectady dissents, arguing that the district's establishment had a valid secular purpose, "to protect the children from the psychological and emotional trauma caused by exposure to integrated classes."

1993   The state court of appeals, in a 4–2 decision yielding four separate opinions, upholds Kahn and rules that the establishment of the Kiryas Joel school district amounts to an impermissible endorsement of religion. The main opinion, written by Judge George Bundy Smith, declares the school district in violation of the First Amendment.

By deciding the case solely on the federal Constitution, the state court leaves the issue on the doorstep of the US Supreme Court. Justice Clarence Thomas issues a temporary stay to keep the district open while the case is litigated.

1994   Lawyers Jay Worona of the New York State School Boards Association, Nat Lewin for Kiryas Joel, Lawrence Reich for the Monroe-Woodbury Central School District, and Assistant Attorney General Julie Mereson for the state argue before the Supreme Court. Worona, assisted by attorney

Pilar Sokol, contends that Kiryas Joel is unconstitutional. The others argue in favor of the special school district.

The Supreme Court, by a 6–3 vote, upholds the original decision by Kahn and shoots down Kiryas Joel. The court declines an opportunity to tinker with the *Lemon* test, its standard for determining when a governmental action violates the constitutionally mandated separation of church and state.

The New York State Legislature enacts and Governor Cuomo signs a new law establishing a school district for Kiryas Joel. This time, the law doesn't specify that it is designed just to benefit the religious enclave of Kiryas Joel—although it's self-evident, since no other community could meet the criteria.

State supreme court justice Joseph Harris in Albany issues a procedural opinion allowing the school district to remain open and predicting that this time around, Kiryas Joel would prevail.

1995   Justice Kahn, reviewing the second legislative attempt to create a special school district for Kiryas Joel, finds that the legislature now got it right.

1997   The New York Court of Appeals says Kahn got it wrong and concludes the second law is an unconstitutional sham.

In *Agostini v. Felton*, the US Supreme Court overrules *Aguilar v. Felton* and decides that public school teachers can instruct at religious schools as long as the material is secular and does not result in "excessive entanglement" between government and religion.

Governor George Pataki and the legislature enact yet another law establishing a school district for Kiryas Joel, this one capable of applying to only one other municipality in the state.

1998   Albany-based state supreme court justice Joseph Teresi finds the third effort to create a special school district for Kiryas Joel unconstitutional.

The appellate division of the state supreme court affirms Teresi.

1999   The New York Court of Appeals, in a 4–3 decision, concludes that the third law is as much an unconstitutional sham as the first two.

A fourth bill is passed allowing Kiryas Joel to create a school district. Since this one applies to any municipality with between ten thousand and twenty-five thousand residents contained within a larger school district, the law is not effectively challenged. The Kiryas Joel school district has operated under this framework ever since.

Supreme Court Religion/Education Establishment Clause Jurisprudence

1908   *Quick Bear v. Leupp*, 210 US 50. The case dealt with Indian funds held in trust by Congress and used to pay a Catholic Indian mission to provide schools. The court decided that this did not constitute a violation of the Establishment Clause.

1930   *Cochran v. Louisiana State Board of Education*, 281 US 370. At issue was whether Louisiana could provide textbooks to all students, including those in parochial schools. The court held for the first time that indirect aid could be provided to religious schools based on a "child benefit" theory.

1947   *Everson v. Board of Education*, 330 US 1. In this key decision, a 5–4 Supreme Court held for the first time that the Establishment Clause is one of the liberties secured by the Due Process Clause of the Fourteenth Amendment—meaning that all government activity, be it at the federal, state, or local level, must conform to the constrictions of the Establishment Clause. It was a case in which a New Jersey school district authorized reimbursing parents for the cost of bus transportation to and from school.

1948   *McCollum v. Board of Education*, 333 US 203. The State of Illinois provided religious instruction in public schools but allowed children who were not interested to be reassigned to classes where religion was not taught. By an 8–1 margin, the justices held that the religious instruction nonetheless violated the First Amendment.

1952   *Zorach v. Clauson*, 343 US 306. Question: Did a New York State program permitting students enrolled in out-of-school religious education programs, while nonparticipants remained in school under the state's mandatory education requirements, violate the Establishment Clause? Answer: No, because the program was offered off school grounds.

1962   *Engel v. Vitale*, 370 US 421. This dealt with a nondenominational prayer composed by the New York Board of

Regents to be recited every morning in public schools. It read, "Almighty God, we acknowledge our dependence upon Thee, and beg Thy blessings upon us, our parents, our teachers and our country." The court ruled the practice unconstitutional.

1963   *Abington School District v. Schemmp*, 374 US 203. A Pennsylvania statute required the reading of ten verses from the Bible in public schools; Maryland permitted a daily recitation of the Lord's Prayer in schools. The court found them both unconstitutional.

1968   *Board of Education v. Allen*, 392 US 236. A New York law permitted public schools to loan textbooks to all students, free of charge, in public or parochial schools. The court upheld the practice, finding that it benefited families with children in parochial schools, and not the schools themselves.

Flast v. Cohen, 392 US 83. This decision established that taxpayers have a right to bring a federal court action challenging an alleged violation of the Establishment Clause. Here, Congress had appropriated money to assist private and public schools, including parochial schools. Chief Justice Earl Warren said in the majority opinion, "Our history vividly illustrates that one of the specific evils feared by those who drafted the Establishment Clause and fought for its adoption was that the taxing and spending power would be used to favor one religion over another or to support religion in general." In a concurrence, Justice Potter Stewart added, "Every taxpayer can claim a personal constitutional right not to be taxed for the support of a religious institution."

1970   *Walz v. Tax Commission*, 397 US 664. Can New York State exempt religious institutions from taxation without violating the Establishment Clause? Yes, because the exemption was offered to nonreligious institutions as well, and taxing religious institutions would unconstitutionally entangle the state in religion.

1971   *Lemon v. Kurtzman*, 403 US 602. In this watershed case, a dispute involving state aid to help parochial schools pay their teachers, the court enacted a three-part litmus test for Establishment Clause analysis: (1) the law must have a secular purpose, (2) the law may neither advance nor inhibit religion, and (3) the law must not excessively entangle religion and government.

   Tilton v. Richardson, 403 US 672. In the first application of the *Lemon* test, the court generally upheld a federal program providing public funds for the construction of facilities in religious institutions of higher learning. The court said the arrangement had not excessively entangled church and state since the buildings were not used for religious purposes.

1972   *Wisconsin v. Yoder*, 406 US 205. The court held that Amish children could be exempt from compulsory school attendance after eighth grade.

   Essex v. Wolman, 409 US 808. Based on the *Lemon* test, the court said that an Ohio statute providing grants to reimburse parents for parochial school tuition was unconstitutional.

1973   *Levitt v. Committee for Public Education & Religious Liberty*, 413 US 472; *Committee for Public Education & Religious*

Liberty v. Nyquist, 413 US 756; *Sloan v. Lemon*, 413 US 825. In this trio of cases, the court struck down state laws providing direct aid to parochial schools and/or tuition reimbursements and tax breaks for parents of parochial school children.

1976   *Roemer v. Maryland Public Works Board*, 426 US 736. "We are asked once again to police the constitutional boundary between church and state," began the opinion by Justice Harry Blackmun. Here, the court upheld a Maryland law providing grants to private, religious-affiliated colleges to be used for nonsectarian purposes.

1977   *New York v. Cathedral Academy*, 434 US 125. After the 1973 *Levitt* decision, which said the state couldn't give direct aid to parochial schools, the New York State Legislature passed a law allowing parochial schools to be reimbursed for expenses incurred before *Levitt* was decided. The court disallowed it.

1980   *Committee for Public Education and Religious Liberty v. Regan*, 444 US 646. At issue was the constitutionality of a New York statute appropriating public funds to reimburse religious-related and secular nonpublic schools for conducting state-mandated testing. The court said the initiative was constitutional under the *Lemon* test, because it had a secular purpose, its primary effect did not advance religion, and it did not entangle the state with organized religion.

Stone v. Graham, 449 US 39. The court struck down a Kentucky law requiring the placement of the Ten Commandments in all public school classrooms. It was unimpressed with a disclaimer at the bottom of the display contending that the commandments had a secular purpose and were the basis for the nation's legal tradition.

1983   *Mueller v. Allen*, 463 US 388. The court upheld a Minnesota statute providing a tax deduction for tuition, textbooks, and transportation for children to attend public, private, or sectarian schools. It said that as long as the benefit to religious schools was indirect, parents of students in religious schools could not be denied a benefit offered to parents in other schools.

1985   *School District of the City of Grand Rapids v. Ball*, 473 US 373. A Michigan program provided funding for special education programs in nonpublic schools, allowing for public school special education teachers to be sent to religious schools. The court found the program violated the *Lemon* test in that it advanced religion.

    Aguilar v. Felton, 473 US 402. Initially, and based on the *Grand Rapids* case, the court struck down a program in which federal funds were used to pay the salaries of teachers providing special education services to children in parochial schools. But it overruled itself twelve years later in *Agostini v. Felton* (see next page).

1990   *Board of Education of the West Side Community Schools v. Mergens*, 496 US 226. In this case, students at a public high school wanted to form an extracurricular religious club to meet on school grounds, a privilege afforded to other groups. The court held that the Federal Equal Access Act prohibits schools from denying student groups the use of the premises based on the religious nature of the meetings.

1992 *Lee v. Weisman*, 505 US 577. In this Rhode Island case, principals were granted permission to invite members of the clergy to give invocations at middle and high school graduations. Since the principal selected the clergy and controlled the content of the prayer, the court said it was unconstitutional.

1993 *Lamb's Chapel v. Center Moriches Union Free School District*, 508 US 384. Here, a religious group wanted to show a religious film at a public school when the school was not being used, a privilege offered to other organizations. The court said it was wrong for the school to deny the request to present a religious film, because the school board had created an "open forum" for the community and could not discriminate based on religion.

1994 *Board of Education of Kiryas Joel Village School District v. Grumet*, 512 US 687. The court ruled unconstitutional the creation of a separate religious school district to receive state and federal financial assistance to educate children with disabilities in the village of Kiryas Joel.

1997 *Agostini v. Felton*, 521 US 203. The court overruled its 1985 decision in *Aguilar v. Felton* and held that public school teachers could instruct at religious schools as long as the material was secular and did not result in "excessive entanglement" between government and religion.

2000   *Santa Fe Independent School District v. Doe,* 530 US 290.
The court shot down as unconstitutional a school district's
policy allowing student-led prayer at football games.

Mitchell v. Helms, 530 US 793. By a 6–3 margin, the court
upheld a program that provided for the loan of equipment
and resources to religious schools under the Education Consolidation and Improvement Act of 1981.

2002   *Zelman v. Simmons-Harris,* 536 US 639. In this landmark
ruling, the 5–4 court upheld a Cleveland voucher program
providing publicly funded scholarships to low-income and
inner-city families so their children could attend private
schools, including those operated by religious entities.

2004   *Locke v. Davey,* 540 US 712. The court held that the state
of Washington did not violate the Constitution by denying state funding to college students pursuing a degree in
theology.

NOTES

Prologue

"We want isolation" . . . Don Lattin, "Church-State Conflict in Jewish Town," *San Francisco Chronicle*, March 25, 1994.

the US Supreme Court, in Aguilar v. Felton . . . Aguilar v. Felton, 473 US 402 (1985).

"We look different . . ." Lattin, "Church-State Conflict."

1. A New Homeland

When Ann Krawet and her husband . . . Everything in this chapter attributed to Ann Krawet is taken from an interview with her by the author.

As was Sotirios "Steve" Lagakos . . . Interview with Sotirios Lagakos by the author.

Those who had warned about the Satmar . . . Daniel D. Alexander, "Political Influence on the Resident Hasidic Community on the East Ramapo Central School District," doctoral dissertation, New York University, 1982.

2. Who Moves In?

"None of our children can ride . . ." Clipping from *Middletown Times-Herald-Record*, 1986, author's collection.

"They would go out to lunch . . ." Don Lattin, "Church-State Conflict in Jewish Town," *San Francisco Chronicle*, March 25, 1994.

"My child was learning about . . ." Timothy Phelps, "Church v. State: Satmar School's Public Funds Use Goes to High Court," *Newsday*, March 27, 1994.

Alexander had written his doctoral dissertation . . . Daniel D. Alexander, "Political Influence on the Resident Hasidic Community on the East Ramapo Central School District," doctoral dissertation, New York University, 1982.

3. Who Governs?

Richard Nixon once said . . . John M. Caher, *King of the Mountain: The Rise, Fall, and Redemption of Chief Judge Sol Wachtler* (Amherst, NY: Prometheus Books, 1998).

"Whatever it takes, you send . . ." Interview with George Pataki by the author.

"The beauty of the leadership system" . . . Interview with Mel Miller by the author.

4. Who Educates?

Brown v. Board of Education in the 1950s . . . Brown v. Board of Education, 347 US 483 (1954).

5. Who Is Worshipped?

"Because we hold it for a fundamental and undeniable truth . . ." For the full text, see James Madison, *The Writings of James Madison*, vol. 2, *Correspondence, 1783–1787* (New York: Putnam, 1901), http://oll.libertyfund.org/titles/madison-the-writings-vol-2-1783-1787.

"Well aware . . . that Almighty God . . ." For the full text, see Nancy Verell, "Virginia Statute for Religious Freedom," Monticello official website, September 30, 2014, www.monticello.org/site/research-and-collections/virginia-statute-religious-freedom.

"It does me no injury for my neighbor . . ." Rebecca Bowman, "Jefferson's Religious Beliefs," Monticello official website, August 1997, www.monticello.org/site/research-and-collections/jeffersons-religious-beliefs.

In Reynolds v. United States, the Supreme Court held . . . Reynolds v. United States, 98 US 145 (1878).

in the 1940s, the Court returned . . . Everson v. Board of Education, 330 US 1 (1947).

In the 1960s the Supreme Court expanded . . . Engel v. Vitale, 370 US 421 (1962).

In 1968 the court overturned a law . . . Epperson v. Arkansas, 393 US 97 (1968).

the 1971 case of Lemon v. Kurtzman . . . Lemon v. Kurtzman, 403 US 602 (1971).

"The same authority which . . ." Madison, *Writings*, vol. 2.

the Supreme Court's momentous decision . . . Brown v. Board of Education, 347 US 483 (1954).

7. Who Is Our Adversary?

Lewin told a story from his clerkship . . . Related by Nathan Lewin, who consented to an extensive interview by the author.

"make social isolation a goal..." A copy of Jay Worona's 1990 brief was provided by the New York State School Boards Association.

Jay relied on the 1971 US Supreme Court precedent... Lemon v. Kurtzman, 403 US 602 (1971).

8. Here Comes the Judge

He put enormous effort into crafting... Grumet v. Education Department, 151 Misc.2d 60 (1992).

"residents of the Village of Kiryas Joel..." Ibid.

"The intent of the Legislature..." Ibid.

9. Establishment

Steve knew we were right, legally and morally... Everything in this chapter attributed to Steve Benardo stems from an extensive interview he granted the author.

10. Reviewing the Decision

"The creation of a public school..." All briefs quoted in this chapter were provided by the New York State School Boards Association.

"Regardless of whether the public school..." Grumet v. Board of Education, 187 A.D.2d 16 (1992).

"The school district's supervision and control..." Lee v. Weisman, 505 US 577 (1992).

11. Does It Pass the Test?

"If this were a religious gerrymander..." All quotes from the oral arguments were transcribed from video recordings obtained from the archives of Albany Law School, Albany, NY.

"Because special services are already available..." Grumet v. Board of Education, 81 N.Y.2d 518 (1993).

"In the first place, it is to be remarked..." James Madison, "The Same Subject Continued: The Union as a Safeguard Against Domestic Faction and Insurrection," *Federalist* 10, November 23, 1787, http://thomas.loc.gov/home /histdox/fed_10.html.

"We have a plan for her future..." Ari I. Goldman, "A Hasidic Village Frets over Its School's Future," *New York Times*, July 8, 1993.

"It became impossible"... Ibid.

"If this case went the other way . . ." Ari I. Goldman, "New York Court Prohibits Hasidic Public School," *New York Times*, July 7, 1993.

12. Would the Supreme Court Care?

Steve Benardo was in his office . . . Interview with Steve Benardo by the author.

"The Appellate Division affirmed . . ." Grumet v. Board of Education, 81 N.Y.2d 518 (1993). Emphasis added.

"We believe that the [New York Court of Appeals] . . ." From Lawrence Reich's motion, provided by the New York State School Boards Association.

While briefly disrupted in the 1960s . . . See Baker v. Carr, 369 US 186 (1962).

13. The Supreme Court Opens the Door

"Yesterday I entered an interim stay . . ." The glimpses of the inner workings of the court come from the writings and notes of Justice Blackmun, Harry A. Blackmun Papers, Library of Congress, Washington, DC.

best known for his opinion in Roe . . . Roe v. Wade, 410 US 113 (1973).

Stevens, a Ford appointee . . . "John Paul Stevens," Biography.com, accessed September 18, 2015, www.biography.com/people/john-paul-stevens-9494379.

constitutional protection for abortion rights . . . Planned Parenthood v. Casey, 505 US 833 (1992).

against prayer in school ceremonies . . . Lee v. Weisman, 505 US 577 (1992).

Souter detested Washington, DC . . . Jeffrey Toobin, *The Nine: Inside the Secret World of the Supreme Court* (New York: Doubleday, 2007).

"To the argument made by . . ." William Rehnquist, "A Random Thought on the Segregation Cases," 1952, www.pbs.org/wnet/supremecourt/rights/print /sources_document7.html.

In 2012 the former president confirmed . . . Joanna Malloy, "Bill Clinton Reveals for First Time That Former New York Gov. Mario Cuomo Rejected Supreme Court Nomination," *New York Daily News*, June 6, 2012.

"has the makings of a potentially" . . . Linda Greenhouse, "God and Country: A School Case Goes to the Heart of a Great Issue," *New York Times*, December 5, 1993.

For example, if a law against narcotics . . . Employment Division, Department of Human Resources of Oregon v. Smith, 494 US 872 (1990).

Wisconsin v. Yoder, the Supreme Court ruling . . . Wisconsin v. Yoder, 406 US 205 (1972).

"barely coherent, making the validity . . ." Greenhouse, "God and Country."

"The problem isn't the solution . . ." From Marc Stern's brief, provided by the New York State School Boards Association.

14. Strange Bedfellows

"Everybody has a stake . . ." Interview with Marc Stern by the author.

"Basically what I learned was . . ." Interview with Jay Worona by the author.

15. May It Please the Court

"almost bombastically pretentious" . . . "Homes of the Court," Supreme Court Historical Society official website, accessed September 18, 2015, www .supremecourthistory.org/history-of-the-court/home-of-the-court/.

"We'll hear argument now in Number 93-517 . . ." The entire transcript of the argument, from which all related quotes used in this chapter were taken, is available at the Oyez Project, www.oyez.org/cases/1990-1999/1993/1993_93_517.

"Nino is ruffled" . . . Harry A. Blackmun Papers, Library of Congress, Washington, DC.

"The central question in the case . . ." Ana Puga, "Jewish Group Argues for School; High Court Gets Church-State Case," *Boston Globe*, March 31, 1994.

the court seemed "befuddled" . . . William Freivogel, "School Issue Seems to Befuddle Court," *St. Louis Post-Dispatch*, April 4, 1994.

I was quoted extensively in an article . . . Martha M. Canan, "Public Funding to Accommodate Religious Views at Stake in High Court Case," *Bond Buyer*, March 31, 1994.

"A one-hour hearing . . ." Lyle Denniston, "Court Wary of Jewish Village School," *Chicago Sun-Times*, March 31, 1994.

Interestingly, the same article . . . Lyle Denniston, "Jewish Village Getting Supreme Negative Vibes; Justices Show Little Support in Hearing," *Houston Chronicle*, March 31, 1994.

"sounded as though they wanted . . ." David G. Savage, "Justices Ponder School District for Hasidim," *Los Angeles Times*, March 31, 1994.

"While the Court could use this case . . ." Linda Greenhouse, "Justices, at Hearing on New York Case, Raise Pointed Questions over Church-State Linkage," *New York Times*, March 31, 1994.

Joan Biskupic of the Washington Post . . . Joan Biskupic, "High Court Considers Hasidic School Case," *Washington Post*, March 31, 1994.

"Although Lewin seemed in danger of losing . . ." Timothy M. Phelps, "Court Hears Hasids' Arguments; Mixing Church, State at Issue," *Newsday*, March 31, 1994.

the justices "were unusually blunt . . ." Tony Mauro, "Hasidic District Faces Sharp Questions," *USA Today*, March 31, 1994.

"that the nation's founders wisely banned" . . . "Respect Church-State Line," *USA Today*, March 31, 1994.

"It doesn't hurt to be accommodating" . . . Sister Mary Ann Walsh, "Respect Needs of Kids," *USA Today*, March 31, 1994.

Nat Lewin and I faced off . . . ABC World News Tonight, March 30, 1994, transcript 4063.

"There are thousands of school districts . . ." "Church vs. State," *MacNeil/Lehrer NewsHour,* March 30, 1994, transcript 4896.

16. Judicial Deliberations

On Friday April 1, 1994, the justices gathered . . . The glimpses of the inner workings of the court come from the writings and notes of Justice Blackmun, Harry A. Blackmun Papers, Library of Congress, Washington, DC.

had the votes to overrule Aguilar . . . See Agostini v. Felton, 521 US 203 (1997).

"all the lower courts—both state and federal . . ." Interview with Marc Stern by the author.

17. Supremely Decided

an unacceptable "fusion" of church and state . . . Board of Education of Kiryas Joel Village School District v. Grumet, 512 US 687 (1994).

18. Déjà Vu

"It is disappointing that a governor . . ." The quote is from an op-ed article I wrote for *Newsday,* "Cuomo Should Stop Building Ghetto Walls," which was published August 31, 1994.

"The trick for negotiators [was] to craft . . ." The quote was included in a decision of the appellate division, third department, by Justice Thomas Mercure. See Grumet v. Cuomo, 225 A.D.2d 4 (1996).

"personally disappointed in the utter disrespect . . ." James Dao, "Albany in Accord on School District for Hasidic Group," *New York Times,* July 2, 1994.

To me, the law was all too reminiscent . . . Brown v. Board of Education, 347 US 483 (1954).

"The swift election-year move . . ." "A Poor Solution for Kiryas Joel," *New York Times,* July 28, 1994.

"an insult to the democratic process" . . . Clipping from Gannett News Service, 1994, author's collection.

"State residents should be questioning . . ." "Catering to Religious Sect Was Big Albany Mistake," *Buffalo News,* July 8, 1994.

"It looks like the New York Legislature is basically . . ." Clipping from Associated Press, 1994, author's collection.

"With the right motivation, the Governor . . ." Clipping from *Rochester Democrat and Chronicle,* July 1994, author's collection.

the new law provided a *"religious-neutral process"*... Grumet v. Cuomo, 162 Misc.2d 913 (1994).

"decided that when the legislature dressed..." John Caher, "Justice Harris Hands Kiryas Joel Its First Victory," *Albany Times Union*, August 11, 1994.

"a sneaky way to do what the First Amendment..." "Kiryas Joel: Still Wrong," *Albany Times Union*, March 10, 1995.

"In determining whether the current law..." Grumet v. Cuomo, 225 A.D.2d 4 (1996).

"singling out the Village of Kiryas Joel..." Grumet v. Cuomo, 90 N.Y.2d 57 (1997).

the high court, on April 15, 1997, decided... Agostini v. Felton, 521 US 203 (1997).

overturning its 1985 decision... Aguilar v. Felton, 473 US 402 (1985).

"The sponsors of the latest bill..." Raymond Hernandez, "Albany Vote Defies Courts Again to Back a Hasidic School District," *New York Times*, August 4, 1997.

During legislative debate, Assemblyman Joe Lentol... Ibid.

"The first time I saw this bill..." Ibid.

"Kiryas Joel's leaders have once again..." Clipping from *Middletown Times-Herald-Record*, 1997, author's collection.

"show some respect" for the New York Court of Appeals... Clipping from Gannett News Service, 1997, author's collection.

"Once again, the New York State Legislature..." American Jewish Congress, "AJCongress Criticizes New York State Legislature for Again Creating School District in Kiryas Joel," PRNewswire, August 4, 1997, www.prnewswire.com /news-releases/ajcongress-criticizes-new-york-state-legislature-for-again -creating-school-district-in-kiryas-joel-74880477.html.

"We conclude with an observation..." Grumet v. Pataki, 93 N.Y.2d 677 (1999).

As of this writing, the Kiryas Joel... See the FAQ on the Kiryas Joel official website, www.kjvoice.com/faq.asp.

Epilogue

a population of around twenty-two thousand... Census figures at US Census Bureau official website, http://quickfacts.census.gov/qfd/states/36/3639853 .html. Note also that 60.5 percent of the population was under the age of eighteen, and a language other than English was spoken in 92 percent of the households.

Consider this July 2015 headline... Bill Mahoney, "Filings Show Kiryas Joel Money Flowed to Cuomo After Veto," *Capital New York*, July 17, 2015, www.capitalnewyork.com/article/albany/2015/07/8572342 /filings-show-kiryas-joel-money-flowed-cuomo-after-veto.

For example, look at the court's... Burwell v. Hobby Lobby, 573 US _ (2014).

an Upstate New York town's practice . . . Town of Greece v. Galloway, 572 US _ (2014).

"I think the main fight is to . . ." Valerie Richardson, "Scalia Defends Keeping God, Religion in Public Square," *Washington Times*, October 1, 2014.

segment of public radio's This American Life . . . Audio of the program is available on *This American Life* official website, www.thisamericanlife.org/radio-archives/episode/534/a-not-so-simple-majority; the transcript is at www.thisamericanlife.org/radio-archives/episode/534/transcript.

"Dear fellow taxpayer in the East Ramapo . . ." Ibid. Used with permission.

INDEX

ABOUT THE AUTHORS

Louis Grumet

 Lou Grumet was the plaintiff in *Board of Education of Kiryas Joel Village School District v. Grumet,* the case that challenged the establishment of a special school district for a religious sect and led to a landmark US Supreme Court decision. At the time, Grumet was executive director of the New York State School Boards Association. He was formerly assistant commissioner for the education of children with handicapping conditions for the New York State Education Department, and was instrumental in establishing the department's role in enforcing quality standards for the education of children with disabilities. Prior to that, he served as special assistant to then–New York secretary of state Mario Cuomo and as Cuomo's representative in matters dealing with disabled individuals. He was also executive director of the New York State Society of Certified Public Accountants, where he helped the state redesign and upgrade its accountability and ethics standards for the profession. He has written extensively on issues of education and governmental ethics and had an article published on

the Kiryas Joel case in the May 2011 issue of the *New York State Bar Journal*.

Grumet earned his juris doctor from New York University Law School, his master's degree in public administration from the University of Pittsburgh, and his bachelor's in public policy from George Washington University. He was awarded the Distinguished Service Award by Americans United for Separation of Church and State, as well as the New York State Civil Liberties Union, in 1995.

John M. Caher

John M. Caher has been a professional writer for three decades, specializing in legal reportage. His reporting has garnered more than twenty awards, including prestigious honors from the American Bar Association, the New York State Bar Association, and the Erie County Bar Association. Caher is the author or coauthor of five other books, including *Personal Bankruptcy Laws for Dummies*, *King of the Mountain*, and *A Time for Reflection*. He was a reporter with the *New York Law Journal* for ten years and, previously, a reporter and editor with the *Albany Times Union*, where he was likely the first newsperson to grasp the legal and political significance of the Kiryas Joel case. Formerly communications director for the New York State Division of Criminal Justice Services, Caher is currently the senior adviser for strategic communications with the New York State Unified Court System.

Caher holds a journalism degree from Syracuse University and a master's degree in technical communications/graphics from Rensselaer Polytechnic Institute. He lives in Clifton Park, New York. Caher and his wife, Kathleen, are the parents of three wonderful, intelligent, principled, beautiful daughters—Erin, Kerry, and Norah.